THE total actor

THE total actor

Raymond Rizzo

John Jay College of Criminal Justice
of the City University of New York

THE ODYSSEY PRESS

a division of The Bobbs-Merrill Company, Inc.
INDIANAPOLIS

To my parents four:
natural, Mary and Pat;
adoptive, Bee and Frank
—all of whom I adore

The Bobbs-Merrill Company, Inc.
4300 West 62nd Street
Indianapolis, Indiana 46268

First Edition
First Printing 1975
Designed by Betty Binns
Photographs by Howard Dando; Model, Hilde Morales

Library of Congress Cataloging in Publication Data

Rizzo, Raymond.
The total actor.

Includes bibliographies and index.
1. Acting. I. Title.
PN2061.R54 792′.028 74-28493
ISBN 0-672-63276-4

Contents

List of exercises, vii
Preface, ix

1 *The total actor* 1

2 *Work on oneself: relaxation* 9

RELAXATION: THE RATIONALE, *10*
TENSION AND BODY GEOGRAPHY, *11*
YOGA, *16*

3 *Work on oneself: concentration and meditation* 50

4 *The total actor and his voice: voice production* 56

PITCH PLACEMENT, *60*
CONTROLLING THE VOICE QUALITY, *62*
THE NASAL VOICE IN CHARACTER WORK, *63*
THE FRONTAL VOICE IN CHARACTER WORK, *65*
THE CHEST VOICE IN CHARACTER WORK, *66*
THE HEAD VOICE IN CHARACTER WORK, *67*

5 *The total actor and his voice: diction* 69

READING SELECTIONS, *82*

6 *Acting: imagination, memory, senses* 93

IMAGINATION, *93*
MEMORY, *95*
SENSES, *97*

7 *Acting is doing* 107

PREPARATION FOR THE ONE-BEAT PROBLEM, *111*

HOW TO CREATE A ONE-BEAT PROBLEM, *114*

EXAMPLE OF A ONE-BEAT PROBLEM BASED ON GIVEN CIRCUMSTANCES, *115*

8 *Emotional problems* 121

HOW TO SET UP IMPROVISATIONS TO SOLVE EMOTIONAL PROBLEMS, *125*

9 *Total acting for total characterization* 128

SUGGESTED GUIDELINES FOR BUILDING A CHARACTER, *129*

ADDITIONAL HINTS FOR BUILDING A CHARACTER, *134*

10 *Shakespeare, Stanislavski, and you* 149

BODY, VOICE, ACTIONS, EMOTIONS, *150*

SUGGESTED PREPARATION FOR SHAKESPEAREAN SCENES, *162*

11 *Style* 221

12 *What are you going to do now?* 228

***Suggested Readings in the Theater*, 243**

Exercises

Chapter two *9*

RELAXATION THROUGH CONTRAST (1), *12*
RELAXATION THROUGH CONTRAST (2), *13*
RELAXATION THROUGH MASSAGE, *14*
RELAXATION THROUGH CONTROLLED BREATHING, *15*
YOGA, *16*
Controlled breathing, 19 The tree, 20 Balanced breathing, 22 The cobra, 24 The bow, 27 The folded leaf, 29 Reverse folded leaf, 31 Preparation for headstand, 33 The candle: shoulder stand, 34 The folded candle, 36 Head stand, 38 Head to knee, 40 The stomach lift, 42 Eye exercises, 44 The lotus, 46 The modified lotus, 48

Chapter three *50*

CONCENTRATION, *52*
MEDITATION, *53*
MEDITATION ON A ROLE, *54*

Chapter four *56*

RELAXATION EXERCISE: THE RAG DOLL, *58*
VOCALIZING WITH CONTROLLED DEEP BREATHING (1), *59*
VOCALIZING WITH CONTROLLED DEEP BREATHING (2), *60*
THE ROCKET EXERCISE, *61*
NASALITY EXERCISES (1–4), *65*
FRONTAL VOICE EXERCISES (1–3), *66*
CHEST VOICE EXERCISES (1–4), *66*
HEAD VOICE EXERCISES (1–4), *67*
VOICE VARIETY EXERCISE, *68*

Chapter five *69*

EXERCISE FOR THE LIPS, *72*
EXERCISE FOR THE TONGUE (1), *76*

EXERCISE FOR THE TONGUE (2), *77*
EXERCISE FOR THE TONGUE (3), *77*
EXERCISE FOR THE TONGUE (4), *78*
VOCALIZATION, *78*
CHANTING EXERCISE, *81*

Chapter six *93*

SEEING EXERCISES (1–10), *98*
LISTENING EXERCISES (1–7), *100*
TOUCHING EXERCISES (1–4), *102*
SMELLING EXERCISES (1–2), *103*
TASTING EXERCISES (1–2), *103*
SENSE MEMORY EXERCISES (1–4), *103*

Chapter seven *107*

SCORING ACTIONS, *110*
SCORING BEATS, *111*
MAKING UP THE ONE-BEAT PROBLEM, *117*
MOTIVATING AN ACTION, *118*
FINDING AN ACTION, *118*
FILLING IN THE GIVEN CIRCUMSTANCES, *119*

Chapter eight *121*

THE EMPTY CHAIR EXERCISE, *126*
THE EMOTIONAL IMPROVISATION, *127*

Chapter nine *128*

SENSE MEMORY EXERCISE FOR CHARACTERIZATION, *136*
IMPROVISATION FOR CHARACTERIZATION (1–3), *136*
READINGS: *Spoon River Anthology, 136*

Chapter ten *149*

READING: *Macbeth, 163*
READING: *Julius Caesar, 172*
READING: *Twelfth Night, 175*
READING: *Romeo and Juliet, 183*
READING: *Henry V, 191*
READING: *Antony and Cleopatra, 197*
READING: *The Taming of the Shrew, 203*
READING: *Richard III, 209*

Preface

Acting students in America have been, for some time, the innocent victims of an internecine struggle between Method and non-Method acting cliques. If, for example, they accidentally have non-Method acting teachers, then Stanislavski and his System are automatically labelled nonsense and are not even examined. Just the opposite happens when a Method man refuses to consider the importance of the acting externals and concentrates solely on the "inner psychological life." In each case the acting student is shortchanged. The war between Method and non-Method partisans was born of a misunderstanding of what the Stanislavski System—which gave birth to the American "Method"—is all about. *The Total Actor* is directed to the important task of ending the conflict by attempting to bring together the "inner" or "internal" Method people and the "outer" or "external" non-Method people in a synthesis. "Inner" or "internal," wherever mentioned in this book, refer to those interior, psychological, or emotional preparations which an actor makes; "outer" or "external" refer to those preparations having to do with his voice, body movement, and so on.

In his important book, *Method or Madness,* Robert Lewis discusses the lopsided Method training of actors in America. The Method, as it has been taught here, is lopsided because it develops only half the actor: the internal, psychological part. Lewis' contention, with which I agree, is that one of the reasons this happened is because the translation of Stanislavski's *An Actor Prepares,* which deals with the inner workings of the actor, was published in this country in 1936; then, not until thirteen years later, in 1949, was his complementary volume, *Building a Character,* published—the book which deals with the actor's external development. In the important years between 1936 and 1949, the American "Method" was developed, its emphasis on training of the actor's "inner" qualities.

Another important purpose of this book is to try to make Stanislavski's system accessible. It is a rare student who can read Stanislavski and come away with a working grasp of his system. Yet the system is of immense value to the actor. The combination of the difficulty of Stanislavski's books and their value explains why there are so many explicators of his system. *An Actor Prepares, Building a Character,* and *My Life in Art* are almost like the esoteric books of the Bible; they have many explicators, and each explicator is surrounded by his own cult.

It should be said in Stanislavski's defense that he objected to any attempt to codify his system. In 1938, two years before his death, he said to the Moscow Art Theatre Company, "There can be no question of 'your' or 'my' system. There is only one system—creative organic nature. There is no other system. And we must remember that this so-called system (let us not talk of the system, but of the nature of creative art) does not remain stationary. It changes every day."[1] It has been said by one of his associates, "He was continually moving ahead. His directorial approach was never dogmatic. He never limited himself to the same method of rehearsing. If the established method of work did not help to create the life of a certain play, everything had to be changed and the search for a new approach begun."[2]

[1] Constantin Stanislavsky, *Stanislavsky on the Art of the Stage,* ed. David Magarshack (New York: Hill and Wang, 1961), p. 1.

[2] Nikolai M. Gorchakov, *Stanislavski Directs* (New York: Funk and Wagnalls, 1954), p. 393.

Stanislavski himself never intended to stress one half of the actor's development and to neglect the other; he knew that both are indispensible, both equally important. But the damage was done, and for over thirty years the self-indulgent mumbler has been presented to the public as the quintessential Method actor, in spite of the public's instinctive knowledge that something was amiss.

This book, accordingly, attempts to supply training for the total actor. The Yoga exercises in Chapter Two are used because they combine internal and external work. Vocal exercises here will involve character work. The acting exercises use the total actor. An actor cannot be divided into body, voice, and psyche and survive. He possesses not three separate instruments, but one, his total self, and he must be master of his entire harmoniously tuned instrument.

Inspiration, accordingly, can never be a substitute for acquired technique. A pianist must practice scales, and as he does his fingering exercises, he can't be involved with thinking about a sonata. But some day, if he becomes an artist, he will use his expert fingering to play a sonata and express, through those fingers, more than just technique. It is the same with the actor. His body and his vocal technique must be melded with his intelligence and imagination to create the acting moments that will make a memorable performance.

Anyone who has read Stanislavski, then, comes to the realization that he was interested first of all in experimentation and growth. He would certainly, for instance, approve of the work being done in the Polish State Theatre by Jerzy Grotowski and his company. Grotowski acknowledges his debt to Stanislavski, but only as the point for his own departure. Stanislavski would have endorsed this attitude.

We Americans, too, must take what is meaningful to us from Stanislavski's system, and build from it. We are far more sophisticated today, for instance, in our psychological knowledge than was Stanislavski. Much of what was complex theory to a handful of specialists in Stanislavski's time is now common knowledge to educated American actors. Many teachers of the "Method" in America today also stress the importance of the cultural differences between Russia and America, and advocate an adapted "American Method."

To the American adaptation, Stanislavski would certainly have agreed. Part of his genius lay in his humility. When Stella Adler visited him in 1934 in Paris and complained that using the System had begun to worry her and that she had lost her joy in acting, he responded, "If the System does not help you, forget it." He added, however, "But perhaps you do not use it properly." For five weeks, then, he worked with Adler on a scene; the result was that when she returned to the Group Theatre in New York, the actors of the Group began to put far less emphasis on the exercises of affective memory, and far more on the given circumstances of the play.[1] The affective memory exercises provide a method of using one's past emotions as material for creating a role, a practice almost abandoned now. The given circumstances, on the other hand, help the actor to find the psychological life and the physical actions of his character; they are the answers to the questions who the character is, what he wants, why he wants it, how he will get it, where and when he is (see p. 113).

It should be noted that the words Stanislavski used about his system were not "Follow it," but "Use it," and that the System is obviously extremely fluid; how can one ever be sure that the proper emphasis is placed on each part? The System is not static and mechanical, but organic and capable of growth. For this reason, I add to the System the use of Yoga exercises (Chapter Two) as a natural means of obtaining depth relaxation and body plasticity. If practiced in the private and relaxed environment of his home—and strictly at his option—these exercises will enable the student to achieve greater relaxation and control, but they are offered only as an option.

The best way to use this book is to apply Stanislavski's implied hint: Only if it works for you, use it—but use it properly. Acting is an art, not a science. Each actor is a complex, sensitive human being, and no one acting rule can possibly apply for all. But remember that in your development as an actor you may feel short-circuited by the very elements of the work you need most and it is at this time that you should have confidence in your teacher's judgment. The performing artist needs an observer to pass judgment on his work.

The important goal is not that you should learn to follow the

[1] Christine Edwards, *The Stanislavski Heritage* (New York: New York University Press, 1965), p. 246.

steps of any system slavishly, but that you should become *total actors,* contributing to the American theater. I want you to achieve a fully-developed acting talent, to conquer the problems of style, to learn to act not just to entertain, inform, or move but to give your audiences an insight into life. What is theater but an attempt to solve the mystery of our existence?

So let us now address ourselves to the task of creating total actors for a country that must return to theater in order to better understand itself in a changing world. I believe that the alchemy wrought by the live actor is as necessary to our cultural survival as is pure air and water to our biological survival.

Without my wife's encouragement and help, this book could not have been written. My debt to Betty Warburton Rizzo can't be expressed in words. She is truly my best friend of over 28 years. In acknowledging contributions to this book, I would like to add sincere thanks to Howard Dando, photographer, and Hilde Morales, model.

It remains only for me to acknowledge that as I wrote this book I became aware more acutely than ever of the great debt I owe all my former teachers. I would like especially to thank Milton Smith of Columbia College, Sanford Meisner of the Neighborhood Playhouse, Stella Adler, Uta Hagen, and Robert Lewis. If they should happen to read this book, they will undoubtedly hear many echoes of their own voices from classes of many years ago.

THE total actor

1

The total actor

To begin, I will ask you to consider the problem of yourself as an actor from two points of view: The first is more difficult, requiring insight into your motives for entering theater. The second involves your understanding of the demands made on the actor by the legitimate stage, in contrast to those made by movies and by television. It also involves your taking an honest look at a legitimate theater that is atrophying rapidly; American theater is not, at present, in a very impressive state of health.

What *are* your motives for entering theater? You may want to brush the question aside ("Is that important?"). It is important to know why you want to do anything, because if you are doing what appears to be the right thing, but for the wrong reasons, you should reconsider both your motive and your action. You should approach acting honestly, and to do this you must apply the Delphic oracle's advice, "Know thyself."

Acting schools and college drama departments function very well as homes for runaways, orphans, the maladjusted. The runaway is the person fleeing from failure in another area. When asked why he wants to be an actor, he says something like, "Well, I thought I wanted to be an engineer, but I couldn't do the math." The orphan is the martyr cut off by his family because he wants to act. Intelligent parents, acquainted with the statistics on the employment and per-capita income of actors, are right to be dubious about an acting career, but the orphan's martyrdom is rewarding to him: It punishes his family, sustains his ambition, and makes him a figure of romantic interest. One type of maladjusted person is the victim of a vain, self-seeking, self-engrossed personality and needs constant attention and adulation. This may be either the loudmouth who dominates the scene, or the moody introvert who also takes center stage effectively. For all these people, acting is a neurotic addiction.

Then, rare as he is, there is the natural genius, the person born to act. If you are such an actor, we can only hope that you don't squander your talent or fall into the hands of some ambitious theatrical agent who might use it to your disadvantage.

Finally, between these extremes are the many students who have acted the leads in high school or college productions. The leading parts probably have been won in stiff competition, the reward of playing them a memorable experience. These young actors determine to prolong the pleasure of being on stage, and if they have aptitude, intelligence, and the ability to work hard, nothing should prevent them from trying. If you are among them, act! But do it totally, not half-heartedly.

There may be as many reasons to act as there are people who want to act, and though I would not tell anyone not to act, I would caution all comers at least to be honest about their original motives. This book is directed toward the serious actor, not the dilettante, words not to be equated with "professional" or "amateur," for the amateur may be serious in his approach to acting, and the professional may be frivolous.

The original motive for an action may change, once you are involved in the activity. You may start with an impure, unbalanced motivation and then find a balanced, true perspective, or you may quit, as so many do, after you find out that acting isn't the solution to your problems, or that your success isn't commensurate with your estimation of your talents.

While you are thinking about the reasons why you want to act, be warned about the charlatans who will exploit you in your state of confusion by enrolling you into a program for which you are not suited, or which simply takes your money. Before you attend an acting school which does not grant degrees, check the school out with the Better Business Bureau, or Actors' Equity, or the American National Theater Academy. Don't give your money up too quickly. Don't pay for the entire course in advance. First ask to audit a class or to pay for one lesson. If possible, follow the same advice for degree-granting institutions. Remember, any university you attend is only as good as the department you need.

Be careful about the schools of acting that give auditions for an entrance requirement. Although some schools use the auditions genuinely, turning away the less talented, many accept all comers; the auditions are just a trick to make the student feel that getting in is difficult.

Even the honest acting teacher may unwittingly harm you. There once was a teacher who told a very young actor that the greatest service he could render the theater would be to abandon the study of acting immediately. The student failed to heed the advice, though he seemed to this one critic to be devoid of talent; and the theater later gained the services of Alec Guiness.

Because of this cautionary tale, I am always careful not to discourage aspiring actors. The actor who fails as Macbeth may be a gifted comedian—and vice versa. If you don't belong in the theater, you will find out in time. You alone must decide what you want to do. The X factor for any actor may be, as it was for Guiness, dedication, will, intelligence.

You must understand that you will have to work very hard. Acting is a performing art. You readily admit that long and tedious hours of training precede competent dancing, singing, or the playing of an instrument. Yet when it comes to acting, many seem to believe that success is all a matter of talent, of inspiration. Many acting teachers say it over and over again: "Actors are born."

I accept the statement conditionally: Acting potential is there at birth. But what about Alec Guiness? The conscientious teacher who told him to quit was unaware of his hidden potential, his strong motivation, his eagerness to accept the discipline that would develop his hidden talent.

Stanislavski himself is a similar case. At the outset of his career, Stanislavski was a self-confessed clumsy ham actor. Imitating one of the best roles of his favorite actor "perfectly," Stanislavski once felt inspired, but the more his inspiration excited him, "the more the audience criticized my rapid patter, my incoherent diction, my hoarse voice, my murmuring speech, my rapid gestures, my strained and exaggerated efforts."[1] It was the lack of acting ability not only in himself, but also in so many actors around him, that led to his patient study of the art of acting in such geniuses as Salvini and Duse, and thus to his development of the System.

You will never excel without discipline. Today, to become a total actor, you need as much dedicated discipline for your body as a dancer needs. You need as much vocal discipline for your speaking voice as a singer needs. Like a writer or painter, you must discipline yourself to observe and use the life around you. And serious actors, like serious singers and dancers, need discipline in their personal habits; smoking, eating, drinking, and sleeping all must be controlled.

Understanding yourself and your motives is, of course, important for a young actor; but next to that, I think, you need to have a realistic understanding of the demands of the theater, of movies, of television. Their demands differ.

The most exacting form is theater. In theater you can't easily fake technique. In the audience-performer relationship, the distinction between real life and performance, or heightened life, is constantly being played on. In the actor's second-by-second existence on stage, he is always being scrutinized. The demand by the more knowing in the audience for truthful yet intensified stage life is unrelenting; to ignore it "cannot but make the judicious grieve; the censure of the which one must, in your allowance, o'erweigh a whole theatre of others" (*Hamlet, III, ii*). Performing onstage is like making a movie without any breaks, cuts, or retakes.

I don't mean to imply that even an acting genius fills every

[1] Constantin Stanislavski, *My Life in Art*, p. 65. Copyright 1948, Elizabeth Reynolds Hapsgood. All excerpts from this volume reprinted with the permission of the Publisher, Theatre Arts Books, New York, and Geoffrey Bles Limited.

second truthfully and fully. That's impossible. But the more skilled the actor, the more insightful moments he can give the audience.

Some critics despair that an audience cannot really discriminate between good and bad acting. I disagree. I think the critics fail to realize that most audiences are both charitable and patient, determined, perhaps, to salvage as much enjoyment from a committed evening as possible. But great acting is recognized and rewarded by being remembered; or how else did Tommaso Salvini, Eleonora Duse, Laurette Taylor, Sarah Siddons, and David Garrick achieve their fame? Mediocrity may be applauded for effort, but it is forgotten by the time the audience reaches the street.

Film acting is easier. Many people don't know that you don't have to be a trained actor to star in a movie. Vittorio deSica picked a shoemaker with a delicately expressive face to play the lead in his *Bicycle Thief*. The movie was a success, and the shoemaker thought he was an actor—but no one hired him for another film. Films deal in closeups and nuances. I have heard an outstanding teacher of acting roundly declare that his most celebrated pupil, now a Hollywood superstar, is no actor at all. "As a student he couldn't project past the second row; now on a twenty foot screen he lifts an eyebrow and the emotion hits the back wall!" Timothy Bottoms, young lead actor in *The Last Picture Show,* has announced in print that he would like to take acting lessons some day because he doesn't yet know what he is doing!

None of these three film stars could have acted a lead role in a stage play and have sustained the part.

To act on stage, you need talent and much technical training. To act in movies or television, now very similar media, you need a personality and a face which projects moods in closeups. Jose Ferrer once summed it all up by saying that the screen is a personality medium and the stage is an acting medium.

Finally, it is important to give you an honest and realistic picture of the economics of the theater. Fifteen years ago a brilliant actress, acclaimed and famous for her work on Broadway, told me at the end of a summer stock engagement that she would then be applying for unemployment insurance. I was dumbfounded, but she explained that for years no plays had been written with parts for her.

It is important that you understand this unpleasant fact about acting in America: You will find it almost impossible to earn a living as a Broadway actor. The Broadway theaters are dwindling in number. In the past forty years, hundreds of theaters hiring thousands of people have shrunk to a mere handful, which hire at any one given time only ten percent of the membership of Actors' Equity. A study made by O. Glenn Saxon has revealed that of the sixty-six playhouses on Broadway in 1931, only thirty-three remained in 1960. Whereas 264 plays were produced on Broadway in 1928, fifty-seven were produced in 1960. Total attendance at the theater fell from 12,300,000 to 8,100,000 between 1930 and 1960.[1] In the past decade, the situation has not changed.

Furthermore, the Broadway theater damns you when you are most successful by condemning you to repeat over and over again the same performance, eight times a week, week in and week out. Alan Arkin won't go to see a Broadway show more than two months old because the actors soon begin to parrot their once-living performances. It is in this situation that a method of acting is absolutely necessary to the actor if he is to sustain his role with living roots.

New York's off-Broadway theaters, once proudly independent and artistically free, now imitate their big sisters on Broadway by repeating the performance of hits until every penny is realized for the investors. At this writing, *The Fantasticks* is celebrating its twelfth year of continuous performance at the same theater. To an unknown, the thought of a lead in such a hit is a dream come true. But the dream becomes a nightmare once the actor finds himself condemned to its endless repetitions.

I think you must ask yourself quite seriously whether or not you wish to train for a theater in such condition. To add to the depressing picture on and off-Broadway, summer stock—the traditional training ground of young actors—is now in a serious decline. This leaves only the regional theaters, for which Robert Brustein of Yale tells his drama students that they are training. He tells them this because there is no other serious theater in which they can practice their profession. But

[1] Edwin Duerr, *The Length and Depth of Acting* (New York: Holt, Rinehart and Winston, 1962), p. 492.

how many good regional theaters are in operation? The Arena Stage in Washington, the Tyrone Guthrie Theater in Minneapolis, the New York Shakespeare Festival are a few of a dozen or more that appear to be alive and well.

And although the regional theater picture is the most hopeful in the country at this time, it too is not without blemish. In 1967 Richard Schechner wrote

> The past six months have not been happy ones for the regional theatre. Resignations, firings, and administrative turmoil have shaken theatres in Philadelphia, Pittsburgh, New Haven, Providence, and Baltimore. Herbert Blau has left Lincoln Center. The artistic excellence and excitement we hoped for in the regional theatre have generally not materialized; the ensemble companies we dreamed of have not come into being; the financial security of steady patronage has not developed; subscription audiences have proven to be mixed blessings.[1]

The remarks were a preface to a comment by Andre Gregory, former Artistic Director of the Theatre of the Living Arts in Philadelphia, who had just been fired because he produced *Beclch*, by Rochelle Owens. Although the board of directors had by contract allowed Mr. Gregory to produce one American play of his own choice, and although he had sandwiched *Beclch* between *Room Service* and *The Time of Your Life*, he had not been able to make the play palatable. When Mr. Gregory's board of directors suggested that he wait before producing such American plays, Gregory replied

> Wait to do the new plays until the writers have become so discouraged from not having their plays done that they are no longer playwrights? If we wait until the communities are "ready," the regional theatre will disintegrate; it is already so badly compromised that most theatres have lost their integrity and their contact with the world around them.[2]

Regional theater, of course, should not only be fearlessly producing avant-garde American plays, it should also be producing the classics.

[1] Richard Schechner, *Tulane Drama Review* 11 (Summer, 1967): No. 4, p. 18.
[2] Ibid., p. 20.

There are two positive approaches to pursuing an acting career. The first is to prepare yourself for a multimedia profession. Be prepared to pay dues to three unions: Actors' Equity, the American Federation of Television Actors, and the Screen Actors' Guild. Remember that if you are a trained stage actor, you will be professionally equipped to work in the movies and in television; it won't work in reverse.

While you are at it, learn to sing—if you have any voice at all—and to dance, or at least to "move," as actors put it, because these talents may keep you working when all else fails. But always remember the difference between the art of the theater, which is the art of interpreting life, and the craft of entertaining, which is the craft of titillating the bored pleasure seeker.

The second approach you can take to the actors' problems is to look for regional theater and not only to act in it, but to help create it. In fact, in order to give yourself the acting experiences you need, never overlook the possibility of producing your own plays, creating your own theater.

To sum up, before you begin to study acting, know yourself and your own motives, know the theater in which you will be working, and, just as important, know the theater in which you *ought* to be working. Then compromise as little as possible.

2

Work on oneself: relaxation

Chapters Two and Three, dealing with "Work on Oneself," are perhaps the most important in this book. As demonstrated in Robert Lewis' chart of the Stanislavski System in *Method or Madness,* "Work on Oneself" is the foundation upon which all of the actor's discipline rests.

Work on oneself, of course, means work on the total actor. It means that you must broaden your intellectual and cultural horizons; you must read important books, learn to know—from art books and museums—great art, listen to great music. It means you must constantly observe the life about you. And it means you must learn to relax and to move fluidly, to speak with a full-toned and interesting voice, above all to use body and voice truthfully under the given circumstances of the play.

In an attempt to clarify the ambiguities of which Stanislavski has so frequently been accused,[1] I will make every attempt to give a clear

[1] As an example, see Stanislavski's *Building A Character* (New York: Theatre Arts Books, 1949), Chapters 4 and 5, where a clear work program is never provided.

and practical guide for the work plan presented here. The work plan will include exercises for both the inner and the outer actor, but not in exclusive terms. The yoga exercises presented for external physical discipline will at the same time require inner psychological involvement. This plan is in response to Lewis' plea for an approach that can bridge the gap between the Method actor, preoccupied primarily with the inner actor, and the stylistic actor, frequently accused of being exclusively external.

In an interview in 1964, Lewis commented

> The speech and voice teachers have to get together with the acting teachers, re-examine their exercises, and involve them with simple acting problems so that they are learned as part of the movement, the inner movement of acting. . . . The body must be used in the exercise to express some inner wish so that it gets tied in with the acting process.[1]

In this chapter on relaxation we are concerned with the very beginning of the struggle to achieve technique. Acting is not a science, but some order is necessary if we are to rise above what St.-Denis calls "the mud of naturalism."[2] You will do well, therefore, to remind yourself again and again that technique must come before inspiration.

Relaxation: the rationale

What is so important about relaxation? An actor uses his entire body to express his inner feelings. Then shouldn't his whole body be a totally relaxed instrument ready to interpret the slightest emotional nuance through a truthful action? And should not his body be as well disciplined as the pianist's trained fingers? Stanislavski certainly thought so:

> In Duse, Yermolova, Fedotova, Savina, Salvini, Chaliapin, Rossi, as well as in the actors of our Theatre when they appeared to best

[1] Robert Lewis, "Would You Please Talk to Those People?" *Tulane Drama Review*, 9 (Winter, 1964): No. 2, p. 101.

[2] Michael St.-Denis, *Theatre: The Rediscovery of Style* (New York: Theatre Arts, 1960), p. 89.

> advantage in their roles, I felt the presence of something that was common to them all, something by which they reminded me of each other. What was this quality, common to all great talents? It was easiest of all for me to notice this likeness in their physical freedom, in the lack of all strain. Their bodies were at the call and beck of the inner demands of their wills.[1]

Stage relaxation does not mean, of course, a condition resembling that of a limp rag. For the stage, the state of relaxation can be learned from a cat. Note a cat with an interest in hunting insects. She is at rest, and every fiber of her body is loose, when suddenly she sees a moth fly by. Now she is at attention, poised, concentrating on the flight of the moth. Her muscles are ready to act, her brain is calculating and recalculating the distance between the moth and herself, and as the moth moves, her body awaits the command to jump. At this moment let us freeze her image. The state of the animal can be described as prepared relaxation. If the cat were improperly poised, she would fall in her leap. She springs, releasing energy; in midair her muscles are relaxed; when she lands, her muscles work again.

The application is obvious. The actor, too, must concentrate on his action on stage, just as the cat concentrates on the moth. Then, if his body is properly trained, his muscles will take care of themselves.

Tension and body geography

Here is a second application to the rule, "know thyself": before you can learn to relax your body, you must learn its geography. How is relaxation to be achieved? Not through the command, "Relax! Relax!" This approach will only create more tension. You can learn to relax, however, by learning to know your body better. In this first lesson in relaxation, the key word is "contrast." You must first learn to recognize the difference between a tense muscle and a relaxed muscle.

To prepare for your lesson, you need only two simple props: a mat or a blanket folded into a long mat, and a quiet room. Avoid over-

[1] *My Life in Art,* p. 463.

head lighting which creates tension; dim, indirect lighting is best. Wear no belts, no tight waistbands, no girdles, bras, shoes, or elastic stockings. Think of the state of freedom your body exults in as you drop away your clothes at the end of a day. If you have privacy, work without clothes, or, if you prefer, wear a loose garment. For group work you can use shorts, bathing suits, or leotards.

RELAXATION THROUGH CONTRAST *(1)*

1 Lie down on the mat on your back, placing your arms at your sides.

2 Close your eyes, but not tightly. Don't try, as yet, to relax.

3 Starting with the muscles of your left foot, tighten that foot as if you were grabbing an object with your toes. Tighten it so hard that you can feel the tension burn. Hold the contraction for a slow count of five.

4 Release the muscles quickly. What you now experience is a state of relaxation. Do it again! Memorize that contrasting sensation.

5 Tilt your left foot towards you as hard as you can. This will tighten the calf muscle. Hold for a count of five. Release. Try to keep all the rest of your body neutral.

6 Tighten the left thigh muscle. Hold for five. Release. Take your time. You cannot rush to meet relaxation.

7 Tighten the left buttock. You will feel it lift your body. Hold for five. Release.

8 Starting with your *right* foot, repeat steps 3 through 7.

9 With your left hand, make a fist. Tighten it hard. Hold for five. Release.

11 Raise your forearm to tighten your bicep. Hold for five. Release.

12 Starting with your *right* hand, repeat steps 9 through 11.

13 Tighten your abdominal muscles. If you experience difficulty here, raise both legs off the ground. Hold for five. Release.

14 Tighten your chest muscles. If you experience difficulty, raise both arms toward one another. Hold for five. Release.

15 Tighten your back muscles. If you find this difficult, try to push your shoulder blades into the mat. Hold for five. Release.

16 The muscles in the small of the back are hard to contract. Turn onto your stomach. Push your pelvis into the mat. Hold for five. Release.

17 Get onto your back. Lift up your head. Tighten your neck muscles and hold for five. Release. (Warning: do not drop your head on release; lower it gently.)

18 Distort your face into a mask of tragedy. Your neck muscles will tighten too. Hold for five. Release.

19 Tighten your eye muscles and forehead. You may feel your scalp move over your skull. Hold for five. Release.

20 Tighten the muscles at the back of the neck. Your ears should move downwards towards the floor. Hold for five. Release.

In performing these exercises, you may have experienced some difficulty with some particular part of the body. Some people, for instance, cannot move their ears at all. This is not important. The important lesson to learn is how to get rid of tension through contrast. Hold and release!

Once you have really mastered this exercise, you need no longer perform it. At that point you will receive frequent messages during the day from tense muscles. Respond with the proper contrast. Tighten, hold, release. Both on stage and off, an attitude of prepared relaxation will stand you in good stead.

RELAXATION THROUGH CONTRAST *(2)*

1 Sit on the floor and, bending your knees, pull your thighs up to your chest.

2 Wrap your arms around your legs.

3 Bury your face between your legs.

4 Now contract every muscle you can—in your belly, shoulders, arms, hands, buttocks, legs, feet, face, and eyes.

5 Continue this all-over contraction until it really hurts. If some parts start to relax, tighten them up harder. Hold for at least a minute.

6 Suddenly release every muscle in an explosion. Stretch out on your back, extending yourself as far as you can. Try to feel as if your joints are about to unhinge. Open your eyes wide and stick out your tongue. Hold this reverse position for a minute.

7 Let go. Relax every muscle.

The wave of relaxation that you now experience, following the two different states of tension, is similar to that experienced in the last exercise. You have progressed from voluntary contraction, or tension, to release, or relaxation.

RELAXATION THROUGH MASSAGE

Massage as therapy for tension was used long before sensitivity groups were formed. You can work in pairs, or three or four people can massage one subject. Use a little baby oil or mineral oil to cut down on the friction between hands and body. The person receiving the massage can tell you when the amount of pressure is too much or too little. Start with a gentle firm touch. If you are massaging an arm or a leg, rub towards the heart. Sometimes massaging sensitive areas such as the hands or feet or back of the neck is extremely beneficial in helping the whole body to relax.

When you are massaged, use your newfound sense of relaxation. Hang loose; let the massage work. Don't fight the manipulations, and don't try to help either. You will notice that whether you are receiving or giving the massage, you and your partner will develop the ability to communicate without words. You will instinctively hit the muscle that needs work, with just the right pressure.

Some massage techniques are: (a) kneading, used on large muscles of the arms, legs, and buttocks, as if they were a mass of clay; (b) pressing your thumbs with firm, gentle pressure into the feet, hands, upper and lower back, and neck muscles; (c) chopping with the blades of the hands on large areas like thigh and back and stomach muscles; (d) tapping with relaxed finger tips on sensitive areas, around the face and head.

There is an endless variety of methods which you will find yourself using which are not mentioned here.

Finally, consider that the touching involved in massage can be a beginning to learning how to work off a fellow actor, for it involves interaction, communication. It is not that you will be touching one another continually in plays, though sometimes, of course, you will, but that you will be working off one another continually—verbally, visually, psychologically. When you massage, try to do so with sensitivity to the other's needs. Respond and adjust to the other's physical signals.

RELAXATION THROUGH CONTROLLED DEEP BREATHING

Deep and controlled breathing helps you to relax because deep breathing slows down the heart beat and the body's metabolism.

1 Lie on the floor as in the first exercise, Relaxation through contrast (1). Place both hands on your diaphragm (stomach) immediately below the rib cage.

2 Exhale slowly, feeling your hands fall, counting from one to ten, allowing one second for each number. Do not speed up. You may be able to complete a count of four, or eight. No matter.

3 When your lungs have emptied, count at the same pace to four.

4 Slowly inhale, counting as above. Do not let the air rush in. Your count may reach four, six, eight, ten, or more. When your lungs are filled, you will then proceed to the next step.

5 Hold your breath again for a count that is twice as long as your inhalation count. If you inhaled for eight seconds, then hold for sixteen.

6 Now once again exhale slowly for the same count as in Step 2.

Yoga

Yoga discipline can help you to become physically free and at the same time to learn muscle control. It can give you a free, calm, flexible, strong body prepared to act as your instrument. It can also help you to develop the powerful concentration needed on stage. Finally, yoga exercises lead to meditation, which will develop your inner consciousness, your sense of an inner reality. This can lead to a development of your personality and offer you an oasis with which you can, for example, prepare yourself before going on stage. In the words of Christine Edwards, "When Stanislavsky established a studio for the Habima Players from Palestine, he placed it under the direction of Vakhtangov. . . . Vakhtangov was strongly influenced by Tibetan philosophy and interested in Yoga, and he employed it in teaching acting. This was also true of Stanislavsky and Chekhov."[1]

Here is involved the "art of self-observation" mentioned by Stanislavski:

> And to teach the student the art of self-observation, the studio must teach him the laws of correct breathing, the correct position of the body, concentration and watchful discrimination.
>
> My whole system is based on this. With this the studio must begin the training of its student-actors. And the first lessons in breathing must become the foundation of the development of that introspective attention on which all the work in the art of the stage must be built."[2]

An actor who does not learn to feed his soul, mind, and heart regularly will—like a sunless and waterless plant—shrivel and die. Dead actors are those automatons who, like zombies, go through a series of conditioned reflexes and stage tricks having nothing to do with life and nothing to say to the living.

Yoga is ideally suited to help the actor combine inner psychological actions with outer physical actions. Even so, the exercises in this chapter are offered as options to be practiced only if you find them helpful.

[1] Edwards, *Stanislavski Heritage*, p. 124.
[2] Stanislavski, *Art of the Stage*, pp. 116–17.

The basis of yoga is rhythmic breathing. Yoga breathing is rhythmic because it is controlled, and thus directly related to the mind, the will, the emotions. Controlled breathing can affect your metabolism. It can slow your heartbeat noticeably and calm your entire body.

Of course, yoga involves not only controlled breathing, but also controlled body positions. This is important to the actor for several reasons. Besides increasing his body control, it can improve his health and prolong his years of vitality. Each yoga position is designed to stimulate a specific gland and to keep it functioning. Old age overcomes sedentery people sooner because their muscles and glands atrophy from lack of stimulation. Yoga positions exercise the muscles, too, and keep them in tone; and they keep the spine flexible. Serious yoga practioners in their seventies and eighties are still flexible and active. For the actor who has left the compulsory dance class behind after drama school, and who is slowly going to pot, yoga can be a boon, for it can be done anywhere. No need for a gym, a dance studio, gadgets or specialists. All you need is a blanket and a private room.

Before beginning the specific exercises, I want to explain more fully how to approach yoga. First, try to do the impossible and banish the concept of success from your mind. Success is a word of primary importance in the Western world, but in the world of yoga it has no meaning. When you attempt a posture or rhythmic breathing cycle, do not watch yourself or rate yourself on your performance, but simply perform the action at hand. Make no judgments. Did you try? That is enough. "But I didn't do it right!" What a splendid time for you to absorb another important acting rule: Never judge yourself.

Do the action with complete concentration on your posture and your rhythmic breathing. Nothing else matters. There is no failure, no success. In time, your control of posture will develop, but no matter; do what you can at the moment.

Another important concept in yoga is that you are not performing a gymnastic feat, and, unlike the performer of Western gymnastics, you will not get pulled into a dizzying cycle in search of perfection. When the gymnast has done twenty push-ups, he typically tries for two more. Young gymnasts have reached over a hundred push-ups. This sort of competition with one's own performance does not exist in yoga. You perform each posture two, three, or four times, depending on yourself, and never more.

Yoga, however, is not a faddist's game. It must be done regularly and made a part of your life. Don't be a fanatic about it and terrorize your co-habitors with your regime. If you miss a day, no harm, but try not to miss two.

I suggest that the best time for yoga is morning, but find the time that is best for you. If you can't get started in the morning, do it later. Never, however, practice yoga immediately after eating. Wait at least three hours before attempting the exercises.

If you get interested in yoga, there are many excellent books on the subject, and many teachers. Here is a word of caution about both: Remember who you are; work from your own reality. I assume you are a Westerner. Do *not* try to adopt wholly an Eastern method of yoga discipline. The yoga presented here is Westernized.

Do not force the body into any position. I have seen many yoga books that tell you to push down on your knees, to bounce them, until you can do a perfect lotus position. This is potentially harmful and dangerous. We Westerners are used to sitting in chairs and our knees are not accustomed to squatting on the floor. I have heard of many enthusiastic Americans who have "bounced" their knees out of joint or weakened the complex cartileges around the knees.

You may be able to get into the lotus easily and with no trouble. But if you can't, do a *modified* lotus without forcing yourself. Do a lotus that will not hurt or force the knees and do it with no shame. Be moderate; develop gradually.

1 Lie on your back on a folded blanket or a mat on the floor. Place one hand on your stomach for the first few cycles to check your diaphragm's action. (The diaphragm is the wide muscle that pushes air out of your lungs, creating a vacuum, when you exhale. When you inhale, air pressure fills the lungs.)

2 Exhale completely. Your stomach should drop lower when you do this (down, not in), and when you have completed the action, hold it for four seconds.

3 Now slowly let your diaphragm expand, which will permit you to inhale. As your diaphragm expands, your hand will rise. This action should take 6, 8, 10, or 12 seconds, depending on your lung capacity and the control you exert over the rate of expansion.

4 Once your lungs are filled, hold your breath for a count of 12, 18, 20, or 24.

5 Again you will exhale slowly by pushing the air out of your lungs with a count of 6, 8, 10, or 12.

When you practice this exercise, you will soon establish a tempo. Exhale, 4, 6, or 8; hold 4. Inhale 6, 8, 10, 12; hold for 18, 20, or for 24. Remember that a longer count is no more "successful" than a shorter count. Women, for instance, should not expect as much diaphragmatic action because their breathing is more in the chest. It is important that you learn to achieve controlled breathing.

If you can achieve control over your breathing, the basic function of life, you are on the way to controlling your body. The actor may well ask himself, what is the breathing rate of someone who is angry, drunk, dull, hurried, dying, meditating, very old, very young, and so on.

Yoga breathing will continue to be used in the subsequent exercises.

THE TREE

For this exercise, you may at first need the help of a chair or a wall.

1 Fix your eyes on a distant point to help keep your balance. Raise your right foot, grasping that ankle with your right hand. Place your right heel as high as possible into your crotch, your entire foot lying firmly against your inner left thigh muscle. (Barefeet and very short pants or tights will help your foot to stay in position.) Place both arms at your sides.

2 Empty your lungs as in breathing exercise, step 2.

3 As you slowly begin the count for inhalation, slowly raise your arms in a wide arc from your sides until they meet over your head, palm to palm, ending inhalation.

4 Hold your breath. Extend arms fully above your head, palms touching. Ideally, you are in perfect control of your body; you should feel the grace and power of your mastery.

5 Exhale, your arms slowly descending vertically, palms together, near your face until they reach your chest, as in prayer. When your lungs are empty, drop arms to your side, starting again.

6 Do three times, then switch feet and repeat.

When you first do this exercise, all effort and concentration probably will be spent on the physical discipline, and you may laugh at the comments about grace and power in step 4. But as you achieve balance and confidence, you can work on inner concentration, which later may help in your search for psycho-physical chain reactions.

Psycho-physical postures.

The following are suggested images to accompany the tree exercise.

I hold myself strong. Tall. Unconquerable! A tree on a mountain top; I sway! I am just—fair in all things. I am a bird—I fly! Soar!

What other images can you think of? Do not ask why or where you are and what you want until later. And at this point, no vocalization is required. Later you can combine physical and vocal exercises to express inner psychological states.

1 Start in a standing position, feet close together, arms at your sides.

2 As you slowly inhale, roll from your heels to the balls of your feet. Inhale and roll slowly until you have inhaled deeply.

3 As you slowly exhale, lower your heels to the floor.

4 Repeat three times. To start, exhale 4, 6, 8, 10 seconds; inhale 4, 6, 8, 10; hold 6, 8, 10, 12.

5 Place your left foot behind your right leg, and catch it there above the ankle. You are now balanced on one foot. Repeat the exercise twice.

6 Place your right foot behind your left leg so that you are now balanced on your left foot. Repeat exercise twice.

Like the tree, this exercise imparts to you the sense of inner psychic balance that an actor on stage must have. Learn to recognize the state. Achievement of this condition will help eliminate any sense of insecurity you feel on stage. Remember, when you can manage on one leg or on one foot, you are inner-balanced as well.

Finally, remember that each exercise helps to firm the body muscles. This exercise is excellent for the arches of your foot, and it also conditions and strengthens the ankles and lower calf muscles.

Psycho-physical postures.

As if I were a skier launching forward into the air (extend your arms as you roll forward). As if I were standing on a tightwire. As if I were balancing myself a hundred feet above the ground. As if I were a weather vane—the wind blows me. As if I were a merry-go-round horse. As if I were a ballet dancer.

Supply your own inner image. What do *you* want to express?

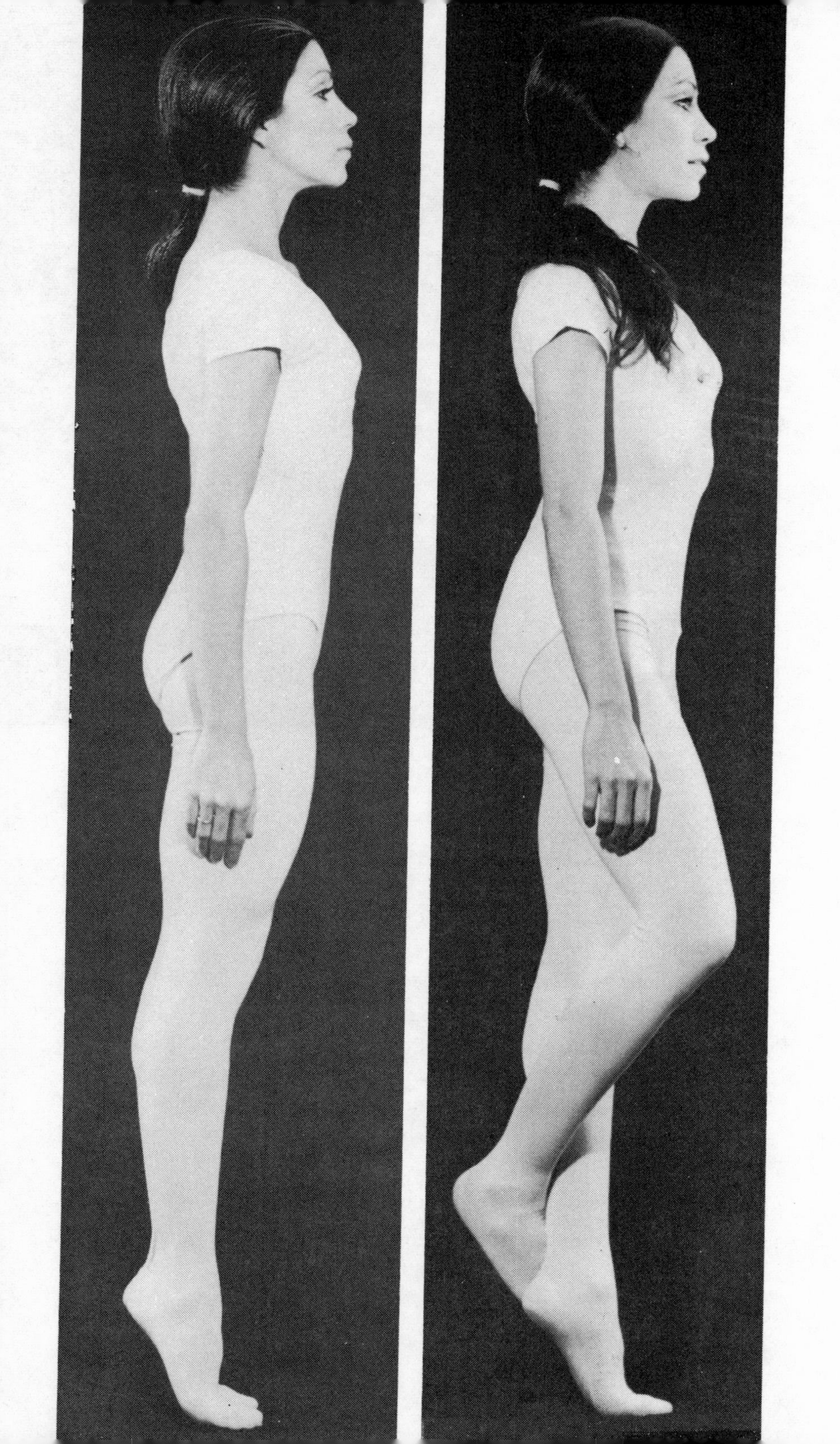

THE COBRA

1 Lie on your stomach. Feel every part of your body making contact with the earth.

2 Place your hands under your shoulders, arms folded parallel to your sides, chin resting lightly on the floor. Check muscles for total relaxation: neck, abdomen, legs.

3 Coordinate breathing and movement. Empty lungs on exhalation count; hold for four seconds.

4 Begin inhalation, slowly raising your head, letting your head lead your chest up, slowly extending arms; keep pelvis in contact with the ground. Experience will enable you to time the entire movement, so that with arms fully extended and head raised—looking at the ceiling —your lungs will be full.

5 Hold inhalation, always with pelvis touching the ground.

6 As you feel the need and begin to exhale, *slowly* descend until, chin touching the ground, your lungs are empty.

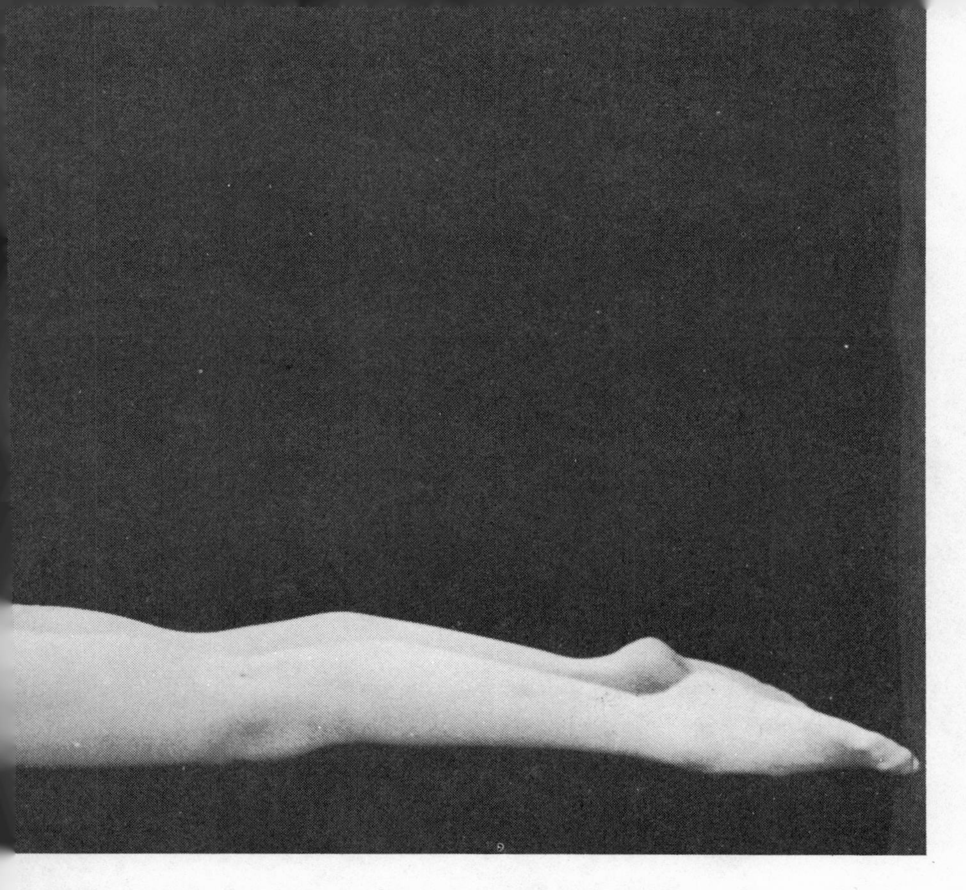

Warning: Never force any position beyond comfort. At first you may feel that you are hardly getting off the floor and can hold the position for only a few seconds, but in time you will hold it longer. If you feel tired after this or *any* exercise, do not rush on. A deep breath will slow your heartbeat.

The cobra, excellent for expanding the chest and developing the bust, is also unsurpassable preparation for vocal exercises, where chest breathing is needed for proper voice support. It also limbers the spinal cord and firms the stomach, neck, and back muscles. According to yoga experts, it stimulates the thymus gland, which helps keep hot heads cooler.

Psycho-physical postures.

As if I were the rising sun. Or Atlas, lifting the world. A resurrection! A phoenix! As if I were praying. I praise the Life Force. As if I were caught in a trap—I want to escape!

THE BOW

In attempting this exercise, do not be discouraged if your knees don't get off the ground. Remember, the effort is all that matters. Before starting this rather strenuous exercise, go through a breathing cycle (see *Controlled breathing*, p. 15).

1 Lie on your stomach. Bending your knees, place your heels on your buttocks. With your hands, reach back and grab your ankles; get a good grip.

2 Complete a breathing cycle, ending in an inhalation, before you start any physical action.

3 With your lungs filled with air, hold your breath and lift your ankles away from your head. Pull with your arms, arching the body into a bow. Hold until the need for exhalation dictates.

4 Slowly release the ankles and return to a flat stomach position. A deep breath will slow your heartbeat.

5 Repeat two or three times. When in the bow, try to rock yourself. Keep head well back.

This is an excellent exercise for strengthening the stomach muscles, the neck muscles, the arm and leg muscles. It develops the chest and is also excellent for developing the bust.

Psycho-physical postures.

As if I were at the breaking point—but I won't quit! As if I were a wheel (rock back and forth). As if I were holding on for my life. As if I were a harp. As if I were a bow—an arrow will be shot from me.

THE FOLDED LEAF

1 Sit back on your feet, placing your buttocks on your heels.

2 Fold your arms behind your back, holding your left elbow with your right hand and holding your right elbow with your left hand. At first you will feel some discomfort in your feet because they are not used to this pressure; but it will soon pass. Adjust your feet until you feel comfortable.

3 Exhale first.

4 Looking straight ahead, inhale slowly and fully.

5 Hold your breath as long as possible without strain.

6 On exhalation, slowly lower your forehead to rest between your knees. Hold the exhalation.

7 On the inhalation, rise in disciplined tempo to the upright position, looking straight ahead.

8 Repeat three times.

This exercise is excellent for keeping the spinal cord flexible.

Psycho-physical postures.

As if a tidal wave were coming—I bend forward to protect myself; it passes over me. As if I see something crawling on the floor—I bend to meet it. As if I were going to be punished—I bend over for the whiplash. As if I were bowing to a superior force—I am humble. As if I were hurt—my wound hurts less when I fold over.

REVERSE FOLDED LEAF

1 Start in the same position as the preceding exercise, positioning your buttocks on your heels. Now use your hands to lower your trunk backward. Arching both your back and neck, place the back of your head on the floor.

2 Empty your lungs and then inhale. Hold. Then exhale. Try to experience the sensation of your stomach's touching your backbone.

3 Repeat three times.

This exercise keeps the spine flexible, strengthens the stomach walls, and prepares the feet for more walking.

Psycho-physical postures.

As if I were vulnerable—I expose my stomach. As if I were an arch—in a church. As if I were a bridge over a small pond. As if I were offering myself to an outside force—I am open. As if I were a high diver doing a backward somersault off a cliff.

PREPARATION FOR HEADSTAND

This exercise is restful and is a necessary preparation for the headstand.

1 Seated in the folded leaf position, interlace the fingers of the hands and make a cup of the palms.

2 Bend forward until your head is on the floor and your elbows form a tripod with your head.

3 Slowly rise onto your toes so that you form an inverted V. If necessary, walk in on your toes to elevate your buttocks higher.

4 Begin the breathing cycle. Exhale. Inhale. Hold. Exhale.

5 Repeat three times.

In this position you can feel gravity pulling on your diaphragm, which will help you to get a deep breath. Feel the weight of your body on your head as you walk your feet in closer to your head. You are almost standing on your head.

This exercise stretches the back muscles of the legs, and is excellent for keeping the diaphragm in top condition for vocal work. It is also a fine exercise for helping you to relax and can be used when tension strikes.

Psycho-physical postures.

As if I were a ball flying through space. As if I were a shelter, a tent; everything under me is safe. As if I were hiding like an ostrich. As if I were a porpoise breaking water—I love to swim! As if I were a child about to try my first somersault.

THE CANDLE: THE SHOULDER STAND

This is another preparation for the headstand. Like the previous preparation, it accustoms you to the upside-down position without forcing you to worry about balance.

1 Lie flat on your back.

2 Raise your legs and place your hands under your buttocks to support the weight of your body as you lift your legs straight up. Your weight is now on your shoulders and your chin is pressed to your chest if you are truly straightened in a vertical column. Point your toes. Your hands should be pressing into your back with your arms forming stabilizing supports. Enjoy the sensation of an upside-down world.

3 Do three to five full breathing cycles. Do not rush the breathing. Keep your balance as you control the breathing.

This exercise rests your heart and relieves your inner organs from the usual pull of gravity. After a long rehearsal, when you are really tired, do a few preparatory breathing cycles on your back, and then get into the candle. You will feel instantly refreshed. Those of you who suffer from headaches can try this exercise for banishing them; it is often very effective.

Psycho-physical postures.

As if I were in a dark room—I am a candle, the flame leaping from my heart to my feet. As if I were a flagpole. As if I were a pair of scissors, I open and close my legs. As if I were a totem pole—a ceremony takes place around me. As if I were a blade of grass.

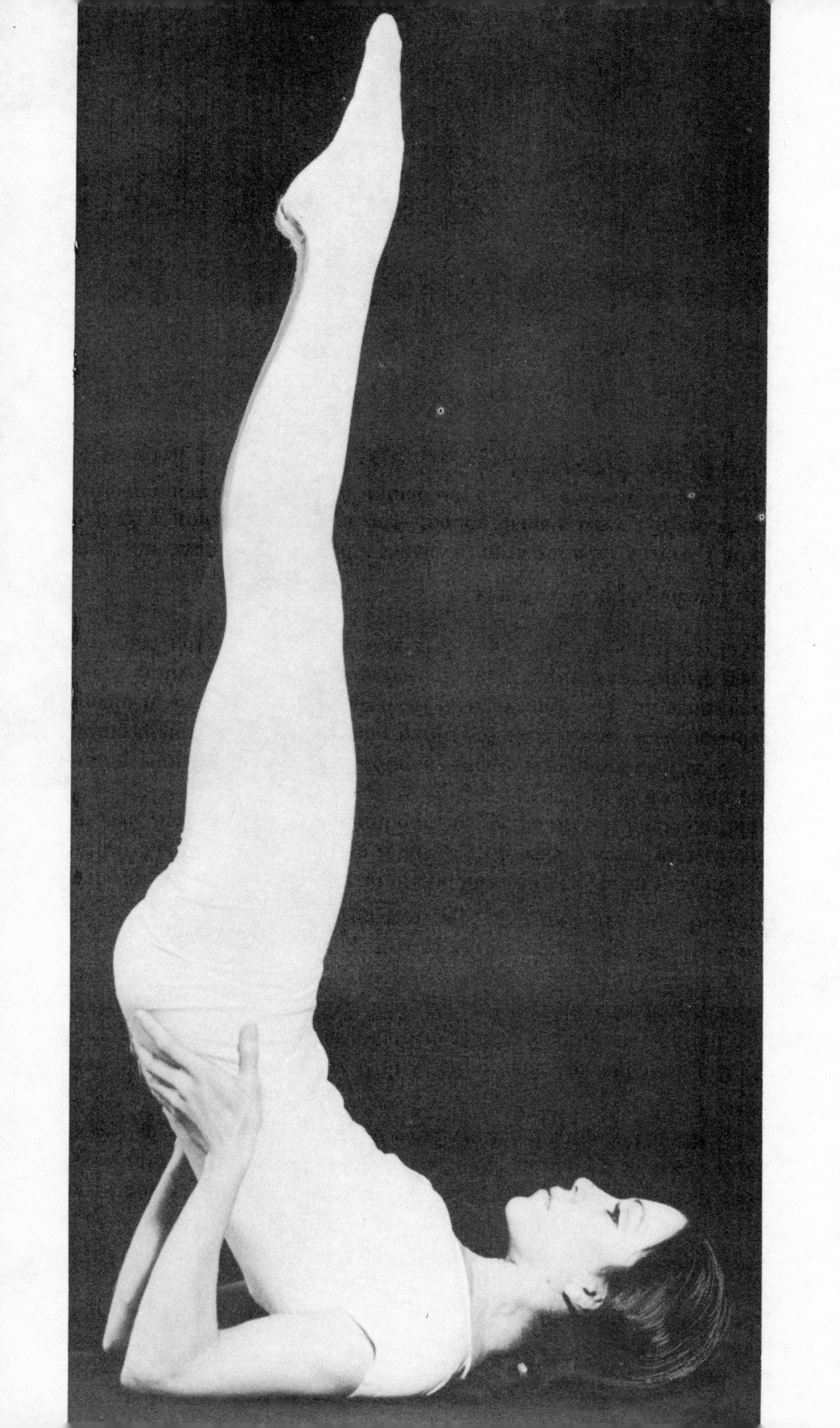

THE FOLDED CANDLE

The folded candle begins from the candle. Go straight from one exercise to the other without stopping. There are two versions of the folded candle. In the first:

1 Lower your body from the candle position by bending at the waist, keeping your legs straight until the toes touch the ground behind your head. You will feel some pull on the upper thigh muscles. Don't force your toes to touch the ground if you're uncomfortable. Eventually your toes will lightly touch the ground with ease.

2 Exhale as you fold over on your diaphragm. Stay in the position with your toes on the ground for the short time in which your lungs are empty. On inhalation, extend your legs again until you are once more in a vertical position.

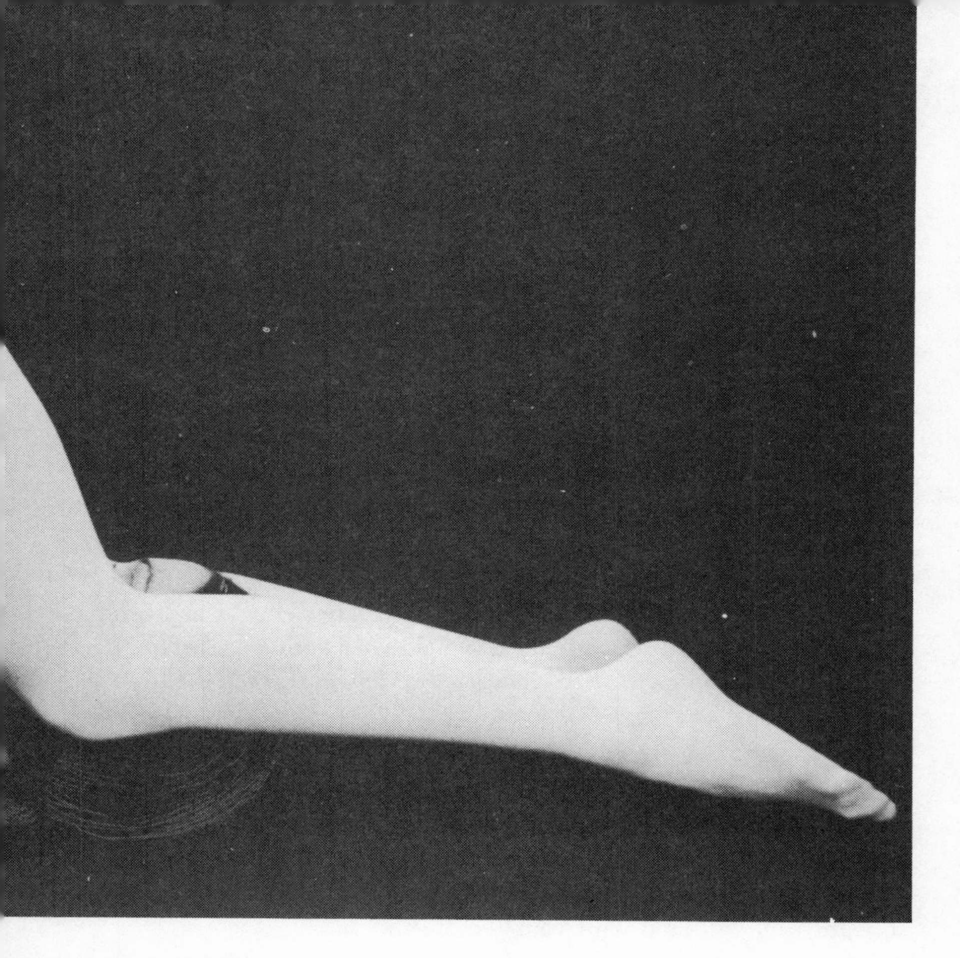

3 Repeat three times. Then slowly lower your body, extending your legs forward until you are again flat on your back. Rest.

Second version: As you slowly lower your feet, bend your legs. With your hands behind your head, grasp your feet. You are now bent into a ball. Then do steps 2 and 3, above.

No exercise can flex your vertebrae as these can. So far as old age is measured by a stiff spine, this exercise will keep you supple and young. It will also flatten the stomach muscles and strengthen the arms and legs.

Psycho-physical postures.

As if I were a rock. As if I were a cannonball about to explode. As if I were a piece of rubber. As if I were a jack knife—my legs are the blade. As if I were a crane—my feet raise and lower a weight.

HEAD STAND

Use a wall to lean against, if you have never done a head stand before. Place a folded pad or a pillow for a head rest on your mat, about twenty inches from the wall.

1 Kneel, facing the wall. Make a cup of your hands by interlacing the fingers. Place your cupped hands before you on your pillow, and the back of your head snugly in the cup so that your forehead seems to be touching the ground. Don't place your head *on* your hands; this will only crush your fingers.

2 From this kneeling position, straighten your legs until you are on your toes. Walk your feet towards your head. Your elbows and head form a perfect tripod which will easily hold your body in a firm vertical position, but spreading the elbows too wide will weaken the tripod base.

3 Get your feet up against the wall. If you need help getting your feet into the air, and a friend or instructor is not available, kick gently to help pull yourself up. You will feel the weight of your body on your head. Don't be frightened; you have safely done the shoulder stand. If you tilt backwards, your feet will find the wall. If you tilt forward, you will land with your feet on the mat.

4 On your head, establish the breathing cycle. If you can go through one, two or three cycles at first, this is excellent. You will shortly be able to extend the time you can stand on your head to three, five, or ten minutes.

Head standing strengthens the muscles of the neck, arms, stomach, and back, and relaxes the throat (later you can use this position to vocalize in). The brain benefits from the increased supply of blood. Yoga disciples claim that many unused areas of the brain will respond to this exercise, and that you will be rewarded with a better memory.

Psycho-physical postures.

As if I were a creature from a planet where people stand on their heads. As if I were a small animal—this is how I see things. As if I were a windmill—my legs are the blades. As if I were a monument in a capitol city. I am important.

HEAD TO KNEE

1 Lie down on your back. Stretch your arms behind your head on the floor with your thumbs interlocked.

2 Inhale and hold your breath.

3 Rise to a sitting position.

4 On exhalation, make an arc with your arms, thumbs still interlocked, until you can touch your toes.

5 Holding big toes with index fingers, slowly bring your head to your knees. Remain there for a few seconds.

6 Inhale slowly as you sit up again.

7 Now lower your trunk onto your back again.

8 Repeat exercise, with breathing cycle, three times.

Remember never to strain your muscles doing these exercises. Do not force your head down onto your knees. If you can't reach your toes, then hold onto your legs wherever your hands reach. In any case, though, try to keep the legs stiff. If you are in such poor physical condition that you can't do the sit-up, then start from a sitting position.

The exercise benefits your arms, legs, and your stomach muscles.

Psycho-physical postures.

As if I were stretching across a chasm to pull someone to safety. As if I were the moon slowly rising and setting. As if I were rowing a boat—am I exhausted or exhilarated? As if I were presenting a gift to someone. As if I were telling a secret to someone hidden under my legs.

THE STOMACH LIFT

1 Stand with your feet apart.

2 Bending forward from the waist, place your hands on your thighs.

3 Exhale slowly and deeply.

4 Now pull the abdominal muscles in and up, until you form a hollow under your rib cage.

5 Hold this position for as long a period as you comfortably can.

6 Then release muscles slowly. Inhale slowly.

7 Repeat cycle three times.

8 Stand up and relax.

9 Now repeat the exercise, but this time, on step 4, press down on your thighs alternately first with the left hand, then with the right. If you do this before a mirror, you will notice how your abdominal muscles will rotate as your hand pressure goes from left to right.

There is no need to emphasize the importance of strong abdominal and diaphragmatic muscles for the actor. All voice work needs deep diaphragmatic control. This exercise will help you to gain that control so that support of speech passages will come easily and powerfully.

Be sure, however, to do this exercise when the stomach is empty, either before breakfast, or four hours after a meal.

Psycho-physical postures.

As if I were preparing to avoid a sword thrust. As if I were looking at a painting. A race? A fight? As if I were disgusted with someone, I tell him off. As if I were poisoned—I must empty my stomach. As if I were protecting something within me.

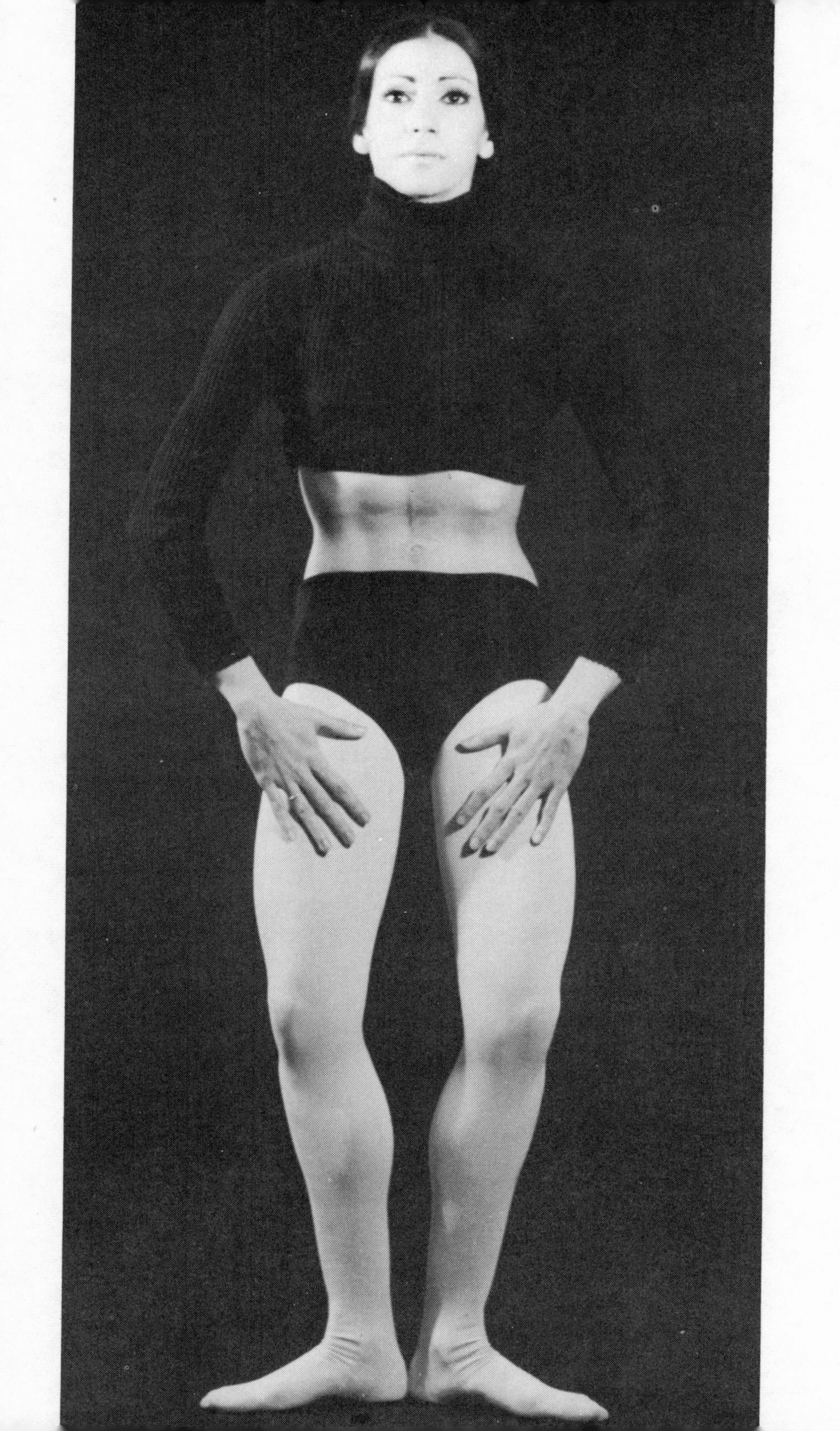

EYE EXERCISES

These exercises may be worked in the exercise series wherever you like.

1 Assume a comfortable lotus position, as described in the next two exercises. Make sure your back is straight, and remember not to move your head in subsequent steps; move only your eyes.

2 Move your eyes all the way to the left, then move them to the right and back. Do this three times.

3 Move your eyes up and down three times.

4 Move your eyes from lower right to upper left and back again three times.

5 Reverse the procedure; move your eyes from lower left to upper right and back again three times.

6 Now move your eyes around in a wide circle, clockwise, three times.

7 Reverse the procedure and move your eyes around in a circle counterclockwise three times.

8 Look at the tip of your nose, then look straight ahead; do this three times.

9 Cross your eyes, looking at the space between your eyes, looking at your upper nose. Now look away. Repeat twice.

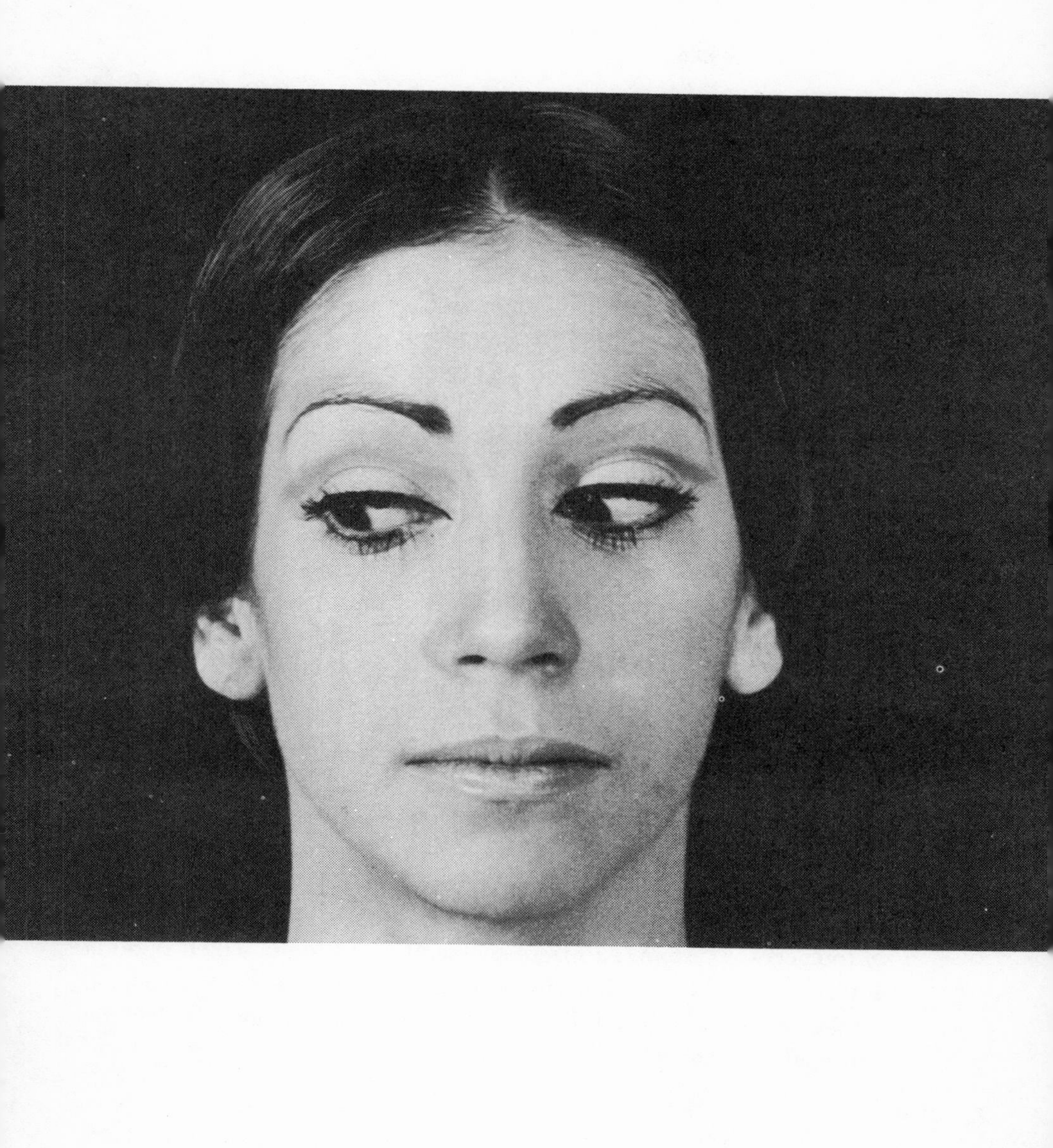

THE LOTUS

The lotus is the crowning point of these exercises. Once through the series you will find yourself willing to rest in the lotus and meditate. Your body will seem to float as if it were truly a lotus blossom on a still pool. The act of meditation is deep and personal, and meditation is necessary for an actor if he is to recharge his emotional, imaginative, and spiritual batteries. The end of a series of yoga positions is an excellent moment for meditation. Your body has been disciplined and is at rest; your mind can work, free of distractions.

What do you meditate about? Some possibilities for actors: (a) your past life; (b) a work of art before you or in your memory; (c) a photograph, a flower, a stone, a view, any object with which you can merge; (d) your role. At such moments insights that are intuitive, wordless, priceless, will flash before you. Meditate on them, put them away in your memory for further use. They must never be exposed by sharing them with others, for they will disintegrate on exposure.

1 Sit on a pillow to help you keep your knees on the ground. Take your left foot and place it on your right thigh so that the sole of your foot is visible. Now take your right foot and place it on your left leg.

In this position the circulation of the blood to the lower half of the body is slowed, because of the compression of the groin by the feet and legs, and as a result, circulation to the thoracic and cerebral areas is increased. Apart from forcing you to sit with a straight back, the important physical effects are ease in breathing and the renewing of the nervous system. This is, of course, the position in which Buddha is pictured, and the position for meditation. But there is no benefit in forcing yourself into a full lotus. If you cannot assume it, try the modified lotus, which follows.

THE MODIFIED LOTUS

Although there are books which instruct you to bounce your legs to stretch the ligaments and muscles so that you can do a full lotus, I do not advise this; there have been instances in which people have damaged themselves trying it. And it does not really matter if you use the full lotus; you can accomplish your purpose just as well with either of the two following versions of the modified lotus:

Version 1. Get on your hands and knees, with knees spread rather wide. Turn your feet parallel to one another and touching. Sit back onto your feet. You may use a cushion either under or over your feet.

Version 2. Kneel on a cushion with your knees forward, over the edge. Tip your knees down onto the floor.

The important concern here is to find a position comfortable for you that will not hurt your feet. Experiment to attain it.

3

Work on oneself: concentration and meditation

Every second you are on stage should be a moment of concentration. In a play you are concentrating on either an object, a sound, a fellow actor, an inner feeling. An undisciplined mind may wander: "How big is the house tonight?" "My voice is certainly sounding good!" "There my friends are, in the third row!" When an actor's mind wanders, he is failing in his craft.

Most people are really unaccustomed to concentrating; those who have learned to concentrate, either from their parents or from exceptional teachers, are truly lucky. They are productive and fulfilled. The ability to concentrate, both deeply and for any length of time, brings accomplishment and power.

A concentrated actor has the power to influence his audience. As Stanislavski said, "The concentration of the creating actor calls out the concentration of the spectator and in this manner forces him to enter into what is passing on the stage, exciting his attention, his imagination, his thinking processes and his emotion." Stanislavski added, "I perceived that creativeness is first of all the complete concentration of the entire nature of the actor."[1]

[1]*My Life in Art,* pp. 464–65.

The ability to concentrate is basic to a truthful approach to acting.

Another acting tool is meditation. Meditation is based on the ability to concentrate, but goes a step beyond concentration. Not everyone will be able to develop the ability to meditate deeply. Most, however, can achieve the ability to meditate to some degree, and can learn to apply meditation to the preparation of a role.

Consider Stanislavski's observation about the acting genius Tomasso Salvini in the role of Othello:

> On the day of a performance he was excited from the very morning, ate very little, and after dinner retired into solitude and received no guests. The performance would begin at eight o'clock, but Salvini was in the theatre at five, that is, three hours before the performance began. He went to his dressing room, removed his overcoat and began to wander about the stage. If any one approached him he would talk a little, then leave his companion, sink into thought, stand in silence, and then lock himself in his dressing room.[1]

Stanislavski proceeds with a fully detailed account of Salvini's method: He would move between his dressing room and the stage, approximately six times, and each time he appeared on stage he was, both internally and externally (in costume), more of Othello and less of Salvini. "He crept into the skin and body of Othello with the aid of some important preparatory toilet of his own artistic soul and body."[2]

To me this testimony strongly suggests that Salvini's preparation had elements of meditation in it.

A restless, tense body is a distraction to the mind; but a relaxed body, calmed by the relaxation exercises, helps the mind to embark on an adventure of concentration and meditation.

As Stanislavski said

> You must know how to focus your attention on the nearest object, without allowing it to be distracted and wander off far away. A constantly flickering light becomes unbearable to human eyes. And

[1] Ibid., p. 273.
[2] Ibid., p. 274.

the distracted attention of an actor is like a flickering light and is unbearable to the spectator. It does not gain the interest of the audience and merely creates a vacuum.

At first you must try to create for yourself the small circle of attention. It helps you, like a small spot of light, to give free play to your intimate feelings and makes you forget the auditorium. This state of mind is called, as we have agreed, public solitude. It is public because the public is with you, and it is solitude because you are separated from the public by the small circle of attention which you have created for yourself. In it you are able to shut yourself up in your solitude at a performance and in the presence of thousands of people.[1]

CONCENTRATION

A quiet place is essential. Usually the same place where you have been practicing your relaxation exercises will do very well.

Begin by doing your relaxation exercises in a comfortable sitting position on a pillow on the floor. Keep your back straight. In this last position, continue to breathe rhythmically, four or five times. Then:

1 Place a candle on a chair or table at about eye level.

2 Return to the sitting position, doing rhythmic breathing.

3 Look into the flame. Keep your eyes from wandering, but do not stare.

4 After a minute or two, close your eyes but still see the flame. Yes, see it with your eyes closed.

5 If the flame disappears, open your eyes and repeat steps 3 and 4 until you can successfully retain the image of the flame with your eyes closed.

Repeat the concentration exercise for a few days until you can, at will, close your eyes and see the flame. When you have succeeded in doing this, your concentration is good.

Now try the same exercise with another object, a picture, a flower,

[1] Stanislavski, *Art of the Stage,* p. 260.

a stone, or anything you feel would make a suitable object for concentration. It is important at this stage that you be involved only with the act of perception. Stay with the same object, such as the candle, until you can successfully close your eyes and retain the inner image. Do not mediate about its meaning; stay with its form only.

Mental activity will certainly interfere with your attempt to concentrate. Like Molly Bloom's, in *Ulysses,* your mind will skip and jump everywhere at first. But stick with the exercise. As you concentrate your attention on the object, remember that the exercise is a preparation for superior acting in two ways. The first is on the simple level of doing an action fully and honestly. You are beginning to develop the concentration you will need in order to create your circle of public solitude. The second way is that you are enlarging yourself, feeding the roots of your personality by absorbing the object observed. This activity leads to meditation. Meditation is an act of thought control, and involves the stimulation of associative ideas.

Meditation is not an act of withdrawal but is rather an act of unfolding, an opening or going forth. Meditation is not for the recluse, fleeing from life. Meditation is a running to life for the fulfillment of one's own reality. It gives an increased awareness of self, born of solitude. In concentration you observe and absorb an object into yourself. Through meditation you become the object, and in some cases see yourself from the object. Meditation leads to the insight that all things are sustained by the same energy. It helps you to identify with the world and in this way to rediscover yourself.

It is always easy to relate Stanislavski's theory of public solitude to meditation. Meditation is a preparatory discipline for public solitude.

MEDITATION

You have just finished your concentration exercise and can successfully see the candle flame, or the other object you have chosen, with your eyes closed.

1 Place the flame within your breast, where your heart is.

2 Meditation is a flow of thought related to one specific object. Remember you are seeking truth and beauty. You must use your own imagination while meditating. What follows is a vague illustration of what you might do for yourself.

Let the flame warm you and send rays of light from within you. Feel the light pulse within you. Feel the truth and beauty of the universe fill you. Speak to the inner light, purge yourself of those elements belonging to the living dead. Seek unity with the life force; feel yourself filling up a reservoir of love and truth.

As you meditate on other objects or pictures, try to channel your thoughts so that they are connected to the life force, which will feed your artistic roots. Meditation will provide the nourishment your spirit needs. Choose objects for meditation which will stimulate wholesome, beautiful thoughts, thoughts that will elevate rather than debase your nature. Negative thoughts are destructive to you. And if you find that an object presents a problem for concentration and meditation, then get rid of it and use another that works well for you.

MEDITATION ON A ROLE

Find a picture of someone that interests you. Place the picture before you and meditate on it. After you have looked at the picture for as long as you find necessary to get the feel of the person, meditate on the following questions of the given circumstances. Ask and answer the questions in the first person singular.

1 Who am I? Let your mind supply you with data gathered from the picture. Get as many small details as possible into your answer. Be creative.

2 What do I want? Create a need for the person. Make the need immediate and imperative.

3 Why do I want it? Create a real psychological basis for your need.

4 How am I going to get it? Make specific plans for fulfilling your need.

5 Where am I? What time is it?

After you have begun studying roles, you can return to this exercise and use it for preparation. Meditate on the given circumstances of the character you are to play. A good time for this exercise is the last thing at night before going to bed; your unconscious mind will continue work on the role while you sleep. Or do the exercise first thing in the morning.

4

The total actor and his voice: voice production

And to one of our home-grown tragedians, who had lost his voice by drinking, and who asked Salvini what was necessary in order to become a tragedian, Salvini answered, "You need only three things: voice, voice, and more voice!" Salvini said this not only to hoarse tragedians, but he repeated it at every opportunity, for . . . he attached a tremendous importance to the voice in tragic roles.

CONSTANTIN STANISLAVSKI[1]

An actor with a poor voice is like a pianist with a poor piano. The voice is one of your most important assets. Walter Kerr, in a column in the Sunday *New York Times,* amusingly described the stopping dead of a Broadway show when the electronic amplification system broke down. The so-called professional actors of the company, each with a dead microphone hidden in his clothing, lacked proper projection technique to proceed without their artificial aids! The hidden dangers of using the microphone should also be understood. In another Broadway playhouse, for example, a young star who was using a mi-

[1] *My Life in Art,* p. 276.

crophone to enhance her mediocre voice, forgot to click it off when she visited the ladies' room off-stage. She treated the entire theater to an amplified version of the accompanying sound effects.

It is important that you be able to escape the electronic shackles which chain American actors today. You may argue, "Why should I develop my voice when an electronic sound chamber can beef it up with fuller tones and project it against the back wall?" What a temptation this solid state gadgetry presents! And besides, in movies and in television, where much of your work will be done (and for more money than you will ever receive in legitimate theater!), the sound man with his boom mike will catch your faintest sigh and magnify it enormously. Yet you must escape the electronic temptation if America is to develop a theater where live actors perform before live audiences. It is, let it be reiterated, mainly to this live actor-audience relationship that this book is directed.

There was a time not too long ago when actors knew that they wouldn't be hired unless their voices projected to the last balcony. There was probably an excess, then, of ranting and bellowing on stage. With the advent of realism, though, and the "slice of life" school, an attempt in the theater was made to reproduce intimate voices speaking in conversational tones. And at least in America, it was then thought that Stanislavski sanctioned the neglect of the voice. Mumbling and the Method were soon melded.

Jerzy Grotowski, in *Towards a Poor Theatre,* presents a solution to the problem.[1] Grotowski considers vocal training most important, and, in perfect agreement with Lewis, has joined vocal with acting training. It is indeed time that the acting teachers in the country involved themselves with voice work. If, as is certainly the case, the voice is vital and cannot be ignored, then let us remove the mystery of vocal work and stop sending the acting students off to the Siberia of the voice class, where all acting ceases.

This chapter is accordingly devoted to an attempt to combine voice work and acting training. The attempt may falter at times; certain exercises, either acting or vocal, are by nature so elementary that

[1] See Jerzy Grotowski, *Towards a Poor Theatre* (New York: Simon and Schuster, 1969), Passim.

one kind excludes the other. But once past the basics, we can make a serious effort to combine acting technique and vocal training.

Do the vocal exercises *after* your relaxation exercises. This will ensure you a completely relaxed body with which to work.

RELAXATION EXERCISE: *The Rag Doll*

1 Unfettered by tight clothing and belts, with your shoes removed, stand with your legs apart, but not too far, so that you have a good sense of balance.

2 Think of a puppet which has had its strings cut. It collapses. In the same way drop your body from the waist so that it folds over, your head hangs limp, and your arms dangle to the ground.

3 If you are doing the exercise in class, the instructor can test your relaxation by lifting and then dropping your arm. If it falls and swings like a pendulum, you are truly relaxed. If it "assists" the instructor by shooting up as he lifts it, or if it remains in the lifted position without dropping, you are tense. Another sign of tension is a stiff neck, which thrusts the head forward. Your head should hang like a ball at the end of the spinal column.

4 If you are doing the exercise in class, the instructor should have you try dropping over several times, to be sure no one is cheating by slowly lowering his body into position. The body must *fall* from the waist, collapsing toward the ground.

5 From the collapsed position, now raise the torso slowly, remembering that the arms and head are still not energized. When you are standing upright, the arms will fall naturally to the sides and the head will be hanging forward on the chest, a dead weight unsupported by any muscle. The instructor can check for relaxation as in step 3.

6 Now rotate the head in as wide a circle as possible. The head should revolve like a ball on a string. Do not raise the shoulders. Be sure the head passes over the right shoulder, the back, the left shoulder, and comes back to a forward position on the chest.

7 Reverse the headroll, doing it in the opposite direction.

8 Repeat steps 6 and 7 several times.

9 If you have come this far successfully, your neck muscles, your face muscles, and your vocal cords are relaxed. You are now ready to try sounding a relaxed vocal instrument.

10 Slowly raise the head, and while doing so, simulate a yawn—or really yawn—and at the same time sound an "ah." Open your mouth as wide as possible. Repeat several times, taking a deep breath with the diaphragm before beginning each "ah." Letting your breath out slowly, sustain each "ah" for as long as you can. You have just heard the most relaxed sound you can make; repeat it so that you can remember what it feels like to make it. If you have been working correctly, you have also heard your voice at its optimum pitch level, the pitch at which you should habitually speak. Try to carry this resonant tone into your everyday speech.

11 After repeating the "ah" sound six to ten times, add an "mmmmmm" to its end. Slowly close the mouth as you form the "m" until your lips are quite closed. Push with your diaphragm so that a good air flow is passing over your vocal cords. If you can feel your lips vibrate and tingle, that is a good sign of facial, as well as tonal relaxation. Taking a deep diaphragmatic breath and slowly closing the mouth to form the "m," repeat "ah . . . . mmmmmmmmm" six times.

VOCALIZING WITH CONTROLLED DEEP BREATHING *(1)*

1 Lie flat on your back.

2 Breathe rhythmically.

3 Initiate a yawn. Really try to yawn. If you can't do it, yawn artificially.

4 While yawning, start the vocal chords vibrating with a sustained "ahhhhhh" sound, and hold until you are out of breath. Do not push the voice up or down. Your tone should be slightly lower than your speaking voice.

5 Repeat five times.

6 Repeat steps 1–4, but close your mouth until the lips meet, adding to the "ahhhhh" sound an "mmmmmmmm." If you do this properly, you will feel a tickling or vibrating sensation in your lips.

VOCALIZING WITH CONTROLLED DEEP BREATHING *(2)*

Repeat steps 2–6 of the above exercise while walking around the room. First use "ahhhhhhh" five times; then add the "mmmmmmm" sound for an additional five times. Vary the speed of your walk from very slow to moderate to fast according to the answers to the questions: Who are you? Why are you walking? Where are you going? What do you want?

In the preceding exercises you have been asked to breathe rhythmically. The breathing is not only diaphragmatic, but thoracic, or from the chest, as well. Do not, however, worry about exactly how to breathe. We all breathe differently because of varying natural attributes.

Pitch placement

Many of you do not use your optimum pitch in speaking; you do not place your voice where it can work best. This in itself will prevent you from being able to project efficiently. Since speech is habitual, many of you get your voices stuck at the wrong pitch level. If this is true for you, your habit must be broken. Caution! Go slowly. A new pitch placement can't be achieved in a day or a week. It will take several months. It has taken your lifetime to establish it where it is.

A simple way to check your optimum pitch level is to use a piano. Start playing notes at a high level which you can reach comfortably with your voice and descend, following the piano, vocally. When you reach the lowest note that you can sound without hurting or losing your voice, then come back up three notes. That last note should be the place of your optimum pitch level. This is the note from which your voice should work as a level of speech. Your voice, of course, will rise and fall from that level.

Approximately nine out of ten people have habitual pitch ranges that are too highly placed. This high placement is the result of tension and robs you of a full-toned and relaxed voice. It also causes vocal fatigue and hoarseness.

THE ROCKET EXERCISE

This exercise is a vocal calisthenic and *must be practiced with caution.* Hoarseness or vocal fatigue will follow if you overdo it at the beginning. If you feel signs of soreness, stop. Practice it for five minutes at first, and gradually increase to ten.

Practicing this exercise will produce noise, so you should find an appropriate place to work and disregard kibitzers. You will have to work, and it will take two months before noticeable results from this exercise appear; but the results, if you do work, will impress you.

mean, main, mine, moan, moon

1 Take a deep diaphragmatic inhalation, release it, inhale again, release, inhale and

2 Without bending back the head, reach for the highest note you can hit *comfortably.*[1] Take the first word, *mean,* and without holding the initial consonant, sliding right into the vowel sound, slide downward at a moderate to fast speed until you reach the lowest note you can hit comfortably where you

3 Press on the final consonant [n] until you are out of breath. Stress the consonant. The final press is most important.

4 Take a deep inhalation and go right into the next word, *main.* Remember that the initial consonant is not to be held; go right into the vowel sound, descend quickly, and stress the final [n].

5 Do the same with *mine, moan,* and *moon.* Repeat from the beginning until you have exercised for the desired amount of time.

[1] If this high note falls within your falsetto range, you will find in gliding downward that you must ride over a vocal range, the nodule on which yodelers work when they yodel. Do not let this phenomenon disturb you.

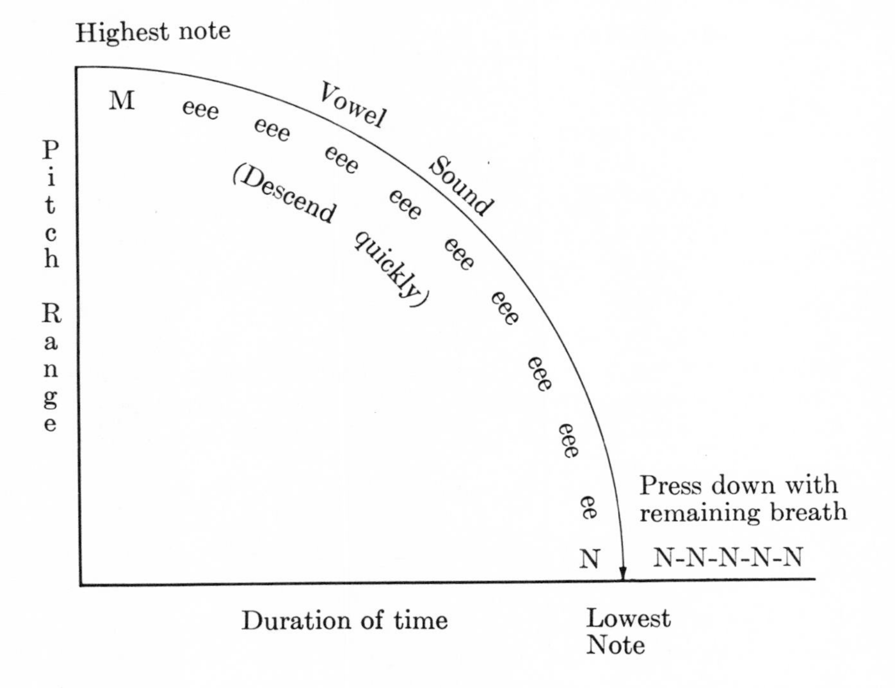

This exercise is designed literally to stretch the vocal cords. If you do not expect results within days or weeks and do not overwork, you will find the results striking.

Controlling the voice quality

You have now explored your vocal range. You should have a good idea where to find your optimal pitch level. Before we analyze different voice placements that can help you in building a character, it is important to discuss your voice in terms of tone or quality.

By this time you are aware that your voice is different from that of other actors; you have your own peculiar vocal signature. Your voice is so distinctive that it can produce a print that will identify you as accurately as a fingerprint. Now, is there anything about this unique voice of yours that needs attention? Some young actors revel in distinctive hoarse voices which, they feel, will get them attention. Remember Lionel Stander in the brilliant film of the thirties, *The Scoundrel?* But chronic hoarseness may mean growths on the vocal chords, and may even, especially if you are a smoker, be an early warning sign of cancer. Similarly, a nasal tone may mean you have an infection of the tonsils, or of the sinuses, or polypi or other nasal growth, or allergic irritations. If you have such symptoms, see a nose and throat specialist. If you are suffering from nasality, and if a specialist has ruled out the above medical causes, chances are you are suffering from acute tension. If your jaw muscle is too tight it will keep the mouth closed too much, and this will result in your voice being forced into the nasal cavities. The relaxation exercises should help you to relax, and the voice exercises in this chapter, particularly the yawning exercise, should relieve the condition.

Finally, do not ignore any prolonged sore throat. Actors tend to believe that a sore throat can result from speaking too much. The fact is, a sore throat from speaking is a sure sign of incorrect speech. If you have learned to use your voice in a relaxed way and in a relaxed body, you can talk all day and not get a sore throat.

The following exercises include work on improvisations, which actually will not be discussed until the chapters on acting. Because of the nature of this book, which includes acting work with voice work, and voice work with acting work, it is impossible to present the exposition in a sequence which is totally self-explanatory. At this point you should either skip ahead to read the material on improvisation (Chapter Eight), or you should postpone the following vocal exercises until after you have done the work on improvisation.

The nasal voice in character work

Let us assume that you are free of bad habits but want to achieve nasality for the sake of a characterization. How can you get a nasal voice if you don't naturally have one?

If you are playing a tense, worried, introspective character, this type of voice, well projected and clearly articulated, can help you to build that character. Or if the character you were trying to create is slow, or stupid, a nasal voice might be useful because the inability to use the velum, or soft palate, is sometimes associated with a sluggish mentality. A sickly person with a cold in the head is a common character in the theater, too. Being able to execute a nasal voice quickly, easily, and convincingly will help solve all these problems.

You can make your voice nasal simply by shutting your jaw and talking through a much smaller mouth opening than usual. You will have to experiment to find the degree of tightness you need.

Another method is to stop the air flow at the back of the throat by raising the tongue and lowering the velum. You can achieve this effect automatically by making the sound "nnnggg." Practice maintaining the effect.

On the other hand, it will be useful if you can learn to control the velum. The velum is that part of your upper mouth known as the soft palate. Place the tip of the tongue where the upper teeth and gums meet. Press as hard as you can and move the tongue back in a curling action. Your tongue will pass over a bump, the gum ridge, then over the hard palate which arches up, and then will reach the soft palate. Attached to the velum is a little piece of flesh that hangs downward, the uvula. You can see the uvula if you use a mirror.

The uvula and velum are a valve that can either open or shut off both the mouth and the nasal passages. When you blow up a balloon, the uvula and velum close off the nasal passages, so that the air rising from your lungs won't escape through your nose. When you "blow" your nose, on the other hand, the valve closes the entrance to your mouth and opens the entrance to your nose. Therefore you can make your voice nasal by pulling down or lowering the velum and keeping it down.

You will have to practice until you can recognize the sensations which accompany a closed velum. Then you will have to practice the technique of speaking while keeping it closed. If you can achieve success here, however, you will be rewarded with a versatile vocal instrument.

NASALITY EXERCISES *(1–4)*

1 Check Chapter Eight to make sure that you make all the proper preparations for the following emotional improvisation.

2 Make up an improvisation based on an emotional problem in which your characterization depends on your speaking with a nasal voice.

3 Make up an improvisation using a bird image for your character. Be a parrot, speaking with a nasal voice. Or be a rooster, a hen, or a pigeon. Do not be too faithful in your image; be selective in choosing physical traits. Keep your nasal voice throughout. Never laugh at the improvisational efforts of others.

4 Find a song or a poem that you especially like. Act it out with a nasal voice. Remember that singing a song is, or should be, acting it.

The frontal voice in character work

When your uvula is in an up position, you are speaking with a frontal voice. To get your uvula into an up position, pretend to blow air into a balloon. You will have to practice speaking while you maintain the uvula in an up position. You will recognize that you are speaking from the front of your mouth. Get the feeling that you are speaking from your front teeth.

The frontal voice might be used by a nosy person, a busybody, a bully, a dominating shrew. Here is where your observation of other people must be put to work; be sensitive to the voices that belong characteristically to different types which you might play. Such observations will be very useful to you in your character work. You will undoubtedly notice that many city dwellers have developed frontal voices. They use their voices like bumpers with which they seem literally to force their ways through dense population! Be careful not to use this voice as a trick. It must grow out of a need arising from the given circumstances.

FRONTAL VOICE EXERCISES *(1–3)*

1 Make up an improvisation based on an emotional problem in which your characterization depends on your speaking with a frontal voice.

2 Make up an improvisation based on an animal. If you choose a dog, project a barking voice. Pick an aggressive animal. Don't be too literal. Be selective in choosing physical traits. Keep vocal and physical traits throughout the entire improvisation.

3 Find a song or a poem that you like. Sing or recite it with a frontal voice. Make sure that you *act* the song as well as the poem.

The chest voice in character work

The fastest and easiest way to establish your chest voice is to do the rocket exercise (Chapter Four). Keep your hand on your chest as you do the exercise, and when you come to the lower part of the scale, you will feel the vibrations in your chest. Here is your chest voice.

Naturally, you can't speak only with your chest voice any more than you can speak only with your head voice, but when you use either one with particular emphasis, the other either does not vibrate, or does not vibrate as fully as usual. *Never* try to force the voice lower for a bigger sound. This kind of forcing can injure the vocal chords. A chest voice can be used when the voice is eased into it. And when you have got your chest voice low, remember to keep it, like Cordelia's, soft and gentle.

CHEST VOICE EXERCISES *(1–4)*

1 Create an improvisation in which two of you are competing barkers at a sideshow. Each of you wants to attract customers to enter his show. Let the other class members react honestly, as customers, to your competition. Fill in the given circumstances before you begin.

Let the competition be keen, and keep your voices placed in the chest. Do not let the excitement or tension drive the voice pitch up.

2 Make up an improvisation based on a gorilla or several gorillas. Move like a gorilla, keeping the voice in the gorilla's chest.

3 Use other animals. Again, don't be too literal. Be very selective in choosing physical traits. Be consistent throughout the improvisation in physical and vocal characteristics.

4 Find a song or a poem that you like. Act it out with a chest voice.

The head voice in character work

This voice is created by using the upper register, or falsetto. Place the voice above the larynx into the head. The uvula should be in an up position, to avoid nasality. Don't let the head voice slip into the mouth. Make the sound of a cat mewing, and you have the right sound. Support the sound with a full column of air from the abdomen. Using this voice is an excellent exercise for expanding your vocal range.

HEAD VOICE EXERCISES *(1–4)*

1 Let a man play a woman whose dinner is overcooked. Her husband comes home too late. Let a woman play the man. Avoid clowning and clichés. Remember that in many countries men play women and women play men in all seriousness.

2 Make up an improvisation based on a snake. Move with the essence of a snake, keeping your voice in your head as you speak.

3 Use other animal images for a head voice. Remember, *no* laughter at the improvisations of others.

4 Find a song or a poem that you like. Act it out with a head voice.

VOICE VARIETY EXERCISE

1 Find fairy tales or fables suitable for reading aloud. Using appropriate voices for the different parts, get involved in the story. For example, in "The Three Billy Goats Gruff," there are three goats—one very young (small voice), one a little bigger (larger voice), and the third quite big (larger voice, still)—all of whom wish to cross the bridge guarded by a very belligerent troll (big voice, but not bigger than that of the biggest goat). For the little goat you might use a head voice; for the middle goat, a nasal voice or frontal voice; and for the biggest goat, a chest voice, full volume. For the troll you might use a frontal voice full volume or a chest voice less than full volume.

"Little Red Riding Hood," "The Three Little Pigs," and many stories from *Aesop's Fables* are excellent for this exercise.

5

The total actor and his voice: diction

What recourse have you in the theatre when the actors pronounce the text in a fashion comparable to your badly printed book, when they drop out whole letters, words, phrases which are often of cardinal importance to the basic structure of the play? You cannot bring back the spoken word, the play plunges forward toward its denouement, leaving you no time to stop and puzzle out what you do not understand. Poor speech creates one misunderstanding after another. It clutters up, befogs, or even conceals the thought, the essence, and even the very plot of the play. The audience will, in the beginning, strain their ears, attention, minds, so as not to miss anything that is going on on the stage; if they cannot follow they begin to fidget, fuss, whisper to each other and finally to cough. . . . One of the means of guarding against such an eventuality is the use of clear, beautiful, vivid speech.

CONSTANTIN STANISLAVSKI[1]

The lip and tongue exercises in this chapter are excerpted from my book, *The Voice as an Instrument*. This book can be consulted for an expanded treatment of vocal development for the performer.

[1] *Building a Character*, p. 83.

An actor cannot consider himself prepared to get on stage if he speaks habitually with a decided regionalism. You cannot drawl a Hamlet, nor can you play a Shavian hero with a Bronx accent.

Accents must, of course, be mastered for certain characterizations,[1] but for the most part American actors must use general American speech, which is spoken throughout America, excluding the South and the Northeast. Speech correction may require careful and persistent practice, but there is no substitute for it:

> Let us say that the pupil could not pronounce the sounds S, KH, and SHTH. Then the teacher would sit down in front of him, open the mouth as wide as possible, and say to the pupil: "Look in my mouth. You see what my tongue is doing; it lies on the roots of my upper teeth. Do the same. Say it. Repeat it ten times. Open your mouth wider, and let me look into it to see if you are doing it correctly."
>
> I have become convinced, from my own experience, that after a week or two of concentration and practice, it is possible to correct the wrongly placed consonants, and to know what to do in order to pronounce them rightly. I passed through the same course and I affirm that the results are wonderful.[2]

Good speech must begin with the speaker's ability to *hear* himself and his own speech defects. You must become a dynamic rather than a passive listener, analyzing as you hear. Listening assumes a major role in speech work. If you wish to correct any decided regionalism that would prove to be an impediment to your speech as an actor, consult my speech book, *The Voice As An Instrument.* There you will find an explanation of the international phonetic alphabet with accurate lip and tongue placement for speaking general American.

But any changes must be made carefully to avoid phoniness. Shaw pointed out this trap in his preface to *Pygmalion:*

> But the thing has to be done scientifically, or the last state of the aspirant may be worse than the first. An honest and natural slum

[1] See John Samuel Keynon and Thomas Albert Knott, *A Pronouncing Dictionary of American English* (Springfield Mass.: G. C. Merriam Company, 1944).

[2] Stanislavski, *My Life in Art,* p. 84.

dialect is more tolerable than the attempt of a phonetically untaught person to imitate the vulgar dialect of the golf club. . . .[1]

Remember not to assume that because you have been speaking English since you were a child, you have mastered its sounds. Approach your language freshly, as if it were a foreign tongue, for when you attempt to produce a General American sound that is not in your habitual repertory of sounds, you will feel that you *are* speaking a foreign tongue. It will not be easy to alter old speech patterns. If you have always, for instance, said *jist* for *just* you will have to learn to hear yourself saying *jist* before you can begin to find out how to alter the sound. The following steps are involved in a change in articulation.

1. Learn how to relax.

2. Exercise your lips and tongue to the point where they can respond easily to instruction as to their proper placement.

3. Learn to associate sound and its written symbols with the placement of tongue and lips necessary to produce it. You must drill as any foreign-language student does in mastering a foreign tongue.

Step 1 has been treated in Chapter Two. The present chapter will undertake to teach step 2.

Remember that the following exercises are comparable to the fingering exercises the pianist or organist must perform on his instrument to master the keyboard. They must be done daily or the muscles will not be trained. Unless the lips and tongue, your articulators, really move when you speak, clear, precise speech is impossible. Since you will be using a mirror to watch your lips and tongue at work, it is important at first to use speech materials that will not distract you.

These exercises aim to help you learn how to move your lips in order to overcome slurring, mumbling, and speaking too fast. Exaggerate lip movement. Use your mirror to watch lip and tongue movement. *Warning: Relax as you work.* Do not contort your face or neck.

The following exercise is made up of nonsense syllables. This frees you from any responsibility to the text.

[1] G. B. Shaw, *Selected Plays* (New York, 1948), I, 194–95.

EXERCISE FOR THE LIPS

1 Exaggerate to extreme as you repeat twenty times:

eeeeeeeeeee-aahhhhhhhhh-oooooooooo

(Lips drawn back—"eeee"; mouth opened wide—"ahhhh"; lips protruding and almost closed—"ooooo.")

2 First pronounce the consonant with closed or nearly closed lips, and then reproduce the "ahhhh" sound of step 1 with a fully opened and relaxed mouth in the following combinations (repeat each line four times):

fah, fah, fah, fah, vah, vah, vah, vah
pah, pah, pah, pah, bah, bah, bah, bah
mah, mah, mah, mah, nah, nah, nah, nah

3 Moving the lips from a closed position to an exaggerated smile position and remembering to move nothing but the lips, repeat rapidly four times each:

me-me-me-me
pree-pree-pree-pree
wee-wee-wee-wee

4 Whisper the following words three times each to exercise lazy lips:

ontological, anachronistically, ecumenical, superfluity, impracticable, lexicographer, irremediable, posthumously, impossibility, impenetrable, schizophrenic, voluptuousness, existentialism, ignominiously, irrevocable, philosophical, polysyllabic, disingenuousness, incalculable, preposterous, antidisestablishmentarianism, supercalifragilisticexpialidocious.

(As the mouth receives very small vibrations from the vocal cords when you whisper, your lips must work exaggeratedly. Remember, whispering is a strain on vocal cords. If you feel any hoarseness, stop.

When you have a sore throat, do not resort to whispering, for it is more taxing than normal speech.)

5 The following verses are from the works of Edward Lear and Lewis Carroll, both masters of the nonsense rhyme. Since the verses are nonsensical, you are free of the necessity to act or to interpret the text. For the moment, as you read them, concentrate on lip action or tongue action alone. Do not, however, think of these exercises as a deviation from your work towards being a total actor. Remember the necessity to learn the fingering of an instrument before you can go on to interpretation. Your control of clear speech will help you to convey your language to your audience.

MR. AND MRS. SPIKKY SPARROW

On a little piece of wood,
Mr. Spikky Sparrow stood;
Mrs. Sparrow sat close by,
A-making of an insect pie,
For her little children five,
In the nest and all alive,

Singing with a cheerful smile
To amuse them all the while,
    Twikky wikky wikky wee,
    Wikky bikky twikky tee,
    Spikky bikky bee!

Mrs. Spikky Sparrow said,
'Spikky, Darling! in my head
Many thoughts of trouble come,
Like to flies upon a plum!
All last night, among the trees,
I heard you cough, I heard you sneeze;
And, thought I, it's come to that
Because he does not wear a hat!

Chippy wippy sikky tee!
Bikky wikky tikky mee!
Spikky chippy wee!

'Not that you are growing old,
But the nights are growing cold.
No one stays out all night long
Without a hat: I'm sure it's wrong!'
Mr. Spikky said, 'How kind,
Dear! you are, to speak your mind!
All your life I wish you luck!
You are! you are a lovely duck!
Witchy witchy witchy wee!
Twitchy witchy witchy bee!
Tikky tikky tee!

'I was also sad, and thinking,
When one day I saw you winking,
And I heard you sniffle-snuffle,
And I saw your feathers ruffle;
To myself I sadly said,
She's neuralgia in her head!
That dear head has nothing on it!
Ought she not to wear a bonnet?
Witchy kitchy kitchy wee?
Spikky wikky mikky bee?
Chippy wippy chee?'

EDWARD LEAR

JABBERWOCKY

'Twas brillig, and the slithy toves
Did gyre and gimble in the wabe:
All mimsy were the borogroves,
And the mome raths outgrabe.

'Beware the Jabberwock, my son!
The jaws that bite, the claws that catch!
Beware the Jubjub bird, and shun
The frumious Bandersnatch!'

He took his vorpal sword in hand:
Long time the manxome foe he sought—
So rested he by the Tumtum tree,
And stood awhile in thought.

And, as in uffish thought he stood,
The Jabberwock, with eyes of flame,
Came whiffling through the tulgey wood,
And burbled as it came!

One, two! One, two! And through and through
The vorpal blade went snicker-snack!
He left it dead, and with its head
He went galumphing back.

'And hast thou slain the Jabberwock?
Come to my arms, my beamish boy!
O frabjous day! Callooh! Callay!'
He chortled in his joy.

'Twas brillig, and the slithy toves
Did gyre and gimble in the wabe:
All mimsy were the borogroves,
And the mome raths outgrabe.

LEWIS CARROLL

THE COURTSHIP OF THE YONGHY-BONGHY-BÓ

On the Coast of Coromandel
Where the early pumpkins blow,
In the middle of the woods
Lived the Yonghy-Bonghy-Bó.

Two old chairs, and half a candle,—
One old jug without a handle;—
These were all his worldly goods:

In the middle of the woods,
These were all the worldly goods,
Of the Yonghy-Bonghy-Bó,
Of the Yonghy-Bonghy-Bó.

Once, among the Bong-trees walking
Where the early pumpkins blow,
To a little heap of stones
Came the Yonghy-Bonghy-Bó.
There he heard a Lady talking,
To some milk-white Hens of Dorking,—
"'Tis the Lady Jingly Jones!
On that little heap of stones
Sits the Lady Jingly Jones!'
Said the Yonghy-Bonghy-Bó,
Said the Yonghy-Bonghy-Bó.

EDWARD LEAR

Using your mirror, you are about to encounter a shy creature, a muscle not used in the light of day, a creature that has almost certainly, until this moment, led an independent life. It is not accustomed to being dominated, but is a coward and will respond quickly to firm discipline. And without a disciplined tongue that is active and responsive in its movement, clearness of speech is impossible. You want energetic lip and tongue movement, however, only if it results in a clear but not overarticulated speech. Now begin to tame that independent creature, remembering that it is a coward and that you must master it to rule over your house of speech.

EXERCISE FOR THE TONGUE *(1)*

1 Open your mouth as wide as possible.

2 Gather and *point* your tongue in the *center* of your mouth open-

ing. (The tongue at first will have a tendency to flatten. Make sure it is not flat, but rounded and pointed; think of gathering or pulling it together.)

3 With the *tip* of the tongue and the tip only, touch the *outside* of your upper lip, the outside of your lower lip, then the left and right sides of the mouth.

4 Repeat for one minute. Keep your mouth open. If it starts to close, hold it open with your hand. If you are one of the rare people who cannot do this exercise because your tongue is literally tied to the bottom of your mouth, perhaps your frenum should be cut to allow the tongue to move more freely. Ask your speech instructor to recommend a good speech clinic where you can be seen by a doctor. Difficulty with consonant sounds in which the tongue has to reach the roof of the mouth is also sometimes due to a frenum that should be cut.

EXERCISE FOR THE TONGUE (2)

1 Looking into the mirror, stretch your tongue until it can almost touch the tip of your nose. One person in a thousand can touch the nose, so don't worry if you don't succeed. *Try* to touch the tip of your nose.

2 Pull the tongue back into the mouth.

3 Again extend the tongue, this time as far down the chin as possible.

4 Repeat steps 1 through 3 as fast as you can until you grow tired, but do them for at least a minute. Have a handkerchief ready to wipe away any excess moisture when you have finished.

EXERCISE FOR THE TONGUE (3)

This is an isometric exercise. Remember Demosthenes, who worked his tongue against pebbles? You will work yours against the roof of your mouth.

1 Keeping your mouth closed, press the tip of your tongue against the roof of your mouth.

2 Start to curl the tongue *slowly,* over the roof of the mouth, pressing up all the time as hard as possible. Once you hit the soft palate, go back to where the teeth meet the gums.

3 Repeat at first for a minute, increasing the time gradually to two minutes. If you are working correctly, you will feel a burning sensation in your tongue.

EXERCISE FOR THE TONGUE *(4)*

1 Open your mouth as wide as possible. Form a large circle with your lips. Now with the tip of your tongue, ride around the rim of the mouth in one direction for one minute, slowly at first, and then faster.

2 Reverse the sweep of your tongue, riding with the tip around your mouth in the opposite direction for one minute, slowly and then faster.

A good variation on following your tongue in the mirror is to close your eyes and follow the movement in your mind. You might try this method on the following exercise, in which the mouth is not open as wide as in the preceding exercises.

VOCALIZATION

1 Repeat each line rapidly four times:

tee-lee tee-lee tee-lee tee-lee
lee-ree lee-ree lee-ree lee-ree
tah-tay-tee-tah tah-tay-tee-tah tah-tay-tee-tah
    tah-tay-tee-tah
lah-lay-lee-lah lah-lay-lee-lah lah-lay-lee-lah
    lah-lay-lee-lah

Notice how your tongue has to move. Go slowly at first, then increase the tempo until you speak the sounds trippingly on the tongue.

2 Repeat each line rapidly four times:

tah tah tah tah
dah dah dah dah
lah lah lah lah
sah sah sah sah
zah zah zah zah

3 Read in an exaggerated articulation, moving the jaw as if you were chewing an apple, and speaking loudly and slowly:

a. The Seven young Parrots had not gone far, when they saw a tree with a single Cherry on it, which the oldest Parrot picked instantly, but the other six, being extremely hungry, tried to get it also. On which all the Seven began to fight, and they scuffled,

and huffled,
and ruffled,
and shuffled,
and puffled,
and muffled,
and buffled,
and duffled,
and fluffled,
and guffled,
and bruffled, and

screamed, and shrieked, and squealed, and squeaked, and clawed, and snapped, and bit, and bumped, and thumped, and dumped, and flumped each other, till they were all torn into little bits. . . . One said this, and another said that, and while they were all quarrelling the Frog hopped away. And when they saw that he was gone, they began to chatter-clatter,

blatter-platter,
patter-blatter,
matter-clatter,
flatter-quatter; more violently

than ever. . . . So after a time [they] said to each other, 'Beyond all doubt this beast must be a Plum-pudding Flea!' On which they incautiously began to sing aloud,

'Plum-pudding Flea,
Plum-pudding Flea,
Wherever you be,
O come to our tree,
And listen, O listen, O listen to me!'

EDWARD LEAR

THE HISTORY OF THE SEVEN FAMILIES
OF THE LAKE PIPPLE-POPPLE

b. Polly, Dolly, Kate and Molly,
All are filled with pride and folly.
Polly tattles, Dolly wriggles,
Katy rattles, Molly giggles;
Whoe'er knew such constant rattling,
Wriggling, giggling, noise and tattling.

MOTHER GOOSE

4 Say each tongue twister three times as rapidly as possible:

a. She makes a proper cup of coffee in a copper coffee pot.
b. A box of biscuits, a box of mixed biscuits, and a biscuit mixer.
c. She sells seashells by the seashore.
d. Sinful Caesar sipped his snifter.
e. Unique New York.
f. Rubber buggy bumpers.
g. Watch the whacky wristwatch.
h. The big black bug bled black blood.
i. Lemon liniment.
j. Strange strategic statistics.
k. Six thick thistle sticks.
l. Purple pickle percolator.

CHANTING EXERCISE

While reading the following passage from Plato, follow these instructions:

1 Hold or stress every consonant that can be held for four seconds. (Remember that plosives, by their very explosive nature, cannot be held, so pronounce but do not hold [p], [b], [t], [d], [k], [g], and the plosive-fricative combinations [*j* as in *judge* and *ch* as in *church*]; the easiest way is to tap four fingers successively and rhythmically on a table, or to hold up your hand and fold the fingers down successively. Remember also to sound the consonants purely, without anticipating the vowels which follow. Say "mmmmmmm" rather than "meeeeee" or "maaaaaa", and "rrrrrrr" rather than "reeeeeee."

2 Hold or stress all vowel sounds which are normally sounded for two seconds, or half as long as consonants. Tap or fold fingers, maintaining a regular rhythm.

3 All words must be chanted exactly as pronounced. This is important, and sometimes difficult. The consonants have been underlined with four lines and the vowels with two. Silent, unpronounced letters have been left unmarked, and plosive and plosive-fricative sounds which cannot be held have been marked with an x.

4 Before beginning the passage, chant sample words:

bath is of
bathe us off

PHAEDO

The body is a source of endless trouble to us by reason of the mere requirement of food; and is liable also to diseases which overtake and impede us in the search after true being; it fills us full of loves, and lusts, and fears, and fancies of all kinds, and endless foolery, and in fact, as men say, takes away from us the power of thinking at all. Whence comes wars, and fighting, and factions? Where but from the body and the lusts of the body? Wars are occasioned by the love of money, and money has to be acquired for the sake and in the service of the body; and by reason of all these impediments we have no time to give to philosophy; and last and worst of all, even if we are at leisure and betake ourselves to some speculation, the body is always breaking in upon us, causing turmoil and confusion in our enquiries, and so amazing us that we are prevented from seeing the truth.

PLATO

Reading selections

It is time to practice your newly-improved diction. The following selections have been made because they are nonsense verses, apparently empty of any logical meaning, and therefore they leave you free to choose any action beats you wish as you read them. Find your own interpretation, and express the inner feelings and thoughts you choose. Remember, no mumbling, no slurring!

LINES READ IN COURT, PURPORTED TO BE BY THE KNAVE

'They told me you had been to her,
    And mentioned me to him:
She gave me a good character,
    But said I could not swim.

He sent them word I had not gone
    (We know it to be true):
If she should push the matter on,
    What would become of you?

I gave her one, they gave him two,
You gave us three or more:
They all returned from him to you,
Though they were mine before.

If I or she should chance to be
Involved in this affair,
He trusts to you to set them free,
Exactly as we were.

My notion was that you had been
(Before she had this fit)
An obstacle that came between
Him, and ourselves, and it.

Don't let him know she liked them best,
For this must ever be
A secret, kept from all the rest,
Between yourself and me.'

LEWIS CARROLL

The following three selections are from *Nonsense Cookery* by Edward Lear.

TO MAKE AN AMBLONGUS PIE

Take four pounds (say four and one-half pounds) of fresh Amblongusses, and put them in a small pipkin.

Cover them with water and boil them for eight hours incessantly, after which add two pints of new milk, and proceed to boil for four hours more.

When you have ascertained that the Amblongusses are quite soft, take them out and place them in a wide pan, taking care to shake them well previously.

Grate some nutmeg over the surface, and cover them carefully with powdered gingerbread, curry-powder, and a sufficient quantity of cayenne pepper.

Remove the pan into the next room, and place it on the floor. Bring it back again, and let it simmer for three-quarters of an hour.

Shake the pan violently till all the Amblongusses have become of a pale purple colour.

Then, having prepared the paste, insert the whole carefully, adding at the same time a small pigeon, two slices of beef, four cauliflowers, and any number of oysters.

Watch patiently till the crust begins to rise, and add a pinch of salt from time to time.

Serve up in a clean dish, and throw the whole out of the window as fast as possible.

TO MAKE CRUMBOBBLIOUS CUTLETS

Procure some strips of beef, and having cut them into the smallest possible slices, proceed to cut them still smaller, eight or perhaps nine times.

When the whole is thus minced, brush it up hastily with a new clothes-brush, and stir round rapidly and capriciously with a salt-spoon or a soup-ladle.

Place the whole in a saucepan, and remove it to a sunny place—say the roof of the house if free from sparrows or other birds—and leave it there for about a week.

At the end of that time, add a little lavender, some oil of almonds, and a few herring-bones; and then cover the whole with four gallons of clarified crumbobblious sauce, when it will be ready for use.

Cut it into the shape of ordinary cutlets, and serve up in a clean tablecloth or dinner-napkin.

TO MAKE GOSKY PATTIES

Take a pig, three or four years of age, and tie him by the off-hind leg to a post. Place five pounds of currants, three of sugar, two pecks of peas, eighteen roast chestnuts, a candle, and six bushels of turnips, within his reach; if he eats these, constantly provide him with more.

Then procure some cream, some slices of Cheshire cheese, four quires of foolscap paper, and a packet of black pins. Work the whole into a paste, and spread it out to dry on a sheet of clean brown waterproof linen.

When the paste is perfectly dry, but not before, proceed to beat the pig violently, with the handle of a large broom. If he squeals, beat him again.

Visit the paste and beat the pig alternately for some days, and ascertain if at the end of that period the whole is about to turn into Gosky Patties.

If it does not then, it never will; and in that case the pig may be let loose, and the whole process may be considered as finished.

The following prologues from *King Henry V* have been chosen because as monologues they demand that you (1) speak clearly and accurately, with energy; and (2) carry out the action of the speech. The very action of all of the following speeches is to *explain,* to *inform,* to *make clear*. Find a simple action like one of these and then stick to it. Really act as an *explainer*. That main line of action will make your words ring true and will keep you from declaiming. Here are acting and speech exercises you can do alone. You are not dependent on an acting partner.

KING HENRY V, I, PROLOGUE

Enter CHORUS

CHORUS

O for a Muse of fire, that would ascend
The brightest heaven of invention,
A kingdom for a stage, princes to act
And monarchs to behold the swelling scene!
Then should the warlike Harry, like himself,
Assume the port of Mars; and at his heels,
Leash'd in like hounds, should famine, sword and fire
Crouch for employment. But pardon, gentles all,
The flat unraised spirits that have dared
On this unworthy scaffold to bring forth
So great an object: can this cockpit hold
The vasty fields of France? or may we cram
Within this wooden O the very casques
That did affright the air at Agincourt?
O, pardon! since a crooked figure may
Attest in little place a million;

And let us, ciphers to this great accompt,
On your imaginary forces work.
Suppose within the girdle of these walls
Are now confined two mighty monarchies,
Whose high upreared and abutting fronts
The perilous narrow ocean parts asunder:
Piece out our imperfections with your thoughts;
Into a thousand parts divide one man,
And make imaginary puissance;
Think, when we talk of horses, that you see them
Printing their proud hoofs i' the receiving earth;
For 'tis your thoughts that now must deck our kings,
Carry them here and there; jumping o'er times,
Turning the accomplishment of many years
Into an hour-glass: for the which supply,
Admit me Chorus to this history;
Who prologue-like your humble patience pray,
Gently to hear, kindly to judge, our play. [*Exit*

KING HENRY V, II, PROLOGUE

Enter CHORUS

CHORUS

Now all the youth of England are on fire,
And silken dalliance in the wardrobe lies:
Now thrive the armorers, and honour's thought
Reigns solely in the breast of every man:
They sell the pasture now to buy the horse,
Following the mirror of all Christian kings,
With winged heels, as English Mercuries.
For now sits Expectation in the air,
And hides a sword from hilts unto the point

With crowns imperial, crowns and coronets,
Promised to Harry and his followers.
The French, advised by good intelligence
Of this most dreadful preparation,
Shake in their fear and with pale policy
Seek to divert the English purposes.
O England! model to thy inward greatness,
Like little body with a mighty heart,
What mightst thou do, that honour would thee do,
Were all thy children kind and natural!
But see thy fault! France hath in thee found out
A nest of hollow bosoms, which he fills
With treacherous crowns; and three corrupted men,
One, Richard Earl of Cambridge, and the second,
Henry Lord Scroop of Masham, and the third,
Sir Thomas Grey, knight, of Northumberland,
Have, for the gilt of France,—O guilt indeed!—
Confirm'd conspiracy with fearful France;
And by their hands this grace of kings must die,
If hell and treason hold their promises,
Ere he take ship for France, and in Southampton.
Linger your patience on; and we'll digest
The abuse of distance; force a play:
The sum is paid; the traitors are agreed;
The king is set from London; and the scene
Is now transported, gentles, to Southampton;
There is the playhouse now, there must you sit:
And thence to France shall we convey you safe,
And bring you back, charming the narrow seas
To give you gentle pass; for, if we may,
We'll not offend one stomach with our play.
But, till the king come forth, and not till then,
Unto Southampton do we shift our scene. [*Exit*

KING HENRY V, III, PROLOGUE

Enter CHORUS

CHORUS

Thus with imagined wing our swift scene flies
In motion of no less celerity
Than that of thought. Suppose that you have seen
The well-appointed king at Hampton pier
Embark his royalty; and his brave fleet
With silken streamers the young Phoebus fanning:
Play with your fancies, and in them behold
Upon the hempen tackle ship-boys climbing;
Hear the shrill whistle which doth order give
To sounds confused; behold the threaden sails,
Borne with the invisible and creeping wind,
Draw the huge bottoms through the furrow'd sea,
Breasting the lofty surge: O, do but think
You stand upon the rivage and behold
A city on the inconstant billows dancing;
For so appears this fleet majestical,
Holding due course to Harfleur. Follow, follow:
Grapple your minds to sternage of this navy,
And leave your England, as dead midnight still,
Guarded with grandsires, babies and old women,
Either past or not arrived to pith and puissance;
For who is he, whose chin is but enrich'd
With one appearing hair, that will not follow
These cull'd and choice-drawn cavaliers to France?
Work, work your thoughts, and therein see a siege;
Behold the ordnance on their carriages,
With fatal mouths gaping on girded Harfleur.
Suppose the ambassador from the French comes
back;
Tells Harry that the king doth offer him
Katharine his daughter, and with her, to dowry,

Some petty and unprofitable dukedoms.
The offer likes not: and the nimble gunner
With linstock now the devilish cannon touches,
[*Alarum, and chambers go off*

And down goes all before them. Still be kind,
And eke out our performance with your mind. [*Exit*

KING HENRY V, IV, PROLOGUE

Enter CHORUS

CHORUS

Now entertain conjecture of a time
When creeping murmur and the poring dark
Fills the wide vessel of the universe.
From camp to camp through the foul womb of
night
The hum of either army stilly sounds,
That the fix'd sentinels almost receive
The secret whispers of each other's watch:
Fire answers fire, and through their paly flames
Each battle sees the other's umber'd face;
Steed threatens steed, in high and boastful neighs
Piercing the night's dull ear; and from the tents
The armourers, accomplishing the knights,
With busy hammers closing rivets up,
Give dreadful note of preparation:
The country cocks do crow, the clocks do toll,
And the third hour of drowsy morning name.
Proud of their numbers and secure in soul,
The confident and over-lusty French
Do the low-rated English play at dice;
And chide the cripple tardy-gaited night
Who, like a foul and ugly witch, doth limp

So tediously away. The poor condemned English,
Like sacrifices, by their watchful fires
Sit patiently and inly ruminate
The morning's danger, and their gesture sad
Investing lank-lean cheeks and war-worn coats
Presenteth them unto the gazing moon
So many horrid ghosts. O now, who will behold
The royal captain of this ruin'd band
Walking from watch to watch, from tent to tent,
Let him cry 'Praise and glory on his head!'
For forth he goes and visits all his host,
Bids them good morrow with a modest smile,
And calls them brothers, friends and countrymen.
Upon his royal face there is no note
How dread an army hath enrounded him;
Nor doth he dedicate one jot of colour
Unto the weary and all-watched night,
But freshly looks and over-bears attaint
With cheerful semblance and sweet majesty;
That every wretch, pining and pale before,
Beholding him, plucks comfort from his looks:
A largess universal like the sun
His liberal eye doth give to every one,
Thawing cold fear, that mean and gentle all
Behold, as may unworthiness define,
A little touch of Harry in the night.
And so our scene must to the battle fly;
Where—O for pity!—we shall much disgrace
With four or five most vile and ragged foils,
Right ill-disposed in brawl ridiculous,
The name of Agincourt. Yet sit and see,
Minding true things by what their mockeries be.

[*Exit*

KING HENRY V, V, PROLOGUE

Enter CHORUS

CHORUS

Vouchsafe to those that have not read the story,
That I may prompt them: and of such as have,
I humbly pray them to admit the excuse
Of time, of numbers and due course of things,
Which cannot in their huge and proper life
Be here presented. Now we bear the king
Toward Calais: grant him there; there seen,
Heave him away upon your winged thoughts
Athwart the sea. Behold, the English beach
Pales in the flood with men, with wives and boys,
Whose shouts and claps out-voice the deep-mouth'd
sea,
Which like a mighty whiffler 'fore the king
Seems to prepare his way: so let him land,
And solemnly see him set on to London.
So swift a pace hath thought, that even now
You may imagine him upon Blackheath;
Where that his lords desire him to have borne
His bruised helmet and his bended sword
Before him through the city: he forbids it,
Being free from vainness and self-glorious pride;
Giving full trophy, signal and ostent
Quite from himself to God. But now behold,
In the quick forge and working-house of thought,
How London doth pour out her citizens!
The mayor and all his brethren in best sort,
Like to the senators of the antique Rome,
With the plebeians swarming at their heels,
Go forth and fetch their conquering Caesar in:

As, by a lower but loving likelihood,
Were now the general of our gracious empress,
As in good time he may, from Ireland coming,
Bringing rebellion broached on his sword,
How many would the peaceful city quit,
To welcome him! much more, and much more
    cause,
Did they this Harry. Now in London place him;
As yet the lamentation of the French
Invites the King of England's stay at home;
The emperor's coming in behalf of French,
To order peace between them; and omit
All the occurrences, whatever chanced,
Till Harry's back return again to France:
There must we bring him; and myself have play'd
The interim, by remembering you 'tis past.
Then brook abridgement, and your eyes advance,
After your thoughts, straight back again to France.

[*Exit*

6

Acting: imagination, memory, senses

> *You as an actor are a complex mechanism. Gordon Craig wanted to dispense with you and replace you with marionettes which could be depended upon to do exactly what the director wanted and to repeat their performances identically each time.*
>
> CONSTANTIN STANISLAVSKI[1]

Imagination

I hope the Craig ambition is frightening to you, not only because you would not like to be made obsolescent by marionettes, but also because you would hate to see the theater lose that rare and illuminating creature, the sensitive and imaginative actor, unpredictable though he may be.

The most mysterious aspect of acting is how you use your imagination and the emotions which your imagination releases. The imagination is fed by the senses and the memory, but how it works, no one

[1] *My Life in Art,* p. 509.

knows. Yet no interpretative artist could function for a second without his imagination.

The playwright De Ghelderode wrote in a letter: "The shriek gushing from the flesh, from agony, ecstacy, or orgasm saves everything. Without shrieks, the theatre is merely chatter: words, words! . . ."[1]

Shrieks are the products of men in states of emotion. Marionettes do not shriek. Stanislavski, Grotowski, and Peter Brook all have sought the Aristotelian goal of catharsis, or emotional purgation. The actors' emotions must release the emotions of the audience.

A fertile imagination, which releases emotion, is the most precious asset you have as an actor. You do, of course, need an excellent voice and an expressive body, but your imagination is that unknown factor, all other talents being equal, that will make you either mediocre or outstanding.

There are those who believe that you are born with an imagination of a certain quality, much like an I.Q., and that there is little or nothing you can do to change it. These are the same people who believe that you can't really make an actor, for an actor is born. Well, genes are important, but so are discipline, desire, and determination. It has been demonstrated that an I.Q. can be raised considerably in cases where the original potential for some reason was not fulfilled. Therefore, even if the quality of your imagination were predetermined by your genetic makeup, who is to say that at this time its full potential has been reached?

The magic of Stanislavski's "as if" can work only on a fertile imagination. Too many of us do not exercise our imaginations enough, and they become lazy and unproductive.

A young child has a strong imagination, a strong sense of make-believe. When you were small, if an older child got carried away with his impersonation of a giant or a bad witch and pursued you too vigorously, you screamed in terror. Your imagination had transformed your friend into a real giant or witch. Remember hiding under your coat at a horror film when your imagination conquered your

[1] Michel de Ghelderode, "To Directors and Actors: Letters, 1948–1959," *Tulane Drama Review* 9 (Summer, 1965): No. 4, p. 56.

sense of disbelief? It is unfortunate that as you mature and want to act, you lose to a great degree this ability to "suspend your disbelief." A good actor must learn, in spite of knowing that he is *not* the character he portrays, to behave exactly "as if" he were.

However, that is only the beginning for your imagination. The imagination must go beyond the given circumstances (see p. 113) of the play as well. It must capture the play's period in a particularized movement and speech, called *style.* The imagination is the well-spring of your talent, and you must make sure that it is fertile and free-flowing.

Memory

Your memory is your bank vault. It is packed with rich sense and emotional memories. Stanislavski tried to solve the problem of how to open the vault at will so that the actor would have access to his memories when he wanted them. It was Pavlov, the Russian scientist, and his study of the conditioned reflex that supplied him with a solution. Pavlov, who worked contemporaneously with Stanislavski, placed a dog in a cage, which had a light above the feeding tray. Every time a bit of food dropped into the tray, the light went on. This procedure was repeated many times until the dog made an association between the light and the food: when the light came on, the dog began to salivate, even when the food did not appear. Pavlov called the dog's salivation a *conditioned reflex.*

Man, like Pavlov's dog, will respond automatically to a stimulus. Stanislavski decided to adapt Pavlov's technique, not in order to elicit automatic responses from the actor, but in order to release emotional memories.

Marcel Proust, in *Remembrance of Things Past,* tells us how he learned the same secret. As a grown man and a writer, he had spent sleepless nights in an effort to recapture, *intellectually,* the elusive memory of certain events of his childhood. He described some of these events, which he remembered fragmentarily. But then one day one of his elusive memories returned in its entirety when

> I raised to my lips a spoonful of the tea in which I had soaked a morsel of the cake [a "petite madeleine"]. No sooner had the warm liquid, and the crumbs with it, touched my palate than a shudder ran through my whole body, and I stopped, intent upon the extraordinary changes that were taking place. An exquisite pleasure had invaded my senses. . . .
>
> And once I had recognized the taste of the crumb of madeleine soaked in her decoction of lime-flowers which my aunt used to give me . . . immediately the old grey house upon the street, where her room was, rose up like the scenery of a theatre to attach itself to the little pavilion, opening onto the garden . . . and with the house the town. . . . In that moment all the flowers in our garden and in M. Swann's park, and the water-lilies on the Vivonne and the good folk of the village and their little dwellings and the parish church and the whole of Combray and of its surroundings, taking their proper shapes and growing solid, sprang into being, town and gardens alike, from my cup of tea.[1]

Ingmar Bergman has adapted this incident in a poignant scene from *Wild Strawberries.* Here an old man returns to his youth in perfect recall when he touches and tastes the wild strawberries that grow in the place where he spent the summers of his childhood. The emotional recall is all the more poignant because the old man's emotional and imaginative life has almost atrophied.

The application to you, as an actor, is obvious. Hundreds and thousands of memories of things past are lying in your head waiting to be summoned up, and with them can come a rich emotional recall to make you a better actor.

But how are you to summon them up? First your abilities to taste, see, hear, smell, and touch must again become as sensitive and as sharp as a child's. Then, through your senses, you can release your past. Unless you become as little children, you cannot enter the kingdom of the theater.

Hermann Hesse tells us of an important day in *Demian:*

> For the first time the outer world was perfectly attuned to the world within; it was a joy to be alive. No house, no shop window, no face

[1] Marcel Proust, *Remembrance of Things Past,* trans. C. K. Scott Moncrieff (New York: Random House, 1934), I, 34, 36.

> disturbed me, everything was as it should be, without any of the flat, humdrum look of the everyday; everything was a part of Nature, expectant and ready to face its destiny with reverence. That was how the world had appeared to me in the mornings when I was a small boy, on the great feast days, at Christmas or Easter. I had forgotten that the world could be so lovely. I had grown accustomed to living within myself. I was resigned to the knowledge that I had lost all appreciation of the outside world, that the loss of its bright colors was an inseparable part of the loss of my childhood, and that, in a certain sense, one had to pay for freedom and maturity of the soul with the renunciation of this cherished aura. But now, overjoyed, I saw that all this had only been buried or clouded over and that it was still possible . . . to see the world shine and to savor the delicious thrill of the child's vision.[1]

In your sensory work, then, you will be working in two ways. You will be trying to get back the child's vividness of sensation. And you will be trying to learn how to use the senses to unlock the vault of memory.

> When from a long-distant past nothing subsists, after the people are dead, after the things are broken and scattered, still, alone, more fragile, but with more vitality, more unsubstantial, more persistent, more faithful, the smell and taste of things remain poised a long time, like souls, ready to remind us, waiting and hoping for their moment, amid the ruins of all the rest; and bear unfaltering, in the tiny and almost impalpable drop of their essence, the vast structure of recollection.[2]

Senses

"You have eyes and yet you can't see!" That statement, by the late Aline Bernstein, a gifted set designer, was once made to a class, of which I was a member. She then described what sounded like a shop out of the Arabian Nights, full of wonderful exotic textures, colors,

[1] Hermann Hesse, *Demian,* trans. Richard and Clara Winston (New York: Harper & Row Bantam, 1970), p. 117.

[2] Proust, *Remembrance of Things Past,* I, 36.

and marvellous objects. When she had finished, she gave us the shop's address: downstairs and down the street, a place we all passed every day without so much as a glance. After the lecture I hurried there to look. She was absolutely right! That was when I learned that observation is an art.

Since that time I've learned that I didn't really know how to listen, either. Few people listen accurately for the structure in a poem, lecture, or piece of music, or for the delicate sounds of nature, for the subtler tones in a speaker's voice. You have ears, and yet you can't hear!

People all over the country are joining sensitivity groups because they feel that they have lost the ability to communicate. Seeing, listening, touching, tasting, and smelling are emphasized at these sessions.

The following exercises are to help you to see accurately and to retain your observations, to hear accurately and to recall sounds, to awaken your senses of touch and taste.

SEEING EXERCISES *(1–10)*

Exercises 1–5 are classroom exercises; exercises 6–10 are individual exercises that you can work on alone.

1 Someday, unexpectedly, have someone from your group leave the room. See how accurately the unprepared class members can describe his clothing. Try again. See how quickly the class can improve in both observation and retention. But do not observe *only* the clothing of other members of the class!

2 Collect objects, one from each class member: pens, rings, cigarette lighters, matches, coins, handkerchiefs, and so on. Place the objects on the floor. Leave them there for thirty seconds. Have each class member pick up his object and pocket it. Call on someone to name all the objects and to describe them in detail. Then change objects and let someone else try. Cut down on observation time to fifteen seconds. Ten seconds.

3 Distribute a bag of oranges to class members. Let each person study his orange very carefully, becoming aware of its every dent and color variation. Mix up all the oranges. Each person must now find his *own* orange. If he has observed well, he will know it without difficulty.

4 Place the group in a circle. Let someone in the group offer an object for the class to work from, a piece of jewelry, an article of clothing, a gadget. The object should be passed around the group. The first person will look at the object, and some part of that object —its shape, color, or use—should start him off on a story. For instance, someone hands him a chain with a green semi-precious stone hanging from it, wrapped in silver bands. His "as if" begins from a sensory impression: "I am walking down a country road surrounded by bright green fields. . . ." He has taken only the greenness from the object. Now he can develop the story freely. At the instructor's word, the object is passed to the next student, who continues the story at a suggestion from the object. Remember that the same object can suggest a thousand different things to a thousand different people, because each person brings a different set of memories to the object. The exercise illustrates the point that Stanislavski found in Pavlov's experiments. The object works on the senses, the senses on the imagination, the imagination on the emotions.

5 Everyone in class is asked to bring in an observed physical characteristic from someone he has studied. Let each person demonstrate the observed physical action. Make sure the action is done fully and in a relaxed way. This exercise is important. Some day a characterization may have you stumped until the sudden recollection of someone's significant physical characteristic will help you solve the problem.

6 At home alone, open a book of fine arts prints. Study one picture for thirty seconds. Close the book. Write down all that you can remember about the picture. Open the book. Compare your notes with what is really there. (Hint: you need a plan for efficient observation. Don't rush around the picture trying frantically to take it all in at once. You can't. Structure your observations. For instance, break the picture down into any obvious geometric pattern. If there are three figures, do they form a triangle? Use that triangle or any other geometric form that you can find. Another method of structuring your observations is to break the picture up into people and objects. Color patterns can be used. How many colors, which dominate? Or is there a story in the picture? Then use the inherent drama in it to help you remember the content. From a structure you can recall with greater accuracy.)

7 Take a new picture. Look at it for ten seconds. Write down your observations. Did you do as well as you did the first time, when you had longer?

8 Remember a room you have been in during the past day or two. Write down all that you can remember about that room. Go back to the room and see how accurately you have reconstructed it.

9 While outside walking, try concentrating on an object, either on the sidewalk or in the sky—say the top of a building. If you truly concentrate, truly observe, others will join you. Or watch you. In life, a person who really concentrates on something is an attention-getter. On stage, the same holds true.

10 Take a discovered physical characteristic which you have observed, and live with it for a day. Use it on the train, in the lunchroom, at home, on a date. Learn to relax with it.

LISTENING EXERCISES *(1–7)*

Many actors are poor listeners. The art of proper listening is so important it is taught as a course in many universities. You can find excellent books on this subject in the library. Good and accurate listening is both rare and fruitful. The good listener will be liked, respected, and successful. An actor who listens well will discover much to feed his acting with.

Exercise 1 is a classroom exercise. Exercises 2–6 may be done either privately or with the class. Exercises 7–8 are to be worked on apart from the class.

1 Blindfold someone. Then make the following sounds:

Tap a table top with your fingers.
Gently slap your palm on someone's cheek.

Rub your hand over different materials.
Drop a comb on the floor. A coin.
Rustle paper.
Handle money.
Unwrap a pack of cigarettes. A candy bar.
Chew peanuts.

Supply as many other different sounds as you can think of. How accurately does the subject hear? As the subject learns to concentrate, is there improvement?

2 Sit with your legs folded comfortably. Close your eyes. Listen to the sounds around you. Identify each sound. Do any of these sounds evoke any emotions in you?

3 Pick a piece of music. Don't limit your listening to music of one period; be particularly catholic. Pick something by Palestrina, Bach, Vivaldi, Haydn, Debussy, Prokofiev, Stravinski, Hindemith. Try the music of less familiar periods, medieval, Elizabethan, as well as the music of India or Japan. Let the music fill you. React emotionally to the music.

Later, if you feel like it, move to the music. March, leap, drift, stretch. Feed off the music. Let it dictate to your moves. If the music changes, then let your movements change too.

4 Listen to the records of great operatic voices. Create a storehouse of aural memories. Stanislavski said, "My impressions of the Italian opera are sealed not alone in my visual or aural memory—for I still feel them physically with my entire nervous system."[1]

Again, he wrote, significantly,

> The strength of the impression left on me by Cotogni in my youth is almost indescribable. In 1910, that is almost forty years after his arrival in Moscow, I was in Rome, walking with a friend through some narrow alley or other. Suddenly from the top story of one of the houses there floated out a note—broad, ringing, stormy, warming, and exciting. And I felt again physically the old, familiar impression.
>
> "Cotogni!", I cried.

[1] *My Life in Art,* p. 32.

"Yes, he lives here," affirmed my friend. "How did you recognize him?" he wondered.

"I *felt* him," I answered. "That note could never be forgotten."[1]

5 There are many excellent records of environmental sounds. There are records of bird calls, surf and sea sounds, whale songs. Seat yourself on the floor on a pillow, your back straight. Breathe deeply and regularly, keeping your eyes closed. Listen passively. Meditate to the sounds. Don't let your mind wander to everyday problems.

6 Read any play and list *all* the sounds that are to be found in the play, from a hammer's pounding to a baby's cry, a woman's sigh, or a siren's wail. List sounds you think should be in the play that aren't mentioned.

7 Have a trusted friend lead you around while you keep your eyes absolutely closed. Take a walk in this manner. Notice how accurate your hearing becomes. Describe what you hear to your friend. He will tell you how accurately you interpret what you hear.

TOUCHING EXERCISES *(1–4)*

When you are on stage, your acting might be helped by your sense of touch. Touching a prop or another actor can evoke a strong emotion. The use of touching, in scenes of love, hate, or tenderness, can be truthful and fulfilling. To fail to develop this sense would be to limit yourself as an actor.

1 Blindfold one person. Place him in a circle of fellow actors. Try to alter your obvious outer garments and jewelry. Change, if possible, your hair styles. How many of you can he identify by touch? Give each person a turn to be blindfolded.

2 Blindfold one person. This time lead him to a table with many different objects on it. Use whatever is available of different sizes and textures: a pen, an eraser, a piece of silk, a blotter, a piece of apple, a piece of chalk, a crayon, and so on. Can he identify the objects? Give each person a turn to be blindfolded.

[1] Ibid., p. 33.

3 Have one person lie on his stomach on the floor. Surround that person with the others, kneeling in a circle. On cue, have everyone touch the person in the center with gentle taps from head to foot. Continue for two or three minutes. Stop. Do it again, using the whole hand and patting harder for one minute. Do not hurt the subject. How does he feel when it's over? How do you feel?

4 Everyone is blindfolded except for guards who must be posted at any dangerous spots. The entire room, or stage setting, is the area to explore. Feel your way around this environment. Live through your fingertips. If you find an object or a person, explore it. Don't move on until you *feel* that there is nothing more to learn.

SMELLING EXERCISES *(1–2)*

1 Blindfold someone. Place different objects near his nose. Without touching, can he identify them? Try a teabag, a pencil, a book, a lipstick, a piece of bread, and so on.

2 Place a strong smelling object in the room: a cut onion, a piece of cheese, a scented handkerchief, a small can of catfood, a stick of incense, cut garlic. Blindfold someone. Can he find it?

TASTING EXERCISES *(1–2)*

1 Get a good solid loaf of black bread at a health food store. Cut it up. Give each person a slice. Smell it, feel it, then chew it slowly and thoroughly. As you do this, look around at others in the group.

2 Blindfold someone. Fill some paper cups with different liquids: coke, tea, water, brandy, lemon juice. The subject should taste each one slowly. The taste should explode in the mouth, on the tongue. How many can the subject identify?

SENSE MEMORY EXERCISES *(1–4)*

Some teachers of the Method are against sense memory exercises, arguing that on stage you will have real props, so why waste time on imaginary props? But that is not the point of these exercises. Of course an actor will have real props in plays—usually. Not always, certainly, in today's theater! However, even if he has real props, he will need the use of his actor's imagination fed by sense memory, because the heavy golden goblet will not really be heavy gold but will be a light papier maché, which he must handle as if it were something quite different. The hot cup of coffee in reality will not be hot, the strong shot of brandy will not be brandy. All these props will have to be handled "as if" they were something else. For this reason, you need the following exercises.

To execute these exercises well, you need to sharpen your ability to observe, and you will need to concentrate. Sloppiness is unforgivable here. Do not rush the exercises, do not take shortcuts, and do not indicate. (Indicating is acting acting; if you were supposed to search for something on stage and only *pretended* to search, you would be indicating.) All actions must be carried out fully.

You will need to do a lot of practicing. Remember, no props may be used. It is necessary to memorize the exact order of all your actions. The order must never vary. On stage all actions are planned and are executed as planned with nothing left to chance.

Much practice will be needed before you will know exactly where in space each object is situated. Objects should always be returned to the same spot. A cabinet door can't shift from one place to another. You must also know the size, shape, and weight of each object. Plan and practice the exercises well. Then watch how poorly the unprepared actor will execute them. In this area, indication is immediately identifiable.

1 Without props, perform these household tasks:

a. Peel potatoes.
b. Shave.
c. Sew a garment.
d. Dust the furniture.
e. Wash your dog.
f. Make a bed.
g. Take a shower.
h. Pack a suitcase.

i. Make a salad, distinguishing vegetables. Mix. Taste.
j. Arrange a bowl of flowers.

Add your own sense memory activities.

2 Try the following activities as if in an outdoor setting. Even though your actions will be broader here, don't forget detail in your work. Do not indicate fatigue. Avoid over-acting.

a. Chop wood.
b. Pick flowers.
c. Push someone on a swing.
d. Dig a hole.
e. Lift a heavy rock.
f. Hang clothes on a line.
g. Make a snow man without gloves on.
h. Fly a kite.
i. Lay a fire and light it in real cold weather.
j. Shoot basketball or swing a baseball bat at pitched balls.

Add your own sense memory activities.

3 For the following exercise, be careful not to indicate, and not to exaggerate what you don't actually recall through sense memory. Above all, don't *act*. Take your time. Concentrate. And remember, no props at all.

a. Taste a lemon.
b. Drink a very hot cup of coffee.
c. Eat something that is hard to bite.
d. Eat something that is very sticky, soft and chewy.
e. Drink a fine brandy; savor it.
f. You are starving and find some dog biscuits. Taste one. Eat it.
g. Cut a watermelon. Give yourself a large slice. Eat it, but don't swallow the pits.

4 This exercise is more difficult. Think before you start!

a. You have a deep cut. Put iodine or alcohol on it. It hurts very much.
b. You have lost your shoes. Your feet are blistered. Every step hurts. You must cross over some very hot sharp rocks and sand.

c. You are cleaning an old attic. You dislodge a hornet's nest. They attack you.
d. You are lost on a camping trip. It is night. You are cold. Find a spot to camp in and unroll your sleeping bag. Light a sterno can and heat some water.
e. Take a bath in a tub of very hot water. Touch the water with your toes, then lower yourself into the tub.

7

Acting is doing

> *Most important is the combination of the incidents of the story. Tragedy [the play] is essentially an imitation not of persons but of action and life, of happiness and misery. All human happiness or misery takes the form of action; the end for which we live is a certain kind of activity, not a quality. Character gives us qualities, but it is in our actions—what we do—that we are happy or the reverse.*
>
> ARISTOTLE
> *De Poetica*, 6, II

Always remember that according to Aristotle, drama is an imitation of life but not life itself. Do not ever forget the word "imitation." The scenery is painted canvas that will rattle if handled too realistically, the king's goblet is not gold, the crown is papier maché. And you must always remember that the onlookers are *there*, though in many styles of theater you will never address them. Don't be impressed by the actor who comes offstage swearing that the audience wasn't there, the stage lights were no longer hot, that he got carried away and succeeded in really living the part. Acting is never really living. It is art and therefore an imitation. A good actor simulating a dying man on stage is apt to be more "real" and more dramatic and certainly more interesting than a man dying in actuality.

But, in imitation of life, acting is doing. This definition, based on Aristotle, is fundamental to the Stanislavski system, which seeks to imitate the truth as found in life.[1]

Too many actors think that acting is feeling and get trapped into contradicting life instead of imitating it. Emoting is not acting. Emoting actors are called indicators, or hams. They do not imitate life truthfully, but *indicate* life by playing emotions. What the actor must do, to be truthful on stage, is to find the action which will express and release his emotion.

In life you always perform actions toward certain goals or for certain purposes. Although some of your actions may have motivations which are "unconscious," although some may have motivations which might not even be adjudged "sane," you never perform an action without some reason.

Furthermore, your actions in life are particular. When you do something, you do it for a *particular* reason. Later in this chapter we will discuss particularization, which is simply the idea that an actor imitating life on stage must do *one* specific action at a time. The reasons for the action must derive from the given circumstances of the play (see p. 113), just as in real life all actions are performed for given reasons under particular circumstances.

Actors, then, must learn to work on specific actions, or on one action at a time, and they must work with the given circumstances. If they do not work in this way, they will fall into the trap of generalization. They will indicate, because they will be playing under generalized circumstances. Typically, such actors will argue that they know the play's given circumstances, and that they know what their actions are, but when you try to pin them down in a particular scene and ask, "Now, what are you doing here?" you will find them at a loss to answer with any logic or accuracy.

On stage, as in life, you must also remember to be in harmony with your universe. A new type of actor, the Method ham actor, has emerged in the past twenty years. This actor is so intent on his own characterization that he forgets all about the meaning and the style

[1] See Francis Fergusson, *The Idea of a Theatre* (Princeton: Princeton University Press, 1951), pp. 250–55, for a discussion of this point.

of the play he is in. He is so interested in his own inner truth, that he forgets to find out if he is false to the main idea of the play. "Falsity under the banner of Truth and Inner Feeling is the most intolerable of pretensions," as Marowitz has remarked.[1]

Another common pitfall for the actor is not false acting but the incorrect interpretation of a role. Stanislavski himself apparently had this experience. When he played Trigorin in Chekhov's *The Seagull,* Chekhov objected:

> "You act magnificently," he [Chekhov] said, "but not my character. I did not write that."
> "What's the matter with it?" I asked.
> "Why, he should have checked trousers and worn-out shoes." That was all he would say in reply to my urgent questioning.
> "Checked trousers . . . and this is how he smokes a cigar. . . ." Here he awkwardly explained his words in gestures.[2]

When Aristotle tells us that "most important is the combination of the incidents," he tells us that the play, as devised by the playwright, has to be inviolable.

An important purpose of this book is to point out a direction that may lead to the unification of the extremes of acting styles to be found in the theater. The introverted actor who mumbles into his navel is as repulsive as the external actor who bays at the moon. The former is unconnected to the play; the latter is unconnected to real life. But there is no reason why the internal and the external cannot be joined to form the total actor dedicated to the art of imitating life through truthful actions.

Here, then, we will start to work on the action itself, the magic "as if," the given circumstances, and other tools that help to discipline the inner actor. But the importance of body and voice, as the instruments for expressing the actor's inner psychological truth, are never to be forgotten. Wherever possible in this book, exercises will be introduced that can capture the totality of the effort an actor must

[1] Charles Marowitz, *The Method as Means: An Acting Survey* (London: Herbert Jenkins, 1961), p. 40.

[2] Constantin Stanislavski, *Stanislavski's Legacy* (New York: Theatre Arts Books, 1968), p. 93.

make. When the wordless one-action problems are presented, do not think for a moment that the word has become less important. You are being taught to concentrate on the single action without the distraction of the word's presence. Later your own words can be added to actions in improvisations, and finally your actions and the playwright's words—and themes—will be united in you, the total actor. Remember that as total actor you can never compromise either life or art by sacrificing either truth for style, or style for truth.

SCORING ACTIONS

"If you analyze human life, you will see that it can be resolved into a series of actions which are simple and can be easily executed."[1] Make a "score" of yesterday. Start at the beginning of the day and list all your actions, from rising to bedtime. Remember to break the actions down when they are complex. What might appear to you at first to be one action, may actually be several distinct actions. You might simply brush your teeth. On the other hand, you might begin to brush your teeth absent-mindedly, and suddenly discover a tender spot, a new cavity. Now you brush carefully, so as not to hurt yourself, and with a new concern for your teeth, remembering that they must be taken care of. Perhaps you worry about the upcoming session with the dentist, and his bill. Or, you brush your teeth absent-mindedly until suddenly you hear something on the radio which angers, irritates, excites, or pleases you. Your brushing takes on a new rhythm. Having lunch with a friend may involve many different actions: What was your relationship to the waitress? What different reactions were evoked in you by your conversation, by your friend's actions?

In this exercise, try to use transitive verbs only, verbs which take objects. Do not describe emotional states using the verb "to be," as, "I was happy." Remember, never act emotions. Emotions cannot be actions; they follow as the result of actions.

In scoring your day, use the first person singular, "I." Never, in developing your understanding of the character you play, speak of

[1] I. Sudakov, "The Creative Process," *Acting, A Handbook of the Stanislavski Method,* comp. Toby Cole (New York: Bonanza Books, 1971), p. 73.

it in the third person, "he," or "she." That will tend to detach you from involvement. The use of the word "I," on the other hand, will be the beginning of getting your mind and your will involved with the emotions.

This fundamental exercise is the very foundation of particularization, or the art of choosing clear actions instead of vague generalized indicated actions, and also of answering in detail the questions of the given circumstances.

Later, when you work on plays, you will work on "beats" which will contain "actions." A beat is a unit of purpose. Let us say that within a play, you have to persuade someone to do something. The scene, or portion of a scene, in which you do your persuading is the "persuasion beat." It may be five or ten pages long, and it may contain several different "actions." You might have as actions, "to threaten," "to flatter," "to bribe," "to seduce," "to convince." When the beat is finished, either you have succeeded or you have failed, but in either case you will go on to a new beat required by the play.

SCORING BEATS

Take the same score you made of yesterday's actions. Now see if you can group the actions into beats. Your grooming actions in the morning, for instance, might combine into one preparation for the day beat. Or let us say you had an encounter with the adjustment department of a large department store. Your actions might have included explaining, pleading, threatening. These actions should now be included in the "getting the refund beat." Try to see the larger patterns in your day.

Preparation for the one-beat problem

You are about to start acting, and must be warned here that acting does not mean what a layman thinks it means. The one-beat problem requires you to concentrate on one beat and one beat only in order to solve a given problem. You will not speak a word, but will act with complete concentration. Be patient! Remember, technique before inspiration.

> What is the essence of the actor's work and of the theatre itself . . . ? The basis of everything is *action*. This may sound like a truism. . . . However, the very fact that these truths enter our consciousness does not assure their proper assimilation. Years are required to understand them properly.[1]

One of the most important contributions Stanislavski made to the theater was the conception of "playing the objective." The purpose is to keep the actor's attention on stage where it belongs and to prevent its straying all over the auditorium. Once the actor becomes aware of the audience, he can fall into the fatal trap of imagining that they came to see *him,* and then he forgets the play, forgets his fellow actors, forgets the long hours of rehearsal. He is off on his own, so crazed by his own delusions that he has forgotten the reality of the play and the truthfulness of his own acting beats, and attempts to display his heart to the audience in order to make the play really clear to them. He begins to overact, or push, and destroys the fabric of the play's reality.

Playing the objective simply means keeping your mind on your action. If you can learn to keep your mind concentrated in your acting objective (the execution, one by one, of your actions and beats), then the chances of your attention being swept away by the lure of the audience will be greatly diminished.

Here are two incidents in which the performance of a one-action problem helped Vsevolod Meyerhold in difficult moments on stage. Meyerhold was not acting properly; he tells us

> Stanislavski stopped me some ten times before he came up on the stage, threw a small piece of paper in my direction, and said: "You go over towards the piano, say your first three words; then you notice the paper, pick it up, proceed to the piano, sit down, unfold the paper, and go on with your lines." It was a great help, and I managed to do what was expected.
>
> You see, I'd only felt foolish saying, "When I was at the military

[1] Cole, *Acting, A Handbook of Stanislavski Method,* p. 71.

> academy." But when I started the speech and then picked up the paper, it was a real action. . . .[1]

Again,

> I didn't have a penny's worth of vitality in me, and kept forcing the lines. No luck. Whereupon Stanislavski gave me an unopened bottle of wine and a corkscrew, saying, "You speak your lines and while you are doing it you open the bottle." Trying to uncork that bottle multiplied the infinitesimal drop of energy in my system and got me into a proper state to do the scene. . . . When confronted with that obstacle, my lines took on the ring of truth.[2]

Your one-beat problem will help to unlock the subtext of the play. The subtext is a synonym for actions or beats. Underneath the words of the script lie buried a series of actions, just as in the scoring exercise (p. 110) you discovered the actions beneath all the dialogue you spoke during the day. Much later we will discuss how words, too, can be actions; but for the present we will concentrate on physical actions.

To solve a one-beat problem, you must fill in the given circumstances, consisting of the answers to the following questions: *Who am I? What do I want? Why do I want it? How am I going to get it? Where am I? When is it?*

If you answer these questions *in detail,* you are particularizing, and you will have all the information needed to concentrate and build your role. Working from the given circumstances is the very heartbeat of the Stanislavski System.

Remember, when you are doing individual work in a one-beat problem, you can decide on the answers to the given circumstances in isolation, but when you are in a play, you certainly cannot. When you are in a play, you must check with the director to see if your work is connected to the main idea of the play as he has worked it out. You must make sure that your given circumstances mesh with the given circumstances of the other actors. If there is a past event which is referred to by the actors but which is not acted in the play,

[1] Vsevolod Meyerhold, "The 225th Studio," *Tulane Drama Review* 9 (Fall, 1964): No. 1, p. 22.

[2] Ibid.

talk it over with the other actors. Discuss the event to clarify what happened. Remember that although this kind of preparatory work is unknown to your audience, and will remain unknown, yet it feeds the roots of the given circumstances, nourishing the inner life of the pasts of both your fellow actors and yourself.

How to create a one-beat problem

1. Pick a problem that you must solve with one main action or beat. Answer all the questions of the given circumstances in detail, but keep the problem uncluttered. *For example,* your parents are sleeping in their bedroom. They are very light sleepers. You must slip in and get your father's car keys from his pocket in order to drive somewhere secretly and rescue your brother. Your main action is: Get the car keys.

2. Pick one or more obstacle actors. In the example given above, they are your sleeping parents. The obstacle actor must cooperate with the actor trying to solve the one-action problem. If you are the sleeping parent in the example above, remember that you are not really sleeping, but you are acting *as if* you were asleep. If you hear a floor board squeak you must not jump up and catch the intruder immediately, thus ending the problem. If you will stir and roll over, then he must concentrate on you, react to your reaction, freeze, remove his shoes, and live out the problem. But if he were to burst into the room yelling, you would have to react truthfully and wake up. Perhaps the intruder has a clever method of stealing the keys while behaving wildly in your room! Be truthful, but be helpful; remember, all good acting is truthful pretending.

The obstacle actors must be instructed about their roles in the conflict. Remember: no conflict, no problem.

3. Don't get theatrical; don't write a play.

4. Remember that you can't speak any words. Don't try to fill in with pantomine!

5. Make sure that your problem can be stated with a transitive verb, and that there is an object of the verb. When you choose a transi-

tive verb, you are choosing a verb that takes an object, and that involves an action: "I hit the dog," "I choose an apple," "I kiss a girl." An intransitive verb will easily lead you into the trap of playing an emotion, for it frequently describes a state of being: "I am happy," "I feel miserable," "I get angry." Do not make your action wishing for something, even though in life people frequently do wish for things. In order to achieve their wishes, they must act. Find yourself an action verb, a transitive verb that takes an object. *For example,* you have to get the car keys!

6. Make sure your problem has a sense of immediacy. You have to get the car keys *now!* Your objective cannot be postponed for any reason. Immediacy must be an important factor in all your improvisational work. It is found in all good plays, as well.

7. Plan your how's (the method of performing the action).

If, in the course of acting out the problem, the obstacle actors foil you, adapt. Try something else. Have a number of how's planned. If one fails, use the next, and so on. The number of how's, or actions, depends on your imagination.

In a play the main action can be broken down into subordinate actions. It is the same in a one-beat problem; the various how's are the subordinate actions.

Remember that all stage action depends on your ability to believe in the given circumstances. To do this easily, you can use the *magic as if*, that is, you must perform the action *as if* it were true. This is what you have done many times as a member of the audience when you have "suspended your disbelief" in order to accept the reality of a given play. You say to yourself, What would I do *if* the following were true?

Example of a one-beat problem based on given circumstances

Who am I? I am twenty-two years old. My family has disowned me for wanting to act. Acting jobs are scarce. Right now I am unemployed. I have no money. My grandfather has recently died. His estate was bought up by an antique dealer, and my grandfather's children have divided the purchase price among themselves. Among my grandfather's possessions was a copy of the *Rosciad,* a verse satire on eighteenth century actors by Churchill, once owned by David Garrick. My grandfather promised me at one time that some day the volume would be mine, but he neglected to give me the gift in his will, and now I am deprived of the volume, which I always loved.

What do I want? Main action: To get the book that is rightfully mine! I want the book promised to me by my grandfather. I have spent many hours studying this book. It has notes in Garrick's handwriting. For me, the book has many important memories attached to it.

Why do I want the book? (The answers to the first and second questions supply the needed information to answer this question. *Why* involves the emotions and supplies the psychological motivation.) It was promised to me! I consider it mine! My grandfather clearly said on many occasions that it was mine! Now my uncles have refused to honor his wishes. I'll show them! As an actor, this book is an inspiration to me. Garrick is one of my heroes. I have spent many hours reading this book. It has emotional attachments for me. It is precious because my grandfather intended it for me, and because it belonged to Garrick. But besides all that, the book has become a secret symbol to me. With it, I know I'll have some of Garrick's good luck. I feel somehow that I must have the book or I will fail as an actor. Nothing can stop me from getting back what is rightfully mine!

How am I going to get the book? (The answer to this question involves the planning of your actions. You might threaten, plead, seduce, and so on. Use transitive verbs only. Have many actions well planned. Remember, the number of how's depends on your imagination. Be prepared to react truthfully to any action on the part of your obstacle actors.) I will go to the auction room on the inspection day and slip the book into a special pocket which I'll have sewn into my jacket. I know there will be people watching (obstacle actors as guards, as well as the management of the auction). I will have to sneak in another old book with the same dimensions. I can appear to be studying the book, and at the right moment, exchange them. If I can't get the book by simple exchange, I'll set a piece of paper on fire in the opposite corner, and when people rush over to it, I'll make the exchange. Or I can ask my girlfriend to faint at the opposite end of the room to cause the necessary diversion.

Where am I? (Place is very important; it will condition all your actions. If you were playing in a play set in the tropics, you would have to be hot, and sweat throughout, even if the theater were air-conditioned. Always adapt to your surroundings.) I am in an auction room filled with many books and other objects, many of which I remember, some of which I know intimately. Some evoke memories. My grandfather's things are here, but all out of context. There are a few other people in the room inspecting his belongings. Guards are watching.

When is it? (Time is important. Actions which are normal at noon might be too noisy at midnight. A tenement in January is not the same environment as that same tenement in July.) It is afternoon, a warm day in spring.

When the time comes to work on scenes and then on entire plays, you will recognize the importance of the given circumstances. Playwriting is a very disciplined form of writing. The hallmark of the art is compression of both time and character. As a result, much of what has happened in the past of the character is a blank to be filled in by the actor. Every play has a blank history consisting of all the events that happened before the curtain goes up. The filling in of this history is the filling in of the given circumstances.

MAKING UP THE ONE-BEAT PROBLEM

Make up your own one-beat problem based on a transitive verb. Be sure there is an object of your action, and, as an actor, relate to that object.

In creating these problems, you are learning to: (1) Supply and use the given circumstances. (2) Concentrate on stage by using objects or your fellow actors. (3) Develop a sense of theatrical truthfulness by doing one main action divided into its smaller units or beats.

(4) Develop a distaste for acting which is only indicated or not connected to a main action.

MOTIVATING AN ACTION

1 Each student in turn should be placed in a pose. At a signal, the actor must motivate that pose with an inner-motivated action.
2 Take turns with your fellow actors. One of you will place all the others into varied positions (avoiding the possibilities for sadistic expression!). At a given signal, the group must try to proceed into a motivated single action that is both believable and understandable to the audience.

FINDING AN ACTION

Reverse the last exercise. Pretend that you are in a play and that your director has no methodical system of work. He relies only on inspiration, and directs in terms of results. In other words, he demands that you project emotions, without giving you actions to perform. If this particular exercise seems too difficult, ask your teacher to help you. Your teacher in this course, remember, stands in the same relationship to you as the director of a play. But if it is possible for you to struggle through the exercise alone, do so, for the time is certain to come when you will meet a director who has no time to feed you proper actions. This harried man will know what he wants from you and will expect you, as an actor, to supply the necessary results immediately. Justify his "result demands" by creating one action to project each of the following emotions:

Be happy!
Be sad!
Be angry!
Be proud!
Be ashamed!
Be shameless!
Be calm!
Be agitated!

FILLING IN THE GIVEN CIRCUMSTANCES

As an actor, it is important that you get to museums, listen to good music, read good books. All these provide ideas which you can use in your work. Ghelderode, for example, was

> . . . inspired to write *Escurial* after I saw two canvases of the Spanish School at the Louvre. An El Greco and a Velasquez on the same wall and not far from each other (this was in 1925–1926). El Greco inspired an anxious, haggard, visible degenerate, pulmonary "King John"—in brief, a beautiful clinical specimen. El Greco's brush brought forth a terrible, disquieting, unforgettable character—and I dreamt of him! Velasquez inspired a magnificent dwarf, swollen with blood and instincts. To bring these two monsters together was all that was needed. The play was the outcome.[1]

An uncultivated actor is a limited actor. And unless you begin to understand different periods in history, the Greek, Elizabethan, Restoration, Victorian periods, for instance, through art, music, and literature, you will not be prepared to act in the different styles of those periods.

1 Find a picture. If you don't live near a museum, use a book of prints. (Please do not resort to calendar art or to *Playboy* for this exercise!) Now become a character in this picture. Create the given circumstances. Discover your main action. Answer all the questions needed to complete the history of the painting. What has happened before this particular scene occurred to make it possible? What *will* happen, now that the picture has come alive?

2 Continue the action shown in the picture. As an example, let us use El Greco's Cardinal Nino De Guevara:

Who am I? I am Nino De Guevara, defender of the faith! My family is a family of aristocrats; but money, land, and the pleasures of the flesh are nothing to me. I gave up courtly life to become a servant of Christ. I have mortified my body to lift up my soul. I have no use for those who do not put the Church first! For my zeal and hard work I have been made a prince of the Church. I must admit that

[1] "To Rene Dupuy," *Tulane Drama Review* 9 (Summer, 1965): No. 4, p. 45.

my aristocratic heritage truly equipped me to be Cardinal of Toledo. My strong desire to destroy all worldly enemies of the Church has won me the title of the Grand Inquisitor!

What do I want? I want to trap this enemy of God whom I am thinking of right now! His name is on this piece of paper which I have just dropped because my hands want to choke his throat. I must control myself for Christ's sake. How I wish I could relax a bit! My legs are like coiled springs; notice how my robe is caught at the base of the chair! I want a confession from this pig, this son of Satan! I want him to admit that he is in league with the devil!

Why do I want this confession? My God in heaven, why do I want to destroy the devil and his agents? Because they go about the world like roaring lions seeking the ruin of souls that Christ yearns to see in Paradise. The devil respects nothing but force. It was God's force that threw Satan out of Heaven. I must imitate God and use force on these diabolical enemies of Christian souls. I must destroy this man or he will destroy God's church and God's children.

How am I going to get this confession? First I will try to trap him with questions about faith. I will see if he knows his Creed, if he will denounce Satan and all his works. But that is not enough! The devil will lie. I must have an exact confession of his sins. Who? When? Where? How many times did you meet? What did you plan? I have the names of others I can use. I can lie for Christ's sake and claim that he has been implicated by others. If he doesn't talk, then torture will get at the truth. Why is it men always tell the truth when you torture them? Oh, what I must do for Christ's love!

Where am I? I am in my country palace, this fortress high on a hill overlooking Toledo, which was my great grandfather's. I made it a gift to the church. The cellar is equipped with the most perfect instruments of torture. This is my home and God's home.

When is it? It is 6:30 A.M. I have just come from a night vigil. I have been fasting. See how thin I am. The sinner has been chained all night to the cell wall and my soul has been chained to a spiritual cell wall. Now we must act! By noon we will have a confession, and more names on pieces of paper. The time to get rid of the devil and all his agents is now!

8

Emotional problems

Actor *What's wrong? I wept but the audience was cold.*
Director *What about the other actors on stage with you, did they weep?*
Actor *I don't recall. I didn't notice.*
Director *Are you telling me that you did not sense whether or not your emotions reached them?*
Actor *I was so excited. I was watching the audience so closely that I did not notice the other actors. I tell you I was playing at such a pitch that I don't remember anything except myself and the audience!*[1]

It is important now to remember that you are building an acting technique to help you become a total actor. Remember that the physical actions you have learned to execute truthfully are to be used for getting at your emotions. Now that you are about to act out emotional problems, you are not to throw away everything that you have learned to this point!

[1] Stanislavski, *Stanislavski's Legacy,* p. 133.

Repeat to yourself that emotions are released through actions. If, as an actor, you rush to play an emotion, you are trying to play results and to become an exhibitionist.

Aristotle, who based drama on action, knew the truth of the psycho-physical process—or involvement of emotion and action—two thousand years before Pavlov and Freud. Sonia Moore, an authority on the Stanislavski System, was asked by the *Tulane Drama Review* editors, "How should the method of physical actions be used during training and during rehearsals?" Her response:

> Students must be taught awareness of the psycho-physical processes of an action. Any exercises have value if students understand their purpose: to become aware of the laws of nature through which we function. They must learn to fulfill the psycho-physical action. In rehearsing a play, an actor must know that an action is his means of building a character; he must be capable of selecting physical actions that express the character and will involve his inner life. Choice of actions is artistic process; only an action that expresses a character is artistic. When an actor masters the choice of actions and is capable of making his creative process understandable to the audience, he becomes a true actor—says Stanislavski.[1]

With this excellent advice in mind, execute your improvisations on emotional problems. There are both benefits and dangers implicit in this sort of exercise.

Among the benefits:

The exercise will help you establish the habit of acting towards goals to fulfill needs. The importance of asking yourself, "What is my objective?" and "What is my action?" cannot be over-stressed.

The exercise also will help you to develop an inner radar system with which you can work off your fellow actors and off objects and keep from acting alone, for yourself only. It will start you on a psychic inventory of yourself, both intellectual and emotional, which will help you to know your own inner resources.

[1] Sonia Moore, "The Method of Physical Actions," *Tulane Drama Review* 9 (Summer, 1965): No. 4, pp. 92–93.

It will function as an emotional calisthenic, which keeps your emotions working.

Finally, it is a sound preparation for the more difficult work which is to follow.

Among the dangers:

Never get the false idea that your acting ability is as good as your improvisational ability. This is not so. Young actors can usually act several years ahead of themselves when they work improvisationally. Don't rush away from a successful improvisation thinking you are ready for Lear, Macbeth, or even a lead in summer stock.

Don't fall in love with your emotional moment. It is important not to get the idea that mere emotionalism is acting. There has been a vogue for Italian filmmakers to capitalize on the Italian temperament by filming grandmothers sobbing over dead bodies, or irate fathers beating shrieking children, all of which is very emotional but certainly not art. Controlled emotion is what you are striving for.

Don't use improvisations as game playing. Improvisations must be well planned and thoroughly criticized immediately afterwards. Approach improvisational work as a discipline which will help you toward specific acting objectives.

Some of you will take to improvisations more readily than others and will have a ball. Others will have some difficulty in using physical actions to unlock your emotions. Be patient, if you find it difficult.

A common trap for students doing improvisations is to fall into the habit of using words instead of actions. Words can be actions when they are connected to the inner purpose. Speak for a purpose, but do not talk instead of doing. Another type of student, the avoider, tends to intellectualize himself out of his needs in order to avoid the conflict he would have to enter if he had to try to fulfill them. This actor finds it easier not to believe in his given circumstances. All the time he's improvising, the audience knows he doesn't really believe in the situation. If you, like the avoider, have the tendency to intellectualize, then try using the magic lever of "as if." Tell yourself you are going to behave "as if" the situation were thus.

Stanislavski tells an anecdote about a nervous young man who, wanting to act, visited a famous actor in his dressing room. The young man stammered, paused, rubbed his hands, and finally, with great effort, made his ambition known. Having listened patiently, the actor then instructed the young man to leave the room and re-enter, duplicating what he had just said and done in an improvisation. The young man, confused, said he couldn't possibly do that again. Then, the great actor told him, he would never be an actor. He was dismissed.[1]

The young man was unable to behave "as if" he were an ambitious novice with the golden opportunity to explain his ambitions to a great actor. But this technique for "acting" one's way through a difficult moment was used by a natural actor, James Boswell, the biographer of the great Dr. Johnson. Boswell, a young Scottish lawyer, was in London to argue his first case before the London bar, and was understandably nervous. How did he control his nervousness? "I drank a couple of large bumpers of white wine," he tells us. "It did me no good. It confused me without inspiriting me. When I got to Westminster Hall, I grew better. I amused my mind, sometimes with the idea of my being an English counsellor, sometimes with the idea of my being a Scots lawyer come up to plead one of the appeals from the court of his country, which was the truth."[2] Behaving as if his own situation were his own distanced Boswell enough from his difficult moment to make him master of it.

Improvisational work for emotional problems can be done in one of two ways. The story line can be provided by the instructor, and the actors can then fill in the given circumstances. Or, the actor can create his own story line. You can decide which way to work. If you are bothered by having to think up a plot situation, ask the instructor for help. Plot lines can be borrowed from plays, history, newspaper stories, from your own imagination. In any case, fill in the given circumstances. Who are you? What do you want? Why do you want what you want? How can you get it? Where are you? When is it?

[1] Stanislavski, *Art of the Stage,* p. 220.

[2] James Boswell, *Boswell for the Defence, 1769–1774,* ed. Wimsatt and Pottle, (New York: McGraw Hill, 1959), p. 114.

How to set up improvisations to solve emotional problems

1. Choose a problem in which you can believe, so that you can work with it.

2. Answer all of the questions of the given circumstances in great detail. You will then have your objective set up and you will know why you want it. Make sure you have several alternative how's in case one or more are thwarted. Always have a sense of immediacy about your improvisation. The action cannot be delayed; it must be performed *now*.

3. Do not ask the obstacle actors what they plan to do. This would negate the whole improvisation. You and your obstacles must work separately from the same story line. This will assure that some kind of spontaneity arises, either from your sharp wit or from your unconscious mind, and spontaneity is one objective of the System.

4. The instructor must be prepared to interfere, if necessary, in case: (a) the improvisation gets too false and is wasting everyone's time (if, for instance, it is all talk and no action); or (b) the improvisation gets too violent and an actor is in physical danger.

I can remember an improvisation during which the actor, in an effort to get money from an actress, had exhausted many how's by pleading, bribing, seducing, joking; finally, he resorted to physical violence by choking. He placed both hands firmly on the actress's neck and began to squeeze. She fought, and he squeezed harder. She continued her action—to resist—and he continued his—to get the money, by choking. Finally, when the actress had turned blue in the face, the instructor yelled, "*Stop!*" The class was absolutely enthralled by the enactment of a murder right before its eyes. The actress, gasping for air, squeaked, "He was killing me!" The instructor answered coldly, "So why didn't you drop dead?"

Perhaps it was no accident that the girl student became a television casting director rather than an actress. And the class learned that on stage when you are seriously strangled, you drop dead. Extreme physical violence is to be avoided.

Before starting work on emotional improvisations, it is important to touch once more on the importance of your intellectual and cultural growth. Improvisations will very quickly unmask and exhaust a shallow mind and personality.

It is unpardonable for a twentieth century actor to be psychologically naive. Modern psychology, of course, like many systems, was tacitly understood long before it was formulated. Sophocles' knowledge of the unconscious may actually have been as profound as Freud's. Shakespeare's understanding of neurotic and psychotic behavior is unparalleled even today. But you ought to be able to express your own knowledge of psychology in modern terms. Psychological conflict is dramatic, the heartbeat of drama. Hedda Gabler, Jocasta, Lear, Willy Loman, Blanche Dubois, Electra, and Hamlet all belong to that endless picture gallery of the family of man, displaying various mental aberrations and emotional drives; you will need to understand them in terms of modern psychology. For this reason, you should read Freud, Jung, and other important authors on psychology.

Some acting students find that emotional release on demand is impossible. This is because they go directly after the emotion and therefore kill it immediately. The following exercise is to help you achieve emotional release without playing the emotion itself. You might think of it like this: Your emotions lie, like oil reserves in the earth, buried deep in your subconscious, and the only way to release them is to drill down with an action. Truthfully performed actions which derive from the given circumstances can release honest emotions.

THE EMPTY CHAIR EXERCISE

This emotional exercise has been used in encounter groups to help people free their feelings.

Place an empty chair in the center of the room or stage. Each member of the group, then, must pick one person with whom he is emotionally involved and imagine that person to be sitting in the chair. Each person in turn advances to the chair to tell the person he imagines to be sitting there exactly what he thinks of him or her. No holds barred, let it all out! Your action, which you must think of in terms of transitive verbs, is to find out the truth, or to get things straight, or to tell that person off!

You should quickly find that the action you have chosen will release your deepest emotions towards the person you have chosen.

THE EMOTIONAL IMPROVISATION

Select actors, fill in the given circumstances, and improvise the following situations:

1 You need the one family car for tonight. Obstacle actor or actors: your parents, who also have to have the car for an important date with your father's boss.

2 You want a specific lead role in a play. You know you can really do the part. This is the last hour of the last day of casting. Obstacle actor: a director who is not planning to use you. His producer has a favorite who is not as good as you are.

3 You need one extra credit to graduate. Convince your teacher he should pass you. Obstacle actor: a tough and honest teacher who has never changed a grade.

4 You need $500 now for an emergency. Obstacle actor: your friend, who has the $500, but has to send it at once to his sick mother.

5 You need the room, which you share with a roommate, for a special date. Obstacle actor: your roommate, who has a cold. It's a freezing winter night and he intends to take a hot bath and go to bed with a hot drink.

6 You have to break off an engagement with the person you are supposed to marry tomorrow. Obstacle actor: your affianced, who has never loved anyone but you and cannot face losing you.

If the above situations don't appeal to you, make up your own emotional improvisation. If you are using something close to you, remember to use the structure of the given circumstances, plus an obstacle actor.

9

Total acting for total characterization

Why should we change into another character when we shall be less attractive in it than in real life? You see, you really love yourself in the part more than you love the part in yourself. That is a mistake. You have capabilities. You can show not only yourself but a role created by you.

STANISLAVSKI[1]

The raw materials for building a character must come from you. But this should not be considered so much a limitation as an invitation to infinite variety.

A small hollow box strung with catgut in the hands of an unmusical person will yield an unbearable screeching but in the hands of a trained musician can produce music. Any untalented person may find fault with his instrument and say that it has built-in limitations. The talented person, however, uses the instrument, even with its limitations, to express a great variety of ideas and moods.

Young actors are very timid when it comes to character work, and

[1] *Building a Character,* p. 20.

the awe they feel at the thought of building a character drives them to seek refuge in clichés and shortcuts.

Remember not to imitate some other actor's imitation of life. An imitation of an imitation will be blurred, weak, even false. Remember that you are your only instrument, and life itself should be your only pattern.

Suggested guidelines for building a character

Don't ever think that you can work in only one possible way. Since the characters in most plays are real men and women, they are made up of inner feelings which are expressed through physical actions, including words. But the manner of your approach to your character must be left up to you. You may start with the "inner feeling" and work outward, or you may reverse the method to start with the outward appearance and the physicalization and work inward to the inner feelings. Use whichever method works best for you, and your method may well change from character to character.

Either approach, however, must be connected to part of the given circumstances. Questions about the given circumstances—divided into "inner" and "outer"—are given below to help you in this approach to characterization. As you become more experienced, the arbitrary divisions into "inner" and "outer" may disappear.

Remember not to answer the questions about the given circumstances until you have read the entire play, preferably several times. Don't attempt character work from one scene; this shortcut will only hurt your work. Connect all acting work to the entire play.

Both plays and characters have dominant ideas which can be discovered in them, though different directors and actors may differ as to the precise dominant idea inherent in each play or character. The play's main idea, as intended by the playwright (and interpreted by the director!) is called the theme of the play. The dominating idea connected to the character is called the spine of the character, and it must be related to the theme of the play. If you are in a full production, your director will tell the entire company what the play is about, and how each part relates to it. As an example, read the interesting "Notebook for *A Streetcar Named Desire*," by the director, Elia Kazan.[1] Kazan decided that the theme of the play was that a "confused bit of light and culture [Blanche] puts out a cry. It is snuffed out by the crude forces of violence, insensibility, and vulgarity [Stanley]." To this theme of the play he related a spine for each character. Blanche: "find protection: the tradition of the old South says that it must be through another person." Stella: "hold onto Stanley (Blanche the antagonist)." Stanley: "keep things his way (Blanche the antagonist)." Mitch: "get away from his Mother (Blanche the lever)." Note that each spine is expressed in a transitive verb—an action!

If you are preparing a scene for production in the classroom and have no director but yourself, you yourself must do this preparatory work. What is the theme of the play? The spine of your character? How do they relate? It is for this reason that you must never read *only* the scene you propose to act.

You know already how to work from the given circumstances, and that is knowing at least half of what you need to know in order to build a character.

Inner connected questions

Who am I? Fill in a complete biography. Particularize and stick to the first person singular throughout.

What do I want? Need is the heartbeat of character work. The answer to this question is usually connected to the theme of the play and to the spine of the character. (See above, Kazan's character spines, which are a response to this question.) Do not go on in your work until you have found your need. But once you think you have found it, do not be afraid to change it, especially if you have found a better way to serve the play.

Why do I want it? This answer will unleash your emotions. You will discover the psychological makeup of your character. Open up, and let the emotions flow. But don't play the emotion! Make sure your

[1] Elia Kazan, "Notebook for *A Streetcar Named Desire*," *Directing the Play*, ed. Toby Cole and Helen Krich Chinoy (New York and Indianapolis: Bobbs-Merrill, 1953), pp. 296–310.

"Why" is connected to your need. Keep your emotions controlled by actions.

Outer connected questions

How do I get what I want? You have already worked on improvisations solving this question, and you know that the answer comes in smaller beats of physical actions. Now, however, you must work on another "how," the character's mannerisms, or the "character how." Laurence Olivier calls his character how's, or physical characterization, his "green umbrella," for it covers his entire character work. The character how, or the character's mannerisms, must become a foundation stone for the smaller "how" beats of physical actions. How, for instance, does your character use his body throughout the play? Does he move quickly or slowly? Is he stiff, awkward, or graceful? Nearsighted? Hard of hearing? Nervous and fidgety? Any specific gestures or noticeable body language? Here animal images can help you. Stanislavski remembers Salvini, playing Othello, in one memorable scene "crying like a tiger in the desert when he has lost his mate." He goes on, "At that moment the likeness of Salvini's Othello to a tiger was self-evident. I understood now that even before, in the embraces of Desdemona and in the subtle, feline manners of the speech in the Senate, even in his very method of walking, I had guessed in him the presence of a beast of prey."[1]

Harold Clurman likes to direct by bestowing on each actor in his play one characteristic gesture which he calls the "psychologic gesture." When he directed Arthur Miller's *Incident at Vichy,* he devised for each actor a spine, in terms of an action, but also a gesture. Lebeau, the painter's, was "arms apart, questioning the world. Then dropping them in discouragement." The police captain's: "A malicious smirk on his face like a man about to play a dirty trick or discover something which will justify his pleasure in punishment. Walks with a noiseless tread." The boy's: "He's bent over in the pose of 'The Thinker,' turned toward the corridor door—*the way out.*"[2]

[1] *My Life in Art,* p. 271.

[2] Harold Clurman, "Director's Notes: *Incident at Vichy,*" *Tulane Drama Review* 9 (Summer, 1965): No. 4, pp. 77–90. Clurman derived his idea of the psychologic gesture from Michael Chekhov.

Another important element of the character how is voice placement. Pick one voice and use it consistently throughout the play as an expression of your character's distinct personality. This is an element of character work much neglected in America, but its importance cannot be over-rated. For a discussion of voice placement, see Chapter Five. If you can learn to free your voice for character work, you will discover that it will enrich and expand your potential for playing many different kinds of people.

Dustin Hoffman, at the outset of his career, did a television role in the play, *Journey of the Fifth Horse,* which earned him a great deal of attention. Here was a young actor unafraid to use a completely nasally placed voice in order to project a character full of tension. The voice, with other carefully selected characteristics, succeeded in making the role a great advertisement of the young actor's talents.

It must be stressed here that both the psychological gesture and voice placement naturally are connected to the given circumstances. Why you make such a movement, assume such a posture, or use such a voice must be justified by what you want and why you want it. How you will obtain your needs will affect your physical and vocal mannerisms.

Where am I? Make sure you understand the time and place you are in. You must, especially, know your stage environment. Stanislavski used to have his sets built around his actors' needs. This probably will not be done for you; in America today, the set is usually thrust upon the actor. But when doing scene work, use props that will help you create the environment necessary for you to create a character. Use a chair, a table, a lamp, a picture, a blanket, anything that will help to make your character feel secure and at home. Is the setting for your scene comfortable or uncomfortable, and why? Is it in the tropics, Siberia, a noisy city apartment, a quiet country retreat? What is going on in the next room? Is someone possibly eavesdropping on you? Is someone dying nearby?

How do you behave when you enter a strange room for the first time? Your behavior is not the same as when you enter a familiar room. An actor unprepared as to place—who has given no thought to this problem—will enter, with complete familiarity, an environment in which supposedly he has never been, because he has been there so often in rehearsal. If, however, place has been established, the set will *always* be strange to him, and *never* familiar.

Study *where* you are in thorough detail, and make sure that you fully understand where the set is located, knowing that this orientation will help to establish your characterization.

When is it? The when of a play involves the period, the season, and the time of day.

Period is vital to a play. The proper accommodation of the actor to the period involves the knowledge of style. Your play may be placed in today's world, or it may be placed between World Wars I and II, or in the Victorian period, the Restoration, Elizabethan, medieval, or classical Greek periods. Any one of these may demand that you act with a certain style. (Style will be discussed at length in Chapter Twelve.) Characters of different periods are affected by that period's customs, conventions, traditions. Costumes and makeup must be authentic. You must learn to handle the swords, fans, togas, capes, canes, snuff boxes, teacups, hoop skirts, dripping lace cuffs, heavy wigs, masks, and other appurtenances given you. Perhaps you may want to use a prop or costume yourself, in order to help in your characterization. The libraries are filled with books on costume that will help you to understand your period. There are also excellent guides to makeup: One is Herman Buchman's *Stage Makeup*, designed to guide the beginner in doing a professional job. Never imagine, however, that makeup and costume will give you a character. They are aids, not solutions; decorations, not foundations. Neither Duse nor Salvini used any makeup at all.

If you are acting in a period play, and are wearing a costume that is heavy or cumbrous by today's standards, don't wait until the dress rehearsal to put it on. Instead, anticipate the problems the costumes create at the dress rehearsal, and wear sheets or old clothes from the Salvation Army at your earliest rehearsals. If you do this, the dress rehearsal will not find you floundering and so distracted by your costume that you can't act. I have seen college productions almost ruined by the arrival of the costumes.

Props can also help in character building. I have heard Robert Lewis tell the anecdote of how, as an actor, he could not solve a characterization problem. Nothing he did, even with the director's help, worked. He had a character background based on a particularized set of given circumstances that would have filled volumes. He tried improvisations of every kind. He tried animal images. Still the characterization eluded him. It was, he felt, dull and lifeless. Then one day on the set he picked up a cane that had been left lying about, and that was it! The minute he picked up the cane, he began to walk in a certain way, to use his voice in a certain way, and all these mannerisms united to create a beautiful characterization. The director promptly warned him not to go back and try to figure out what had happened, but just to go on using the cane. In this case the cane did not create the characterization; it acted as a lightening rod for all the energy of the actor's preparatory work, which had not been done in vain.

Season, too, must be taken into account. Seasons and their climates have a profound psychological effect on plays. Shakespeare consistently used the elements and seasons to reflect inner psychological states of his characters. Even if you are indoors throughout the play, remember to be aware of what season it is outside. And what's the weather?

The time of day is also important. Remember, through your character, to reflect the supposed, not the actual, time of day.

Additional hints for building a character

What hints does the playwright supply you with as you read the play? Physical description? Psychological clues?

What do you (the character) do in the play? Read it carefully! What you do is what you are!

What do the other characters say about you that you can use? (Not all remarks will be useful; the character may be lying).

What do you say about yourself? Can this testimony be trusted? If not, what does that tell you about your character?

Make sure that your character how's, your mannerisms, are connected to character needs. Be very selective. Use mannerisms sparingly and artfully. Perhaps you can adapt Clurman's idea of one main psychological gesture.

Remember the spine of your character. Your main need must be connected to the main idea, or theme, of the play.

In all character-building work, you must not work in a vacuum. You need to relate to the other characters. All the assembled facts of the given circumstances, your biography, must be connected to the whole play.

In summation, you are the instrument. The characters to be played are the score. Instruments can play many different kinds of music, but not *all* music. You with your instrument will be able to play many different kinds of characters, but not all characters.

Frequently, actors of all ages and degrees of experience are upset because a director doesn't see them in some particular part. Usually older actors have learned to be realistic about their limitations. But younger actors are like Don Quixote, anxious to conquer each oncoming character. Don't let the idea of typecasting crush you. After all, your basic personality—that distinctive essence of you, with your hair, height, and vocal quality—can never be utterly erased. "But I can *act* it!" You probably can act the part, but the playwright and the director have particular images in mind for that character and you will find it very difficult to change their minds. Be realistic! If you are male, but 5′4″, blond with blue eyes, and have a high-pitched voice, don't try out for Othello. Yet, Garrick was short, and Salvini somewhat stout. If you can really act, it is possible to overcome physical obstacles.

In order to play as many characters as possible, you should try always to be alert and should constantly observe and absorb the life around you. Be a sponge, soaking up experience from paintings, sculpture, music, the dance, the opera, ballet, the theater; live and read, go to movies, see the best of television. These sources will feed your soul and repay you a hundredfold for your attention. As Marowitz put it, "The resourceful actor, because he has more to draw on, will give the appearance of variety by simply utilising the abundance of his nature. The resourceless actor, unblessed with such abundance, can do no more than exhibit his paucity in half a dozen slightly modified versions. The crime is not acting oneself, but not having enough of oneself to act!"[1]

[1] Marowitz, *The Method as Means,* p. 17.

SENSE MEMORY EXERCISE FOR CHARACTERIZATION

Do a sense memory exercise in a one-beat problem that must be executed with a unique physical characteristic—lameness, near-sightedness, or other traits.

IMPROVISATION FOR CHARACTERIZATION *(1–3)*

1 Create an improvisation with your characterization based on an animal image. Be careful not to be too literal. Select one or two outstanding characteristics of the animal that will help you. For example: a nervous character might well be based on a squirrel, with its quick turns of the head. You might characteristically keep your hand held to your mouth, and nibble at your fingernails.

2 Create an improvisation that needs a special voice placement, plus one of the physical characteristics used above.

3 Solve an emotional improvisation based on complete given circumstances for a character that is psychologically disturbed. Make sure your physical life stems from a neurotic or psychotic root.

READINGS: *Spoon River Anthology*

The following selections from Edgar Lee Masters' *Spoon River Anthology* are particularly suited for the practice of character building. You are spared the necessity of reading entire plays and don't have to make up rehearsal schedules with acting partners. Yet these capsulized monologues still require you to use the following order to build a character:

1 Determine the given circumstances for the inner-connected questions: Who am I? What do I want? Why do I want it?

2 Determine the given circumstances for the outer-connected questions: How am I going to get it? Answer for beats or actions, and for character mannerisms, gesture, bearing, voice placement. Where am I? When is it?

3 If a particular character moves you to improvise a costume or create a makeup, then do so.

The following characters are included here for your convenience. If you exhaust them, you can go to the source, *Spoon River Anthology*.[1] The book presents a gallery of Spoon River people, poets, atheists, artists, doctors, editors, tradesmen, farmers, housewives, lovers, and soldiers, "all, all, sleeping on the hill," all talking from their graves. The poems are short and compact, and therefore challenging to the actor attempting to build a character.

Before beginning your work, here are a couple of warnings. "In trying to get away from the boring monotony of their reading actors ornament their speech, especially if they are reciting poetry. They resort to artificial vocal floweriness, cadences, abrupt lowering and raising of the voice, so characteristic of conventional high-flown elocution, which does nothing whatsoever to convey the emotions germaine to the role, and consequently leaves with more perceptive listeners a sense of falseness."[2] Remember, too, that there is always the temptation not to prepare, the idea that maybe, if you just plunge in and read, that something will happen automatically, a miracle, a perfect reading! The following characterizations were not chosen as readings, so be careful. They are acting problems for character work. Now build a character!

EUGENE CARMAN

Rhodes' slave! Selling shoes and gingham,
Flour and bacon, overalls, clothing, all day
    long
For fourteen hours a day for three hundred and
    thirteen days
For more than twenty years,
Saying "Yes'm" and "Yes, sir" and "Thank
    you"

[1] Edgar Lee Masters, *Spoon River Anthology* (New York: Macmillan, 1915).
[2] Stanislavski, *Stanislavski's Legacy*, p. 190.

A thousand times a day, and all for fifty dollars a
month.
Living in this stinking room in the rattle-trap "Com-
mercial."
And compelled to go to Sunday School, and to
listen
To the Rev. Abner Peet one hundred and four times
a year
For more than an hour at a time,
Because Thomas Rhodes ran the church
As well as the store and the bank.
So while I was tying my neck-tie that morning
I suddenly saw myself in the glass:
My hair all gray, my face like a sodden pie.
So I cursed and cursed: You damned old thing!
You cowardly dog! You rotten pauper!
You Rhodes' slave! Till Roger Baughman
Thought I was having a fight with some one,
And looked through the transom just in time
To see me fall on the floor in a heap
From a broken vein in my head.

To get you started, let's work on the given circumstances for Eugene Carman, using creative imagination to fill in gaps.

Who am I? I am a weak man, full of self-loathing, a store clerk who has worked for peanuts for more than twenty years, all of which time was like serving a jail sentence. I only did it because I felt that life had passed me by when I was jilted by the only girl I ever loved, who ran away with my savings, enough for me to have set myself up in my own business. I entered Rhodes' store, a man too hurt to pick himself up and start again. At the end of twenty years I wake up enough to feel the full brunt of self-loathing, longing for self-destruction that is in me!

What do I want? I want to be free of Rhodes, of the bowing and scraping, and the Sunday school, and the awful room I live in. Death is the only way to freedom for which I have strength. I have nothing to live for, and I am suddenly ashamed of myself. I have just awakened to my state, like a dreamer waking from a nightmare. What escape is there from my nightmare?

How am I going to get my freedom? I can imagine no way, except death.

Where am I? In a dark, smelly, cheap room in a flyspecked firetrap of a hotel on the other side of the tracks. The place stinks of the old spittoons and the piss-stained clothes of old men, the floor creaks, the bed is broken, it's too hot in summer and too cold in winter. I am in hell! I wish I were dead!

When is it? It's time to go to that damned Sunday school. That bastard Rhodes is waiting. I have to go, his beady eyes are waiting to check me in. Damn him! Damn his store! Damn his church! And damn me for getting ready to go there again!

For physical character traits: I am a beaten man, but I must avoid playing a cliché beaten man. First, I am dead within. I don't move fast, I don't speak fast, until I am angry. My head juts forward like a workhorse's. Yes, I am a broken-down workhorse. My stomach protrudes, my lower lip hangs, my eyes are dull. But when suddenly I *see* my gray hair in the mirror—then I explode like a volcano!

Once you have done the proper work on the given circumstances for each character, you will see how to read the lines. Here you would read slowly, deliberately, like an old workhorse, until you reach the line, "I suddenly saw myself in the glass." At this point, you would explode in self-fury. The effect would be highly dramatic, but the drama would be legitimate, because the change would be justified.

Use the same technique on the following excerpts from *Spoon River*. Be both careful and creative.

GEORGINE SAND MINER

A step-mother drove me from home, embittering me.
A squaw-man, a flaneur and dilettante took my virtue.
For years I was his mistress—no one knew.
I learned from him the parasite cunning

With which I moved with the bluffs, like a flea on a
dog.
All the time I was nothing but "very private" with
different men.
Then Daniel, the radical, had me for years.
His sister called me his mistress;
And Daniel wrote me: "Shameful word, soiling our
beautiful love!"
But my anger coiled, preparing its fangs.
My Lesbian friend next took a hand.
She hated Daniel's sister.
And Daniel despised her midget husband.
And she saw a chance for a poisonous thrust:
I must complain to the wife of Daniel's pursuit!
But before I did that I begged him to fly to London
with me.
"Why not stay in the city just as we have?" he
asked.
Then I turned submarine and revenged his repulse
In the arms of my dilettante friend. Then up to the
surface,
Bearing the letter that Daniel wrote me,
To prove my honor was all intact, showing it to his
wife.
My Lesbian friend and everyone.
If Daniel had only shot me dead!
Instead of stripping me naked of lies,
A harlot in body and soul!

PETIT, THE POET

Seeds in a dry pod, tick, tick, tick,
Tick, tick, tick, like mites in a quarrel—
Faint iambics that the full breeze wakens—
But the pine tree makes a symphony thereof.

Triolets, villanelles, rondels, rondeaus.
Ballades by the score with the same old thought:
The snows and the roses of yesterday are vanished;
And what is love but a rose that fades?
Life all around me here in the village:
Tragedy, comedy, valor and truth,
Courage, constancy, heroism, failure—
All in the loom, and oh what patterns!
Woodlands, meadows, streams and rivers—
Blind to all of it all my life long.
Triolets, villanelles, rondels, rondeaus,
Seeds in a dry pod, tick, tick, tick,
Tick, tick, tick, what little iambics,
While Homer and Whitman roared in the pines?

MRS. WILLIAMS

I was the milliner
Talked about, lied about,
Mother of Dora,
Whose strange disappearance
Was charged to her rearing.
My eye quick to beauty
Saw much beside ribbons
And buckles and feathers
And leghorns and felts,
To set off sweet faces,
And dark hair and gold.
One thing I will tell you
And one I will ask:
The stealers of husbands
Wear powder and trinkets,
And fashionable hats.
Wives, wear them yourselves.
Hats may make divorces—

They also prevent them.
Well now, let me ask you:
If all of the children, born here in Spoon River
Had been reared by the County, somewhere on a
    farm;
And the fathers and mothers had been given their
    freedom
To live and enjoy, change mates if they wished,
Do you think that Spoon River
Had been any the worse?

DORA WILLIAMS

When Reuben Pantier ran away and threw me
I went to Springfield. There I met a lush,
Whose father just deceased left him a fortune.
He married me when drunk. My life was wretched.
A year passed and one day they found him dead.
That made me rich. I moved on to Chicago.
After a time met Tyler Rountree, villain.
I moved on to New York. A gray-haired magnate
Went mad about me—so another fortune.
He died one night right in my arms, you know.
(I saw his purple face for years thereafter.)
There was almost a scandal. I moved on,
This time to Paris. I was now a woman,
Insidious, subtle, versed in the world and rich.
My sweet apartment near the Champs Élysées
Became a center for all sorts of people,
Musicians, poets, dandies, artists, nobles,
Where we spoke French and German, Italian, English.
I wed Count Navigato, native of Genoa.
We went to Rome. He poisoned me, I think.
Now in the Campo Santo overlooking

The sea where young Columbus dreamed new worlds,
See what they chiseled: "*Contessa Navigato*
Implora eterna quiete."

HERBERT MARSHALL

All your sorrow, Louise, and hatred of me
Sprang from your delusion that it was wantonness
Of spirit and contempt of your soul's rights
Which made me turn to Annabelle and forsake you.
You really grew to hate me for love of me,
Because I was your soul's happiness,
Formed and tempered
To solve your life for you, and would not.
But you were my misery. If you had been
My happiness would I not have clung to you?
This is life's sorrow:
That one can be happy only where two are;
And that our hearts are drawn to stars
Which want us not.

WILLARD FLUKE

My wife lost her health,
And dwindled until she weighed scarce ninety
pounds.
Then that woman, whom the men
Styled Cleopatra, came along.
And we—we married ones
All broke our vows, myself among the rest.
Years passed and one by one
Death claimed them all in some hideous form,
And I was borne along by dreams
Of God's particular grace for me,

And I began to write, write, write, reams on reams
Of the second coming of Christ.
Then Christ came to me and said,
"Go into the church and stand before the congregation
And confess your sin."
But just as I stood up and began to speak
I saw my little girl, who was sitting in the front seat—
My little girl who was born blind!
After that, all is blackness!

KNOWLT HOHEIMER

I was the first fruits of the battle of Missionary Ridge.
When I felt the bullet enter my heart
I wished I had staid at home and gone to jail
For stealing the hogs of Curl Trenary,
Instead of running away and joining the army.
Rather a thousand times the county jail
Than to lie under this marble figure with wings,
And this granite pedestal
Bearing the words, "*Pro Patria*."
What do they mean, anyway?

DOCTOR MEYERS

No other man, unless it was Doc Hill,
Did more for people in this town than I.
And all the weak, the halt, the improvident
And those who could not pay flocked to me.
I was good-hearted, easy Doctor Meyers.
I was healthy, happy, in comfortable fortune,
Blest with a congenial mate, my children raised,
All wedded, doing well in the world.

And then one night, Minerva, the poetess,
Came to me in her trouble, crying.
I tried to help her out—she died—
They indicted me, the newspapers disgraced me,
My wife perished of a broken heart.
And pneumonia finished me.

MRS. MEYERS

He protested all his life long
The newspapers lied about him villainously;
That he was not at fault for Minerva's fall,
But only tried to help her.
Poor soul so sunk in sin he could not see
That even trying to help her, as he called it,
He had broken the law human and divine.
Passers by, an ancient admonition to you:
If your ways would be ways of pleasantness,
And all your pathways peace,
Love God and keep his commandments.

MINERVA JONES

I am Minerva, the village poetess,
Hooted at, jeered at by the Yahoos of the street
For my heavy body, cock-eye, and rolling walk,
And all the more when "Butch" Weldy
Captured me after a brutal hunt.
He left me to my fate with Doctor Meyers;
And I sank into death, growing numb from the feet up,
Like one stepping deeper and deeper into a stream of ice.
Will some one go to the village newspaper,
And gather into a book the verses I wrote?—
I thirsted so for love!
I hungered so for life!

"INDIGNATION" JONES

You would not believe, would you,
That I came from good Welsh stock?
That I was purer blooded than the white trash here?
And of more direct lineage than the New Englanders
And Virginians of Spoon River?
You would not believe that I had been to school
And read some books.
You saw me only a run-down man,
With matted hair and beard
And ragged clothes.
Sometimes a man's life turns into a cancer
From being bruised and continually bruised,
And swells into a purplish mass,
Like growths on stalks of corn.
Here was I, a carpenter, mired in a bog of life
Into which I walked, thinking it was a meadow,
With a slattern for a wife, and poor Minerva, my daughter,
Whom you tormented and drove to death.
So I crept, crept, like a snail through the days
Of my life.
No more you hear my footsteps in the morning,
Resounding on the hollow sidewalk,
Going to the grocery store for a little corn meal
And a nickel's worth of bacon.

MRS. BENJAMIN PANTIER

I know that he told that I snared his soul
With a snare which bled him to death.
And all the men loved him,
And most of the women pitied him.
But suppose you are really a lady, and have delicate tastes,
And loathe the smell of whiskey and onions.

And the rhythm of Wordsworth's "Ode" runs in your ears,
While he goes about from morning till night
Repeating bits of that common thing;
"Oh, why should the spirit of mortal be proud?"
And then, suppose:
You are a woman well endowed,
And the only man with whom the law and morality
Permit you to have the marital relation
Is the very man that fills you with disgust
Every time you think of it—while you think of it
Every time you see him?
That's why I drove him away from home
To live with his dog in a dingy room
Back of his office.

BENJAMIN PANTIER

Together in this grave lie Benjamin Pantier, attorney at law,
And Nig, his dog, constant companion, solace and friend.
Down the gray road, friends, children, men and women,
Passing one by one out of life, left me till I was alone
With Nig for partner, bed-fellow, comrade in drink.
In the morning of life I knew aspiration and saw glory.
Then she, who survives me, snared my soul
With a snare which bled me to death,
Till I, once strong of will, lay broken, indifferent,
Living with Nig in a room back of a dingy office.
Under my jaw-bone is snuggled the bony nose of Nig—
Our story is lost in silence. Go by, mad world!

OLLIE MCGEE

Have you seen walking through the village
A man with downcast eyes and haggard face?
That is my husband who, by secret cruelty

Never to be told, robbed me of my youth and my beauty;
Till at last, wrinkled and with yellow teeth,
And with broken pride and shameful humility,
I sank into the grave.
But what think you gnaws at my husband's heart?
The face of what I was, the face of what he made me!
These are driving him to the place where I lie.
In death, therefore, I am avenged.

FLETCHER MCGEE

She took my strength by minutes,
She took my life by hours,
She drained me like a fevered moon
That saps the spinning world.
The days went by like shadows,
The minutes wheeled like stars.
She took the pity from my heart,
And made it into smiles.
She was a hunk of sculptor's clay,
My secret thoughts were fingers:
They flew behind her pensive brow
And lined it deep with pain.
They set the lips, and sagged the cheeks,
And drooped the eyes with sorrow.
My soul had entered in the clay,
Fighting like seven devils.
It was not mine, it was not hers;
She held it, but its struggles
Modeled a face she hated,
And a face I feared to see.
I beat the windows, shook the bolts.
I hid me in a corner—
And then she died and haunted me,
And hunted me for life.

10

Shakespeare, Stanislavski, and you

I have already said in the Preface to this book that the early Method practitioners in America, under the influence of Stanislavski's earlier book, *An Actor Prepares,* trained actors to work on "inner feeling" and neglected to train them to express different styles of acting through the externals of diction and body movement. It was therefore thought that classical plays, and those of Shakespeare in particular, were incompatible with the Stanislavski System.

In fact, in *My Life in Art* (p. 350), Stanislavski, with his usual honesty, had made the following confession long before the American dilemma materialized: "Why can I express my perception of Chekhov but not of Shakespeare? . . . apparently it is not the inner feeling itself but the technique of its expression that prevents me from doing in the plays of Shakespeare what we are able to do in Chekhov."

In the course of his soul searching, Stanislavski came up with the answer: technique. He, of course, went on in *Building a Character,* to stress the importance of voice and diction, relaxation, and body movement.

Body, voice, actions, emotions

Shakespeare, as much as any playwright, supplies us with a wealth of material demanding the talents of the total actor. Shakespeare demands full characterization: complete internal feeling expressed through complete external technique. He demands that the words become actions.

The time has come when a truce must be called between the externalists and the internalists. Alone, neither is right; each is partially right and needs to be joined to the other for the fulfillment of the total actor.

Shakespeare himself knew the difference, of course, between the mere speaking of lines, external acting, and the acting of them with true inner feeling. When Hamlet requests the First Player to give him a speech (II, ii), Polonius' comment on the acting is, "Look, whether he has not turned his colour and has tears in's eyes. Prithee, no more." And Hamlet, left alone, repeats,

> . . . that this player here
> But in a fiction, in a dream of passion,
> Could force his soul so to his own conceit
> That from her working all his visage wann'd;
> Tears in his eyes, distraction in's aspect,
> A broken voice, and his whole function suiting
> With forms to his conceit. . . .

Hamlet makes the point to contrast the player's reaction to his own apparent lack of reaction in the face of a real, not a theatrical, outrage. But it is apparent that Shakespeare supported the idea that excellence and truth in acting are to be achieved through action moved by the inner being, not through a passive state or mood.

When he writes, "could force his soul so to his own conceit/ That from her working all his visage wann'd . . . ," he does not, of course, mean by force what we today would mean. For an actor to "force" today means to play an emotion directly, to go after results. In Shakespeare, force means to mold. The actor's intellect forms an image, conceit, which evokes an emotional response which the actor is able to express both physically and truthfully.

"As a matter of fact," Stanislavski has said, "every physical action has an inner psychological action which gives rise to it. And in every psychological inner action there is always a physical action which expresses its psychic nature: the unity between these two is organic action on the stage."[1]

In order further to understand Shakespeare's ideas about acting, let us examine Hamlet's famous speech to the players:

> Speak the speech, I pray you, as I pronounced it to you, trippingly on the tongue: but if you mouth it, as many of your players do, I had as lief the town-crier spoke my lines. Nor do not saw the air too much with your hand, thus; but use all gently: for in the very torrent, tempest, and as I may say, whirlwind of passion, you must acquire and beget a temperance that may give it smoothness. Oh, it offends me to the soul to hear a robustious periwig-pated fellow[2] tear a passion to tatters, to very rags, to split the ears of the groundlings,[3] who, for the most part, are capable of nothing but inexplicable dumb-shows and noise: I would have such a fellow whipped for o'er doing Termagant;[4] it out-herods Herod:[5] pray you, avoid it. (III, ii)

On one level, this is assuredly William Shakespeare, the playwright, addressing the Globe company! The advice of the entire speech, of which this is only the first of three sections, is so comprehensive that it could be expanded into a full-length acting text.

The very first sentence is a diction lesson which we would do well to attend. Stage speech must not be mumbled, and the only way to avoid mumbling is to move the tongue "trippingly." So if you quickly passed by the lip and tongue exercises in Chapter Five of this book, do not delude yourself into believing that you are the exception of centuries. You are merely lazy—as were, apparently, Shakespeare's comrades. For the next line informs us that many of

[1] Gorchakov, *Stanislavski Directs*, p. 119.

[2] Actors in Shakespeare's time wore great wigs and a lot of false hair.

[3] The ground or pit of the theater was a sunken space below stage level. Those who watched the play from it were the groundlings.

[4] Termagant was the name given in old romances to the god of the Saracens, therefore a villainous heathen. He was traditionally played by yelling, ranting, and howling.

[5] Herod, the murderer of the innocents, was a favorite villain in mystery plays. He too was overplayed.

the players spoke poorly: "But if you mouth it, as many of your players do, I had as lief the town-crier spoke my lines." Have you ever heard the town crier in one of those reproduced eighteenth century villages do his bit? His speech is a mass of vowels and consonants melted into a gooey mess.

Nothing is more precious to a playwright than his words. It is no accident, then, that the playwright Shakespeare gave priority to getting his words clearly enunciated. Taking no chances, evidently, Hamlet even pronounces the speech to the players so that they have a model: "Speak the speech, I pray you, as I pronounced it to you."

In the remaining lines of the speech, Shakespeare condemns overacting and indicating. By tearing a passion to tatters, to very rags, the false actor does not build his part truthfully according to nature, but instead destroys any resemblance to truth. He is playing results. For this kind of actor, Shakespeare—like Christ cleansing the temple—resorts to a whip!

Hamlet's advice to the players continues:

> Be not too tame neither, but let your own discretion be your tutor: suit the action to the word, the word to the action; with this special observance, that you o'erstep not the modesty of nature: for anything so overdone is from the purpose of playing, whose end, both at the first and now, was and is, to hold, as 'twere, the mirror up to nature; to show virtue her own feature, scorn her own image, and the very age and body of the time his form and pressure.[1] Now, this overdone, or come tardy off,[2] though it make the unskilful laugh, cannot but make the judicious grieve; the censure of the which one must, in your allowance,[3] o'erweigh a whole theatre of others. Oh, there be players that I have seen play,—and heard others praise, and that highly,—not to speak it profanely, that, neither having the accent of Christians, nor the gait of Christian, pagan, nor man, have so strutted and bellowed, that I have thought some of nature's journeymen had made men, and not made them well, they imitated humanity so abominably.

Shakespeare certainly does not wish the player to cease acting altogether: ". . . let your own discretion be your tutor." You, and you alone, know when your acting is truthful.

[1] Impression.
[2] Or badly done.
[3] By your admission.

"Suit the action to the word, the word to the action." There is a valid distinction between the two directions. Actions, both physical and psychological, can derive from the word. But conversely, the words of the script can be interpreted according to the subtext, or hidden action or beat beneath the lines. If you were to accompany the words, "I could kill you," with a threatening gesture, you would be suiting the action to the word. If, however, your subtext or beat were to express *love* with the words, and if you said them lovingly, actually making love as you spoke them, you would be suiting the words to the action. Such a radical departure from the words, however, is certainly not to be generally recommended unless it is part of the playwright's plan!

The important lesson to learn is that in a well-written play, as in Shakespeare's plays, the words *are* actions, because they are direct expressions of inner actions.

Shakespeare, the poet of nature, is of course in agreement with Stanislavski: Nature is the basis of art. If you are true to nature, an imitator of life, you are true to life. Shakespeare's mirror, of course, is not a reflector of mere externals, but is the magic mirror of the theater which reflects *human* nature—man's inner feelings, his soul. Nature, in Shakespeare's time, meant the laws of the universe which govern man and his world.

Towards the ends of this section, Shakespeare returns to the ridicule of the ham actor, the egomaniac who puts himself before the play, and who in a moment of colossal egoism thinks the audience has come to see and hear him alone. The end of Hamlet's speech condemns these fellows:

> And let those that play your clowns speak no more than is set down for them: for there be of them that will themselves laugh, to set on some quantity of barren spectators to laugh too; though, in the meantime, some necessary question of the play be then to be considered: that's villanous, and shows a most pitiful ambition in the fool that uses it. Go, make you ready.

There are actors who can rehearse with the company and do everything well until opening night; then madness overtakes them and they forget all the values established, all the beats shared with fellow actors, even the theme of the play, in order to show themselves off or to play for a laugh. It is true that this kind of actor can win the praise of the ignorant; but the discerning critic will not be fooled. There should be no mercy for the selfish actor who wins plaudits for himself at the expense of the play. The words "villanous," "fool," and "pitiful" sum him up nicely.

A lot of ink has been spilled over the question of whether Shakespeare knew about Aristotle and his "rules" and ignored them, or didn't know about them at all. His vocabulary in the speech above, stressing the important words "action" and "imitation," would certainly imply that he was familiar with the Aristotelian ideas. But, like the other Elizabethan playwrights, Shakespeare did not apply "the rules" of the unity of action and time suggested by Aristotle. (The rule of the unity of place was not Aristotelian; it was added by the French critics of the seventeenth century but soon was found to be far too constricting.) Subplots proliferated in the Elizabethan theater, and the alternation of comic with tragic bits certainly violated the Aristotelian ideal of unity. As for Aristotle's recommendation that the play ought, as nearly as possible, be contained in one twenty-four hour period, Shakespeare spans sixteen years between Acts III and IV of *The Winter's Tale!*

But never imagine that because Shakespeare did not follow the Greek model of unity of action, he did not understand that very important idea. His plays contain a superb unity of action of a different kind: every action—tragic, comic, plot, or subplot—is connected thematically to the main theme of his play. And there is a superb unity of thought and imagery in each of his plays that becomes fully apparent only after long study of the texts.

The wholesome neglect of the unities of time and place was made possible by the conventions of platform-acting in the Elizabethan theater. The action was continuous; Shakespeare did not break his dramas down into acts and scenes—this was done later. The place was usually indicated in the lines, and the set remained largely undifferentiated by scenes or props. The scene, if important, would be sketched in in words; the time would be mentioned too, if it was important. Because of the beneficial freedom from sets and props, the Shakespearian play originally had a healthy tempo and rhythm that was entirely lost in the nineteenth century, when productions were so cluttered with heavy scenery, realistic props, and unnecessary crowds, that the pure structural components of the plays were buried.

Today we are back to the platform and purity of action of Shakespeare, although occasionally some bright and bored director or designer will come up with a new way to "do" him. The only way to do Shakespeare, however, is with intellectual honesty and no trickery, no special effects. Study his pure structure, and he will reward you a hundred fold.

Time in Shakespeare, however, is unusually compressed by modern standards, and will create an acting problem for you until you learn to deal with it. In Shakespeare you will have only a few lines in which to develop one action or beat, and then you *must* go on to the next beat, and so on. This telescoping of "psychological time" is done to suit the purpose of the play. All plays present a conventional compression of time. The compression is tighter in verse and in non-realistic plays. In a modern, realistic play, you will have far more time, then, for character development, and the acting beats will not come at you with such speed.

Your approach to characterization, however, will be the same as in any other play. Find out about your character by filling in the given circumstances. In Shakespeare's plays, as in all plays, you can find out something about yourself from what other people say and feel about you, but be careful; Shakespeare's characters are true to life and therefore not to be implicitly trusted. X, in speaking about you, will be speaking from his own point of view, which may be totally or partially unreliable. Study the play to find out which characters are to be believed and which are not.

You also must avoid playing the Monday morning quarterback. In other words, don't play the character in the beginning as he is revealed at the end of the play. Your character has to develop throughout the play. One example of character alteration is Salvini's development of Othello, as interpreted by Stanislavski. Stanislavski saw the change in Othello's character as "this ladder down which Othello descended in the full sight of the spectators from the heights of bliss to the depths of destructive passion."[1] Othello begins the play ap-

[1] *My Life in Art,* p. 270.

parently a perfect creation, his reason and his passion in balance. Jealousy poisons Othello's love and then infects and destroys the man. Or think of Hamlet, who enters as a hurt and indecisive boy, but in the course of the play finds himself and is able to act. Or see Lady Macbeth, so sure she can take the consequences of murdering Duncan, yet knowing so little of herself that in the end she is undone by her own daring. Think of the tamed shrew, the Benedict resigned to marriage, the broken Falstaff. But never play your character's ending in the beginning!

Some acquaintance with the conventions of the Elizabethan theater will be helpful to you. Soliloquies often present a problem because they are not a very popular modern convention, though they are certainly to be found in modern theater. Shakespeare writes two basic kinds of soliloquies, neither addressed primarily to the audience. The first is the thinking-out-loud kind of soliloquy, in which the actor's thoughts are spoken aloud, solely so that we can know what they are. We understand that we are listening to his thoughts. The second kind is the monologue of the old, or mentally imbalanced person, who in real life talks to himself. We understand that we are listening to a real speech. Hamlet's "To be or not to be" is an example of the first kind, the porter's speech in *Macbeth* an example of the second. There also is the monologue which is addressed directly to the audience by a character, usually comic, and occasionally by the "prologue." And there is the aside, which can be a remark to someone on stage or to the audience. Some asides are short expository speeches to make matters clearer to the audience, and some, like genuine soliloquies, are revelations of inner thought.

As Shakespeare uses soliloquies and asides to make thoughts visible to us, he uses another convention to make people invisible. Remember that his plays were originally performed on practically naked platforms adorned with few props, and that it was accordingly difficult to hide people on stage—hence the convention of having characters appear on stage and yet be invisible to others, as in the case of Puck, Ariel, and Prospero. Or the character uses a disguise such as a hat, a cloak, or a beard. These conventions help move the plot smoothly, and—like the time and place conventions—are accepted by the audience if taken for granted by the company.

Another of Shakespeare's conventions, of course, is the use of blank verse. Verse is more compressed in meaning than is prose; you will meet more images, and have to make the transition from one beat to another more quickly than in prose drama. But never for a moment think that a verse drama is less "realistic," that it consists of a series of "poems." All speeches are actions, and are responses to the foregoing speeches. Even the soliloquies relate to what precedes and what follows.

As an example, take the soliloquy by Hamlet just after he has dismissed the players:

Now I am alone!

(The first beat is a response to the acting of the player, who has both paled and wept at the fate of Hecuba. He responds.)

O' what a rogue and peasant slave am I!
Is it not monstrous that this player here,
But in a fiction, in a dream of passion,
Could force his soul so to his own conceit
That from her working all his visage wann'd;
Tears in his eyes, distraction in's aspect,
A broken voice, and his whole function suiting
With forms to his conceit? and all for nothing!
For Hecuba![1]
What's Hecuba to him, or he to Hecuba,
That he should weep for her? What would he do,
Had he the motive and the cue for passion
That I have? He would drown the stage with tears
And cleave the general ear with horrid speech,
Make mad the guilty and appal the free,
Confound the ignorant, and amaze indeed
The very faculties of eyes and ears.

(Hamlet now berates himself and takes himself to task.)

Yet I,
A dull and muddy-mettled rascal, peak
Like John-a-dreams,[2] unpregnant[3] of my cause,

[1] Hecuba, the wife of Priam, King of Troy, was the cause of the player's tears in the speech he recited for Hamlet.

[2] A drowsy ninny.

[3] Unmindful.

And can say nothing; no, not for a king,
Upon whose property and most dear life
A damn'd defeat was made. Am I a coward?
Who calls me villain? breaks my pate across?
Plucks off my beard, and blows it in my face?
Tweaks me by the nose? gives me the lie i' the
throat,
As deep as to the lungs? who does me this, ha?
Why, I should take it: for it cannot be
But I am pigeon-liver'd, and lack gall
To make oppression bitter; or, ere this,
I should have fatted all the region kites
With this slave's offal:—bloody, wanton villain!
Remorseless, treacherous, lecherous, kindless[1] villain!
Oh, vengeance!
Why, what an ass am I! This is most brave,
That I, the son of a dear father murder'd,
Prompted to my revenge by heaven and hell,
Must, like a wench, unpack my heart with words,
And fall a-cursing, like a very drab,
A scullion!
Fie upon't! foh!—About, my brain!

(With the last three words, Hamlet shifts to another beat, resolving on action.)

Hum, I have heard
That guilty creatures, sitting at a play,
Have by the very cunning of the scene
Been struck so to the soul that presently
They have proclaim'd their malefactions;
For murder, though it have no tongue, will speak
With most miraculous organ. I'll have these players
Play something like the murder of my father
Before mine uncle: I'll observe his looks;
I'll tent[2] him to the quick: if he but blench,
I know my course.

[1] Ignoring the laws of kind, or kinship.
[2] Probe.

(This next beat is very important. Right after Hamlet's foregoing resolution, comes his doubt. He doubts his own resolution.)

> The spirit that I have seen
> May be the devil; and the devil hath power
> To assume a pleasing shape; yea, and perhaps
> Out of my weakness and my melancholy,
> As he is very potent with such spirits,
> Abuses me to damn me. I'll have grounds
> More relative than this.

(Hamlet again resolves on his course.)

> The play's the thing
> Wherein I'll catch the conscience of the king.

Obviously the soliloquy is not an interpolated fine "set piece" of poetry, but an important transitional moment in the plot, as well as an important piece of characterization.

Another popular misconception about acting Shakespeare is that the words, being poetry, need special handling, special shades of color—a trap marked "external acting." To play Shakespeare, get into the given situation, know the given circumstances, and know what your beat is. What is your action? Why are you doing it? Then trust Shakespeare to supply you with words that will move fast or slow, to fit the proper action and its accompanying emotional life. Each scene does have a built-in rhythm of its own; I will offer you a demonstration of this fact when you work on a scene from *Twelfth Night,* later. But if you have found the right actions and beats, you will be in tune with the playwright's intentions and with the rhythm of the scene.

But it is quite true that even if you are successfully applying the Method to Shakespeare, you will fail if you do not understand the structure of his lines. Shakespeare's line is blank verse, or unrhymed iambic pentameter. An iamb is an unstressed syllable followed by a stressed syllable (υ –), and an iambic pentameter line is a line made up of five iambs, or, usually, ten syllables. If you are unfamiliar with the unstress-stress pattern, just think of the common words "today," or "hello." Each word is a perfect iamb. Most English words of two syllables have the stress on the first syllable, rather than on the second, but when combined properly into a line, the stresses fall properly:

> This castle hath a pleasant seat; the air
>
> Nimbly and sweetly recommends itself
>
> Unto our gentle senses.

Neither castle nor pleasant is an iamb, because the stress is on the first syllable of each word, but the arrangement of the words within the line makes the line properly iambic pentameter, or blank verse. In the second line, note the inversion of the first foot from an iamb (unstress-stress) to a trochee (stress-unstress), which is a standard foot variation in blank verse, particularly in the first foot.

Blank verse is the most "natural" verse form in English. English falls naturally into the stress-unstress rhythm. You frequently speak in iambic and often speak perfect iambic pentameter lines without being aware of it. Dr. Johnson once offered as an example the line, "Lay your knife and fork upon your plate." (The omission of the first short syllable in the first foot is another common variation in the blank verse line.) You speak in natural iambics, and in English, iambs are the rhythmic norm. There's hardly a chance you identified that last sentence as rhythmically identical with two standard lines of blank verse, but:

> You speak in natural iambics, and
>
> In English iambs are the rhythmic norm.

This should convince you that you will be able to speak Shakespeare well and naturally. (These lines, too, scan well as iambics—two lines, followed by "and naturally"). And that is exactly what you should do, with due deference to the fact that you are speaking compressed, multi-imaged language that demands crisp enunciation. Speak Shakespeare naturally, but speak it "trippingly on the tongue."

Another convention which must be mentioned is the Elizabethan convention of altering words to make the lines scan. This should cause you no trouble when Shakespeare either does or does not use an optional contraction to fit the meter, but there may be other adjustments made to fit the exigencies of meter. One syllable may be deleted from a word; when this happens, you must read it naturally as Shakespeare intended it to be read, without violating the metric pattern of the line. Charity may become char'ty, medicine may become "med'cin," prisoner may become "pris'ner," over becomes "o'er," and so on. Words may also have to be expanded to fit the meter. In particular, the ending in "ed" can be pronounced. Thus condemned becomes con-dem-ned. Words like champion, which we would pronounce "champ-yun," become "champ-i-on." You must develop an ear for the underlying rhythm, and those rhythms must remain unviolated, but you must also speak the sentences naturally, as Shakespeare intended them to be spoken.

As in all the performing arts, the *doing* is the most important thing in acting. And in order for you to learn, supervising the doing must be a sensitive intelligent observer-teacher to comment on your performance. Class work is actually only as good as the instructor or observer. His goals, his evaluations, his reactions, can't be planned in a textbook; and they are going to relate to all the complexities of the performance that you bring him in ways which cannot possibly be anticipated here. I can only say that your teacher must be alert to catch shoddy work, such as generalized or indicated acting, ranting in the place of actions, emotions not connected to beats, the development of cliché acting tricks. He must be shrewd, well-informed, an artistically honest person who is also aware that he's dealing with sensitive artists who must be taught with understanding and tact.

Before you begin, with your instructor's help, to solve the following scenes from Shakespeare, here are a number of procedural steps which I would suggest you use. The order is not necessarily important, so that if you want to start work on the last step, rather than the first, go right ahead. Use the formula any way that gets you, the actor, involved in the scene, so that you will be working in a totally honest and totally exciting, and dramatic, manner.

Suggested preparation for shakespearean scenes

Read the entire play. Don't be lazy about it; get into the habit right away of relating your work to the entire play. Learn to connect your part, the spine of your character, to the theme of the play.

Read everything you need to read, in order to understand the people and the period of the play. If you are doing one of Shakespeare's history plays, read his source, Holinshed or Plutarch. Then read a competent historian who is more up to date, so that you really understand what the conflict was all about. But remember to interpret your character from Shakespeare, not from some dissenting historian! Even if Shakespeare's view is not historically accurate, you must act *as if* it were true.

Answer all the questions of the given circumstances. Who am I? What do I want? Why do I want it? How am I going to get it? Where am I? When is it? Remember, always use the first person in discussing your character. What do *I*, not what does *he*, want? Remember that the answer to this question is the main spine, or super-objective, of your part. It will remain the same throughout the play. The smaller units or actions or beats will change from scene to scene. Why do I want it? must involve psychological and emotional motivations. Be sure and find some sense of immediacy. Why do I want it *now*? How am I going to get it? This answer will be described in beats, which will change as the action of the play progresses. The questions Where am I? and When is it? involve your sense of place and time. These are immensely important, because your behavior must be affected by these answers.

If this preceding work is done properly, you will find yourself solving the question of "the missing scene." All plays begin without having shown one or two preceding scenes, and usually other scenes, in the course of the action, take place offstage. Determining the given circumstances will help you fill in that first missing scene, and the use of improvisations can help you fill in the later missing scenes, so that you, the character, are honestly aware of having experienced them. For example, an actor playing Macbeth might profitably do an improvisation of Duncan's murder, a "missing scene." Work out any improvisations which you feel are necessary for your part. Involve other actors who should be involved.

Discuss the preceding work with your fellow actors. You do not act alone. If your work is isolated and does not mesh with the total scene or play, then it will be destructive to the unity of the work.

Be sure to determine what physical characteristics your character has. How do you hold yourself? How do you walk? Have you an animal image for the part that might help? (Shakespeare is very good at suggesting these. Usually each play has characteristic animal images running through it.) Are you lazy? Energetic? Nearsighted? Neat? Dirty? Clean? Hard of hearing? Soft spoken? Here is where your observation of people can be put to good use, helping you to play a characteristic individual, rather than a cliché.

What sort of voice does your character have? Remember that voice placement is vital to character work. Enjoy using voices other than your own normal speaking voice. Be bold. Experiment; now is the time to do it! But avoid slovenliness in your speech.

Solve the problems found in the words you have to speak. Is the imagery clear to you? Consult the glossary for unfamiliar words. Make sure you understand; if *you* don't, your audience won't.

What are the metronomic demands of the script? In other words, *tempo?* Will you be speaking verse or prose? If verse, have you solved the problem of keeping the underlying rhythm true by identifying the words that will have to be expanded or contracted?

Finally, a word about your next part: Don't ever get into a rut by using the answers to the preceding problems over again, just because they worked the last time. Remember, there are ham method actors. Don't work up an inventory of tricks—psychological, physical, or vocal—to resort to. Art is not self-repeating, it is always inventive. Answer the questions and re-do the work, each time. Try something new.

READING: *Macbeth*

Act I, scene iii, and Act IV, scene i, are combined: A heath. Characters: Three witches and Macbeth. (Hecate is not a fourth witch; it is assumed that Hecate is one of the three witches.)

1 Start with the suggested preparation for Shakespearean scenes (see p. 162). Read Holinshed on Macbeth.

2 Make sure that no two actors use the same physicalizations in character work; all three witches must not fall into the same cliché of the bent-over wicked witch. Develop body movements that are weird, distinctive, grotesque, but not clichés. Here is another example of the truth that an actor cannot work and plan in isolation.

3 Develop different voice placements. Avoid the amateurish approach of having all three witches wail in high-pitched voices.

4 Use sheets, old clothing for costumes; props if needed.

ACT I, SCENE iii

Thunder. Enter the three Witches.

First Witch Where hast thou been, sister?
Sec. Witch Killing swine.
Third Witch Sister, where thou?
First Witch A sailor's wife had chestnuts in her
lap,
And mounch'd, and mounch'd, and mounch'd:—
"Give me," quoth I:
"Aroint[1] thee, witch!" the rump-fed ronyon[2] cries.
Her husband's to Aleppo gone, master o' the
Tiger:[3]
But in a sieve I'll thither sail,[4]
And, like a rat without a tail,[5]
I'll do, I'll do, and I'll do.
Sec. Witch I'll give thee a wind.[6]

1 Begone. This and all the other notes to the scenes from Shakespeare used in this book have been adapted from the excellent notes in the edition, *Plays of Shakespeare,* edited and annotated by Charles and Mary Cowden Clarke (London: Cassell, Petter, and Galpin).

2 A scurvy wretch who feeds on scraps.

3 The ship *Tiger* actually made a voyage to Aleppo in 1583.

4 Witches were supposed to be able to sail in sieves.

5 A witch could turn herself into any animal, but the tail would be missing.

6 Winds were articles of trade, and therefore giving one was a kindness.

First Witch Thou art kind.
Third Witch And I another.
First Witch I myself have all the other;
And the very ports they blow,[1]
All the quarters that they know
I' the shipman's card.[2]
I'll drain him dry as hay:
Sleep shall neither night nor day
Hang upon his pent-house lid;
He shall live a man forbid:[3]
Weary seven-nights nine times nine
Shall he dwindle, peak, and pine:
Though his bark cannot be lost,
Yet it shall be temptest-tost.—
Look what I have.
Sec. Witch Show me, show me.
First Witch Here I have a pilot's thumb,
Wreck'd as homeward he did come. [*Drum within.*
Third Witch A drum, a drum!
Macbeth doth come.
All The weird[4] sisters, hand in hand,
Posters of the sea and land,
Thus do go about, about:
Thrice to thine, and thrice to mine,
And thrice again, to make up nine:
Peace!—the charm's wound up.

ACT IV, SCENE i
A dark cave.

Thunder. Enter the three Witches.
First Witch Thrice the brinded cat hath mew'd.

[1] And the very ports they blow to.
[2] In the shipman's chart on which he marks the compass points.
[3] Bewitched.
[4] Witch, or prophetic sisters.

Sec. Witch Thrice; and once the hedge-pig
whin'd.
Third Witch Harper[1] cries:—'tis time, 'tis time.
First Witch Round about the cauldron go;
In the poison'd entrails throw.—
Toad, that under cold stone
Days and nights has thirty-one
Swelter'd venom[2] sleeping got,
Boil thou first i' the charmed pot.
All Double, double toil and trouble;
Fire, burn; and, cauldron, bubble.
Sec. Witch Fillet of a fenny snake,
In the cauldron boil and bake;
Eye of newt, and toe of frog,
Wool of bat, and tongue of dog,
Adder's fork, and blind-worm's sting,
Lizard's leg, and owlet's wing,—
For a charm of powerful trouble,
Like a hell-broth boil and bubble.
All Double, double toil and trouble;
Fire, burn; and, cauldron, bubble.
Third Witch Scale of dragon; tooth of wolf;
Witches' mummy; maw and gulf[3]
Of the ravin'd[4] salt-sea shark;
Root of hemlock digg'd i' the dark;
Liver of blaspheming Jew;
Gall of goat; and slips of yew
Sliver'd[5] in the moon's eclipse;
Nose of Turk, and Tartar's lips,

1 Either a familiar named Harper, or a missprint for 'Harpy.'
2 The toad's venom is secreted from just beneath the skin.
3 Gullet.
4 Ravenous.
5 Sliced.

Finger of birth-strangled babe
Ditch-deliver'd by a drab—
Make the gruel thick and slab:
Add thereto a tiger's chaudron.[1]
For the ingredients of our cauldron.
All Double, double toil and trouble;
Fire, burn; and, cauldron, bubble.
Sec. Witch Cool it with a baboon's blood,
Then the charm is firm and good.

Hec. Oh, well done! I commend your pains;
And every one shall share i' the gains:
And now about the cauldron sing,
Like elves and fairies in a ring,
Enchanting all that you put in.
Sec. Witch By the pricking of my thumbs,
Something wicked this way comes:—
Open, locks,
Whoever knocks!

Enter MACBETH.

Macb. How now, you secret, black, and midnight hags!
What is't you do?
All A deed without a name.
Macb. I cónjure you, by that which you profess
(Howe'er you come to know it), answer me:
Though you untie the winds, and let them fight
Against the churches; though the yesty[2] waves
Confound and swallow navigation up;
Though bladed corn be lodg'd,[3] and trees blown down;

[1] Entrails.
[2] Frothy.
[3] Witches were supposed to be able to move bladed corn from one place to another.

Though castles topple on their warders' heads,
Though palaces and pyramids do slope
Their heads to their foundations; though the treasure
Of Nature's germins[1] tumble all together,
Even till destruction sicken,—answer me
To what I ask you.

First Witch Speak.

Sec. Witch Demand.

Third Witch We'll answer.

First Witch Say, if thou'dst rather hear it from our mouths,
Or from our masters'?

Macb. Call them, let me see them.

First Witch Pour in sow's blood, that hath eaten
Her nine farrow;[2] grease, that's sweaten
From the murderer's gibbet, throw
Into the flame.

All Come, high or low;
Thyself and office deftly show!

Thunder. An Apparition *of an armed Head rises.*[3]

Macb. Tell me, thou unknown power,—

First Witch He knows thy thought:
Hear his speech, but say thou naught.[4]

1 Seeds.

2 Her nine children. Scottish law was that if a pig ate its farrow it was to be stoned to death and not eaten.

3 The three apparitions are symbolic. The first, the Armed Head, symbolizes Macbeth's head, to be cut off by Macduff. The second, the bloody babe, symbolizes Macduff's birth by Caeserian section. The third, the child with a tree, symbolizes Macduff's approach to Dunsinane behind a screen of Birnam Wood.

4 One must be silent during an incantation.

App. Macbeth! Macbeth! Macbeth! beware
Macduff;
Beware the thane of Fife.—Dismiss me:—enough[1]

[*Descends.*

Macb. Whate'er thou art, for thy good caution,
thanks;
Thou hast harp'd my fear aright:[2]—but one word
more,—
First Witch He will not be commanded: here's
another,
More potent than the first.

Thunder. An Apparition *of a bloody Child rises.*

App. Macbeth! Macbeth! Macbeth!—
Macb. Had I three ears, I'd hear thee.[3]
App. Be bloody, bold, and resolute; laugh to
scorn
The power of man, for none of woman born
Shall harm Macbeth.

[*Descends.*

Macb. Then live, Macduff: what need I fear of
thee?
But yet I'll make assurance double sure.
And take a bond of fate: thou shalt not live;
That I may tell pale-hearted fear it lies,
And sleep in spite of thunder.—What is this,

Thunder. An Apparition *of a Child crowned, with a tree in his hand, rises.*

That rises like the issue of a king,
And wears upon his baby brow the round

1 Apparitions were supposedly impatient to be gone, and reluctant to communicate.
2 Thou hast struck the right key-note of my fear.
3 An eager response to the calling of his name three times.

And top of sovereignty?[1]

All Listen, but speak not to it.

App. Be lion-mettled, proud; and take no care
Who chafes, who frets, or where conspirers are:
Macbeth shall never vanquish'd be, until
Great Birnam wood to high Dunsinane hill
Shall come against him.

[*Descends.*

Macb. That will never be:
Who can impress[2] the forest; bid the tree
Unfix his earth-bound root? Sweet bodements!
good!
Rebellious head,[3] rise never, till the wood
Of Birnam rise, and our high-plac'd Macbeth
Shall live the lease of nature, pay his breath
To time and mortal custom.—Yet my heart
Throbs to know one thing: tell me (if your art
Can tell so much), shall Banquo's issue ever
Reign in this kingdom?

All Seek to know no more.

Macb. I will be satisfied:[4] deny me this,
And an eternal curse fall on you! Let me know:—
Why sinks that cauldron? [*hautboys*] and what noise[5]
is this?

First Witch Show!

Sec. Witch Show!

Third Witch Show!

1 The crown that encircles the head, and the ornament that rises from it.

2 Press into his service.

3 Perhaps the first apparition.

4 I must know.

5 Music.

All Show his eyes, and grieve his heart;
Come like shadows, so depart!

Eight Kings appear, and pass over in order, the last with a glass in his hand; BANQUO *following.*

Macb. Thou art too like the spirit of Banquo; down!
Thy crown does sear mine eye-balls:—and thy hair,
Thou other gold-bound brow, is like the first:—
A third is like the former.—Filthy hags!
Why do you show me this?—A fourth?—Start, eyes!—
What! will the line stretch out to the crack of doom?[1]
Another yet?—A seventh?—I'll see no more:—
And yet the eighth appears, who bears a glass[2]
Which shows me many more; and some I see
That two-fold balls and treble sceptres carry:[3]
Horrible sight!—Now, I see, 'tis true;
For the blood-bolter'd[4] Banquo smiles upon me,
And points at them for his.—What! is this so?
First Witch Ay, sir, all this is so:—but why
Stands Macbeth thus amazedly?—
Come, sisters, cheer we up his sprites,[5]
And show the best of our delights:
I'll charm the air to give a sound,
While you perform your antic round;
That this great king may kindly say,
Our duties did his welcome pay.

[1] Doomsday.
[2] A sorcerer's magic mirror.
[3] A compliment to Shakespeare's sovereign, James I.
[4] Blood-smeared.
[5] Spirits.

[*Music. The* Witches *dance, and then vanish.*

Macb. Where are they? Gone?—Let this
pernicious hour
Stand aye accursèd in the calendar!—
Come in, without there!

READING: *Julius Caesar*

Act I, Scene i: A street. Characters: Flavius, Marullus, a carpenter, a cobbler.

1 Start with the suggested preparation for Shakespearean scenes.

2 Read Plutarch's *Lives,* the lives of Julius Caesar, Marcus Antonius, and Marcus Brutus. Depending on the character you play, are you for Caesar or for the murdered Pompey? Get involved, but don't play enthusiasm!

3 Again do a full, rounded job on the physicalization of the characters. Develop real types with full histories. Since the scene is emotionally rather light, concentrate on character problems.

4 How do Flavius and Marullus differ from the two citizens?

5 Work up a simple costume for your character.

ACT I, SCENE i—ROME. *A street.*

Enter FLAVIUS, MARULLUS, *and a throng of* Citizens.

Flav. Hence! home, you idle creatures, get you
home:
Is this a holiday? what! know you not,
Being mechanical, you ought not walk
Upon a labouring day without the sign
Of your profession?—Speak, what trade art thou?

First Cit. Why, sir, a carpenter.

Mar. Where is thy leather apron and thy rule?
What dost thou with thy best apparel on?—
You, sir, what trade are you?

Sec. Cit. Truly, sir, in respect of a fine workman,
I am but, as you would say, a cobbler.

Mar. But what trade art thou? answer me
directly.

Sec. Cit. A trade, sir, that, I hope, I may use
with a safe conscience; which is, indeed, sir, a mender
of bad soles.

Mar. What trade, thou knave? thou naughty
knave, what trade?

Sec. Cit. Nay, I beseech you, sir, be not out with
me: yet, if you be out, sir,[1] I can mend you.

Mar. What meanest thou by that? mend me,
thou saucy fellow!

Sec. Cit. Why, sir, cobble you.

Flav. Thou art a cobbler, art thou?

Sec. Cit. Truly, sir, all that I live by is with the
awl: I meddle with no tradesman's matters, nor
women's matters, but with awl. I am, indeed, sir, a
surgeon to old shoes; when they are in great danger,
I re-cover them. As proper men as ever trod upon
neat's-leather have gone upon my handiwork.

Flav. But wherefore art not in thy shop to-day? Why dost thou
lead these men about the streets?

Sec. Cit. Truly, sir, to wear out their shoes, to get myself into
more work. But, indeed, sir, we make holiday, to see Caesar,
and to rejoice in his triumph.[2]

Mar. Wherefore rejoice? What conquest brings he home?
What tributaries follow him to Rome,
To grace in captive bonds his chariot-wheels?
You blocks, you stones, you worse than senseless things!

[1] Out at toes.

[2] This was in celebration of his having defeated the sons of Pompey at the battle of Munda, in Spain; and of his having been appointed Consul for the next ten years, and Dictator for life.

Oh, you hard hearts, you cruel men of Rome.
Knew you not Pompey? Many a time and oft
Have you climb'd up to walls and battlements,
To towers and windows, yea, to chimney-tops,
Your infants in your arms, and there have sat
The live-long day, with patient expectation,
To see great Pompey pass the streets of Rome:
And when you saw his chariot but appear,
Have you not made a universal shout,
That Tiber trembled underneath her banks,
To hear the replication of your sounds
Made in her concave shores?
And do you now put on your best attire?
And do you now cull out a holiday?
And do you now strew flowers in his way,
That comes in triumph over Pompey's blood?[1]
Be gone!
Run to your houses, fall upon your knees,
Pray to the gods to intermit the plague
That needs must light on this ingratitude.
Flav. Go, go, good countrymen, and, for this fault,
Assemble all the poor men of your sort;
Draw them to Tiber banks, and weep your tears
Into the channel, till the lowest stream
Do kiss the most exalted shores of all.
[*Exeunt* Citizens.
See, whe'r their basest metal be not mov'd;
They vanish tongue-tied in their guiltiness.
Go you down that way towards the Capitol;
This way will I: disrobe the images,
If you do find them deck'd with ceremonies.[2]

[1] Pompey's sons, defeated by Caesar; the elder, Cnaeus Pompey, was beheaded after the battle of Munda.

[2] Ceremonial adornments: scarves or colored draperies.

Mar. May we do so? You know it is the feast of Lupercal.[1]
Flav. It is no matter: let no images
Be hung with Caesar's trophies.[2] I'll about,
And drive away the vulgar from the streets:
So do you too, where you perceive them thick.
These growing feathers pluck'd from Caesar's wing,
Will make him fly an ordinary pitch;
Who else would soar above the view of men,
And keep us all in servile fearfulness.

[*Exeunt.*

READING: *Twelfth Night*

Act II, scene v: Olivia's garden. Characters: Sir Toby Belch, Sir Andrew Aguecheek, Fabian, Maria, Malvolio.

1 Start with the suggested preparation for Shakespearean scenes. This time there is no need to read the background for the play. The source of the play is a number of light Italian works. According to Elizabethan tradition, however, the background of the comedy is not authentically Italian, but a never-never land for the romantic plot and almost straight English for the comic subplot.

2 Tempo, or rhythm, is essential here, as it is for playing any comic scene. Don't ignore the metronomic imperative of the staccato short speeches, some of which are cut off. This scene requires the concentrated diligence of a musician playing in a string quartet. A long, meaningful psychological pause in the middle of these verbal fireworks would destroy the entire scene. Play the tempo and justify it.

3 Remember that acting is character work! Enjoy yourself among Shakespeare's marvellous characters. Develop full physical characteristics—gestures, postures, walks, and so on.

[1] A festival in honor of the god Pan, held every February.

[2] Flavius is answering Marullus' scruples about tearing down the decorations for a religious feast by answering that they are really in honor of Caesar.

4 Vary the voice placements; avoid duplication with the other actors, or the orchestration will be monotonous. Malvolio's voice placement is an interesting problem. A normal full-toned chest voice would not be best for Malvolio. Why?

5 As you avoided clichés in playing the witches in *Macbeth* and the citizens in *Julius Caesar,* avoid playing the clichés of old age. Sir Andrew and Sir Toby are old men but are not lacking in vitality and a lust for life. They are energetic and fun-loving, young in spirit. How are you going to play this combination? (Once again: Acute observation of character in real life will greatly help your acting.)

6 Malvolio must be careful to avoid the trap of joining in the fun against himself. He must not, figuratively, wink at the audience to let them see that he, too, is in on the joke. When playing an ass, you must never admit to being one. Play it truthfully: The more seriously Malvolio takes himself, the funnier he is.

ACT II, SCENE v.

Enter SIR TOBY BELCH, SIR ANDREW AGUECHEEK, *and* FABIAN.

Sir To. Come thy ways, Signior Fabian.

Fab. Nay, I'll come: if I lose a scruple of this sport, let me be boiled to death with melancholy.

Sir To. Wouldst thou not be glad to have the niggardly rascally sheep-biter[1] come by some notable shame?

Fab. I would exult, man: you know, he brought me out o' favour with my lady about a bear-baiting here.

Sir To. To anger him, we'll have the bear again; and we will fool him black and blue:—shall we not, Sir Andrew?

Sir And. An we do not, it is pity of our lives.

Sir To. Here comes the little villain.

Enter MARIA.

How now, my nettle of India!

Mar. Get ye all three into the box-tree: Malvolio's coming down this walk, he has been yonder i' the sun, practising

1 Paltry thief.

behaviour to his own shadow this half hour: observe him, for the love of mockery; for I know this letter will make a contemplative idiot of him. Close, in the name of jesting! [*The men hide themselves.*] Lie thou there [*throws down a letter*]; for here comes the trout that must be caught with tickling.

[*Exit.*

Enter MALVOLIO.

Mal. 'Tis but fortune; all is fortune. Maria once told me she[1] did affect me: and I have heard herself come thus near, that, should she fancy, it should be one of my complexion. Besides, she uses me with a more exalted respect than any one else that follows her. What should I think on't?

Sir To. Here's an overweening rogue!

Fab. Oh, peace! Contemplation makes a rare turkey-cock of him: how he jets[2] under his advanced plumes!

Sir And. 'Slight, I could so beat the rogue!

Sir To. Peace, I say.

Mal. To be Count Malvolio,—

Sir To. Ah, rogue!

Sir And. Pistol him, pistol him.

Sir To. Peace, peace!

Mal. There is example for't; the lady of the Strachy[3] married the yeoman of the wardrobe.

Sir And. Fie on him, Jezebel![4]

Fab. Oh, peace! now he's deeply in: look how imagination blows him.[5]

Mal. Having been three months married to her, sitting in my state,—

[1] Olivia.

[2] Struts.

[3] Perhaps Stracci, meaning rags, tatters.

[4] Sir Andrew knows this is a name of reproach; his applying a woman's name to a man is of a piece with his usual accomplishments.

[5] Swells him.

Sir To. Oh, for a stone-bow,[1] to hit him in the eye!

Mal. Calling my officers about me in my branched velvet gown; having come from a day-bed, where I have left Olivia sleeping,—

Sir To. Fire and brimstone!

Fab. Oh, peace, peace!

Mal. And then to have the humour of state; and after a demure travel of regard,—telling them I know my place, as I would they should do theirs,—to ask for my kinsman Toby,—

Sir To. Bolts and shackles!

Fab. Oh, peace, peace, peace! now, now.

Mal. Seven of my people, with an obedient start, make out for him: I frown the while; and perchance wind up my watch, or play with some rich jewel. Toby approaches; court'sies[2] there to me,—

Sir To. Shall this fellow live?

Fab. Though our silence be drawn from us with cars,[3] yet peace.

Mal. I extend my hand to him thus, quenching my familiar smile with an austere regard of control,—

Sir To. And does not Toby take you a blow of the lips then?

Mal. Saying, "Cousin Toby, my fortunes having cast me on your niece, give me this prerogative of speech,"—

Sir To. What, what?

Mal. "You must amend your drunkenness."

Sir To. Out, scab!

Fab. Nay, patience, or we break the sinews of our plot.

Mal. "Besides, you waste the treasure of your time with a foolish knight,"—

Sir And. That's me, I warrant you.

Mal. "One Sir Andrew,"—

[1] A cross-bow for discharging stones.

[2] Makes a salutation.

[3] Carts—extorted by violence.

Sir And. I knew 'twas I; for many do call me fool.
Mal. [*Seeing the letter.*] What employment have we here?
Fab. Now is the woodcock near the gin.
[MALVOLIO *takes up the letter.*
Sir To. Oh, peace! and the spirit of humours intimate reading aloud to him!
Mal. By my life, this is my lady's hand: these be her very C's, her U's, and her T's; and thus makes she her great P's.[1] It is, in contempt of question, her hand.
Sir And. Her C's, her U's, and her T's: why that?
Mal. [*Reads.*]
To the unknown beloved, this, and my good wishes.
Her very phrases!—By your leave, wax.—Soft!—and the impressure her Lucrece, with which she uses to seal: 'tis my lady. To whom should this be?
Fab. This wins him, liver and all.
Mal. [*Reads.*]

Jove knows, I love:
But who?
Lips do not move;
No man must know.

"No man must know."—What follows? the numbers altered![2]—
"No man must know:"—if this should be thee, Malvolio?
Sir To. Marry, hang thee, brock![3]
Mal. [*Reads.*]

I may command where I adore:
But silence, like a Lucrece's knife,
With bloodless stroke my heart doth gore:
M, O, A, I, doth sway my life.[4]

Fab. A fustian riddle!

[1] As there is no "C" or "P" in the direction of the letter as read by Malvolio, it is possible the address had the words "with Care Present" added, as was the custom at the time.

[2] The versification of the lines is altered in the next stanza.

[3] Badger, then a term of contempt.

[4] Such riddles were then common in love letters.

Sir To. Excellent wench, say I.

Mal. "M, O, A, I, doth sway my life."—Nay, but first, let me see,—let me see,—let me see.

Fab. What a dish of poison has she dressed him!

Sir To. And with what wing the stannyel[1] checks at it!

Mal. "I may command where I adore." Why, she may command me: I serve her; she is my lady. Why, this is evident to any formal capacity;[2] there is no obstruction in this:—and the end,—what should that alphabetical position portend? if I could make that resemble something in me,—Softly!—M, O, A, I,—

Sir To. Oh, ay, make up that:—he is now at a cold scent.

Fab. Sowter[3] will cry upon 't, for all this, though it be as rank as a fox.[4]

Mal. M,—Malvolio;—M,—Why, that begins my name.

Fab. Did not I say he would work it out? the cur is excellent at faults.

Mal. M,—but then there is no consonancy in the sequel; that suffers under probation: A should follow, but O does.

Fab. And O shall end, I hope.[5]

Sir To. Ay, or I'll cudgel him, and make him cry O!

Mal. And then I comes behind.

Fab. Ay, an you had any eye behind you, you might see more detraction at your heels than fortunes before you.

Mal. M, O, A, I;—this simulation is not as the former:—and yet, to crush this a little, it would bow to me, for every one of these letters are in my name. Soft! here follows prose.—[*Reads.*]

1 The stonehawk (trained in falconry) flies at it.

2 Rational capacity.

3 The name of a hound.

4 Since it is as rank as a fox.

5 Meaning that in the end he will cry out in dismay.

If this fall into thy hand, revolve. In my stars I am above
thee: but be not afraid of greatness; some are born great,
some achieve greatness, and some have greatness thrust
upon them. Thy Fates open their hands; let thy blood
and spirit embrace them. And, to inure thyself to what thou
art like to be, cast thy humble slough, and appear fresh.
Be opposite[1] with a kinsman, surly with servants; let thy
tongue tang arguments of state; put thyself into the trick
of singularity: she thus advises thee that sighs for thee.
Remember who commended thy yellow Stockings, and
wished to see thee ever cross-gartered:[2] I say, remember.
Go to, thou art made,[3] if thou desirest to be so; if not,
let me see thee a steward still, the fellow of servants, and
not worthy to touch Fortune's fingers. Farewell. She that
would alter services with thee,

THE FORTUNATE-UNHAPPY.

Daylight and champain[4] discovers not more: this is
open. I will be proud, I will read politic authors. I
will baffle Sir Toby, I will wash off gross acquaintance,
I will be point-device,[5] the very man. I do not
now fool myself, to let imagination jade me; for every
reason excites to this, that my lady loves me. She
did commend my yellow stockings of late, she did
praise my leg being cross-gartered; and in this she
manifests herself to my love, and, with a kind of
injunction, drives me to these habits of her liking.
I thank my stars, I am happy. I will be strange,
stout,[6] in yellow stockings, and cross-gartered,

[1] Contrary.
[2] Wearing garters criss-crossed up the entire leg.
[3] Your fortune is made.
[4] Open country.
[5] Exactly.
[6] Reserved and proud.

even with the swiftness of putting on. Jove and my stars be praised!—here is yet a post-script. [*Reads.*]

Thou canst not choose but know who I am. If thou entertainest my love, let it appear in thy smiling; thy smiles become thee well; therefore in my presence still smile, dear my sweet, I pr'ythee.

Jove, I thank thee.—I will smile: I will do everything that thou wilt have me.

[*Exit.*

Fab. I will not give my part of this sport for a pension of thousands to be paid from the Sophy.[1]

Sir To. I could marry this wench for this device,—

Sir And. So could I too.

Sir To. And ask no other dowry with her but such another jest.

Sir And. Nor I neither.

Fab. Here comes my noble gull-catcher.

Re-enter MARIA.

Sir To. Wilt thou set thy foot o'my neck?

Sir And. Or o' mine either?

Sir To. Shall I play my freedom at tray-trip,[2] and become thy bond-slave?

Sir And. I' faith, or I either?

Sir To. Why, thou hast put him in such a dream, that, when, the image of it leaves him, he must run mad.

Mar. Nay, but say true; does it work upon him?

Sir To. Like aqua-vitae,[3] but with a midwife.

1 The Emperor of Persia.

2 A game like backgammon, played with three dice.

3 Strong waters.

Mar. If you will, then, see the fruits of the sport,
mark his first approach before my lady: he will
come to her in yellow stockings, and 'tis a colour she
abhors, and cross-gartered, a fashion she detests;
and he will smile upon her, which will now be so
unsuitable to her disposition, being addicted to a
melancholy as she is, that it cannot but turn him
into a notable contempt. If you will see it, follow me.

Sir To. To the gates of Tartar,[1] thou most
excellent devil of wit!

Sir And. I'll make one too.

[*Exeunt.*

READING: ***Romeo and Juliet***

Act II, scene ii: A garden; Juliet is in a balcony overlooking it. Characters: Romeo, Juliet.

1 Start with the suggested preparation for Shakespearean scenes. The given circumstances are particularly important in establishing the enmity between the two families.

2 To play this scene properly is a real challenge. The trap this time is not a question of tempo, but of actions. Playing emotions must be avoided. If you do not find the proper actions to play, you will feel like the dog being wagged by its tail.

3 Be careful about the verse, which is quite lovely. Be sure you know which words are contracted and which expanded for the sake of the meter.

4 Where and When are the two questions of the given circumstances that are quite important for this scene.

ACT II, SCENE ii—CAPULET'S *garden.*

Rom. He jests at scars that never felt a wound.[2]—

[1] Tartarus, a region in hell.

[2] In reference to a jest of Mercutio's, about Romeo's love.

[JULIET *appears above at a window.*

But, soft! what light through yonder window
breaks?
It is the east, and Juliet is the sun!—
Arise, fair sun, and kill the envious moon,
Who is already sick and pale with grief,
That thou her maid art far more fair than she:
Be not her maid,[1] since she is envious;
Her vestal livery is but sick and green,
And none but fools do wear it; cast it off.—
It is my lady; oh, it is my love!
Oh, that she knew she were!—
She speaks, yet she says nothing: what of that?
Her eye discourses, I will answer it.—
I am too bold, 'tis not to me she speaks:
Two of the fairest stars in all the heaven,
Having some business, do entreat her eyes
To twinkle in their spheres till they return.
What if her eyes were there, they in her head?
The brightness of her cheek would shame those
stars,
As daylight doth a lamp; her eyes in heaven
Would through the airy region stream so bright,
That birds would sing, and think it were not
night.—
See, how she leans her cheek upon her hand!
Oh, that I were a glove upon that hand,
That I might touch that cheek!

Jul. Ah me!

Rom. She speaks:—
Oh, speak again, bright angel! for thou art
As glorious to this night, being o'er my head,
As is a winged messenger of heaven

[1] Do not be the maid of the vestal, Diana.

Unto the white-upturned wondering eyes
Of mortals, that fall back to gaze on him,
When he bestrides the lazy-pacing clouds,
And sails upon the bosom of the air.

Jul. O Romeo, Romeo! wherefore art thou
Romeo?
Deny thy father, and refuse thy name;
Or, if thou wilt not, be but sworn my love,
And I'll no longer be a Capulet.

Rom. [Aside.] Shall I hear more, or shall I
speak at this?

Jul. 'Tis but thy name that is my enemy;—
Thou art thyself though, not a Montague.
What's Montague? it is nor hand, nor foot,
Nor arm, nor face, nor any other part
Belonging to a man. Oh, be some other name!
What's in a name? that which we call a rose,
By any other name would smell as sweet;
So Romeo would, were he not Romeo call'd,
Retain that dear perfection which he owes,[1]
Without that title:—Romeo, doff thy name;
And for that name, which is no part of thee,
Take all myself.

Rom. I take thee at thy word:
Call me but love, and I'll be new baptis'd;
Henceforth I never will be Romeo.

Jul. What man art thou, that, thus bescreen'd
in night,
So stumblest on my counsel?[2]

Rom. By a name
I know not how to tell thee who I am:
My name, dear saint, is hateful to myself,

[1] Owns.

[2] Secret reflections.

Because it is an enemy to thee;
Had I it written, I would tear the word.
Jul. My ears have not yet drunk a hundred words
Of that tongue's utterance, yet I know the sound:
Art thou not Romeo, and a Montague?
Rom. Neither, fair saint, if either thee dislike.[1]
Jul. How cam'st thou hither, tell me, and wherefore?
The orchard walls are high and hard to climb;
And the place death, considering who thou art,
If any of my kinsmen find thee here.
Rom. With love's light wings did I o'erperch these walls;
For stony limits cannot hold love out:
And what love can do, that dares love attempt;
Therefore thy kinsmen are no let to me.[2]
Jul. If they do see thee, they will murder thee.
Rom. Alack, there lies more peril in thine eye
Than twenty of their swords: look thou but sweet,
And I am proof against their enmity.
Jul. I would not for the world they saw thee here:
Rom. I have night's cloak to hide me from their sight;
And but thou love me,[3] let them find me here:
My life were better ended by their hate,
Than death prorogued,[4] wanting of thy love.
Jul. By whose direction found'st thou out this place?
Rom. By love, who first did prompt me to enquire,
He lent me counsel, and I lent him eyes.

1 If either displease thee.
2 Are no hindrance to me.
3 And unless you love me.
4 Delayed.

I am no pilot; yet, wert thou as far
As that vast shore wash'd with the farthest sea,
I would adventure for such merchandise.
Jul. Thou know'st the mask of night is on my
face,
Else would a maiden blush bepaint my cheek
For that which thou hast heard me speak to-night.
Fain would I dwell on form, fain, fain deny
What I have spoke: but farewell compliment.[1]
Dost thou love me? I know thou wilt say,—Ay;
And I will take thy word: yet, if thou swear'st,
Thou mayst prove false; at lovers' perjuries,
They say, Jove laughs. Oh, gentle Romeo,
If thou dost love, pronounce it faithfully:
Or if thou think'st I am too quickly won,
I'll frown, and be perverse, and say thee nay,
So thou wilt woo; but else, not for the world.
In truth, fair Montague, I am too fond;
And therefore thou mayst think my 'havior light;
But trust me, gentleman, I'll prove more true
Than those that have more cunning to be strange.
I should have been more strange. I must confess,
But that thou overheard'st, ere I was 'ware,
My true love's passion: therefore pardon me;
And not impute this yielding to light love,
Which the dark night hath so discoverèd.
Rom. Lady, by yonder blessèd moon I swear,
That tips with silver all these fruit-tree tops,—
Jul. Oh, swear not by the moon, the inconstant
moon,
That monthly changes her circled orb,
Lest that thy love prove likewise variable.
Rom. What shall I swear by?

[1] Away with affected hesitation!

Jul. Do not swear at all;
Or, if thou wilt, swear by thy gracious self,
Which is the god of my idolatry,
And I'll believe thee.
Rom. If my heart's dear love,—
Jul. Well, do not swear: although I joy in thee,
I have no joy of this contráct to-night:
It is too rash, too unadvis'd, too sudden;
Too like the lightning, which doth cease to be
Ere one can say, It lightens. Sweet, good night!
This bud of love, by summer's ripening breath,
May prove a beauteous flower when next we meet.
Good night, good night! as sweet repose and rest
Come to thy heart as that within thy breast!
Rom. Oh, wilt thou leave me so unsatisfied?
Jul. What satisfaction canst thou have tonight?
Rom. The exchange of thy love's faithful vow for mine.
Jul. I gave thee mine before thou didst request it:
And yet I would it were to give again.
Rom. Wouldst thou withdraw it? for what purpose, love?
Jul. But to be frank, and give it thee again.
And yet I wish but for the thing I have:
My bounty is as boundless as the sea,
My love as deep; the more I give to thee,
The more I have, for both are infinite.

[*Nurse calls within.*

I hear some voice within; dear love, adieu!—
Anon, good nurse!—Sweet Montague, be true.
Stay but a little, I will come again. [*Exit above.*
Rom. Oh, blessèd, blessèd night! I am afeard,
Being in night, all this is but a dream,
Too flattering-sweet to be substantial.

Re-enter JULIET *above.*

Jul. Three words, dear Romeo, and good night indeed.
If that thy bent of love be honourable,
Thy purpose marriage, send me word to-morrow,
By one that I'll procure to come to thee,
Where and what time thou wilt perform the rite;
And all my fortunes at thy foot I'll lay,
And follow thee my lord throughout the world.

Nurse. [*Within.*] Madam!

Jul. I come, anon:—But if thou mean'st not well,
I do beseech thee,—

Nurse [*Within.*] Madam!

Jul. By-and-by, I come:—
To cease thy suit, and leave me to my grief:
To-morrow will I send.

Rom. So thrive my soul,—

Jul. A thousands time good night! [*Exit above.*

Rom. A thousand time the worse, to want thy light.—
Love goes towards love, as schoolboys from their books;
But love from love, toward school with heavy looks.
[*Retiring.*

Re-enter JULIET *above.*

Jul. Hist! Romeo, hist!—Oh, for a falconer's voice,
To lure this tassel-gentle[1] back again!
Bondage is hoarse, and may not speak aloud;
Else would I tear the cave where Echo lies,
And make her airy tongue more hoarse than mine,
With repetition of my Romeo's name. Romeo!

[1] Tiercel-gentle, the male of the goshawk, use in falconry.

Rom. It is my soul that calls upon my name:
How silver-sweet sound lovers' tongues by night,
Like softest music to attending ears!
Jul. Romeo!
Rom. My dear?
Jul. At what o'clock to-morrow
shall I send to thee?
Rom. At the hour of nine.
Jul. I will not fail: tis twenty years till then.
I have forgot why I did call thee back.
Rom. Let me stand here till thou remember it.
Jul. I shall forget, to have thee still stand there,
Remembering how I love thy company.
Rom. And I'll still stay, to have thee still forget,
Forgetting any other home but this.
Jul. 'Tis almost morning; I would have thee gone:
And yet no farther than a wanton's bird;
Who lets it hop a little from her hand,
Like a poor prisoner in his twisted gyves,
And with a silk thread plucks it back again,
So loving-jealous of his liberty.
Rom. I would I were thy bird.
Jul. Sweet, so would I:
Yet I should kill thee with much cherishing.
Good night, good night! parting is such sweet sorrow,
That I shall say good night till it be morrow.
[*Exit above.*
Rom. Sleep dwell upon thine eyes, peace in thy breast!—
Would I were sleep and peace, so sweet to rest!
Hence will I to my ghostly father's cell,
His help to crave, and my dear hap to tell. [*Exit.*

READING: *Henry V*

Act V, scene ii: A room in the palace of the King of France. Characters: Henry, Katharine, Alice.

1 Start with suggested preparations for Shakespearean scenes. Read Holinshed.

2 If you had just played Romeo, what character work would you now need for this kingly lover? How do they differ?

3 In what ways are Juliet and Katharine different? Similar?

4 The built-in tempo is different in this wooing scene from the last. Why? Note how time and place make a big difference.

5 Note that the rough-hewn King Henry speaks in prose rather than in verse. What is the significance of this fact in a love scene? How does the written word help you here?

6 Listening is vital for all actors in this scene. It always is, but why especially here?

7 The actress playing Katharine should wear a long dress.

8 For the actress playing Alice, remember, "There is no such thing as a small part, only small actors." Your main action here is to attend your mistress during a most important interview in which her reputation could be at stake. Play your part without endeavoring to pad it by drawing attention to yourself at the expense of the scene.

ACT V, SCENE ii

K. Hen. Fair Katharine, and most fair!
Will you vouchsafe to teach a soldier terms
Such as will enter at a lady's ear,
And plead his love-suit to her gentle heart?

Kath. Your majesty shall mock at me; I cannot
speak your England.

K. Hen. Oh, fair Katharine, if you will love me
soundly with your French heart, I will be glad to
hear you confess it brokenly with your English
tongue. Do you like me, Kate?

Kath. *Pardonnez-moi,* I cannot tell vat is—"like me."

K. Hen. An angel is like you, Kate, and you are like an angel.

Kath. *Que dit-il? que je suis semblable à les anges?*[1]

Alice. *Oui, vraiment, sauf votre grace, ainsi dit-il.*[2]

K. Hen. I said so, dear Katharine; and I must not blush to affirm it.

Kath. *Oh, bon Dieu! les langues des hommes sont pleines de tromperies.*

K. Hen. What says she, fair one? that the tongues of men are full of deceits?

Alice. *Oui,* dat de tongues of de mans is be full of deceits: dat is de princess.

K. Hen. The princess is the better Englishwoman. I' faith, Kate, my wooing is fit for thy understanding: I am glad thou canst speak no better English; for, if thou couldst, thou wouldst find me such a plain king, that thou wouldst think I had sold my farm to buy my crown. I know no ways to mince it in love, but directly to say,—I love you: then, if you urge me farther than to say,—Do you in faith? I wear out my suit, Give me your answer; i' faith, do; and so clap hands and a bargain: how say you, lady?

Kath. *Sauf votre honneur,* me understand vell.

K. Hen. Marry, if you would put me to verses or to dance for your sake, Kate, why you undid me: for the one, I have neither words no measure; and for the other, I have no strength in measure,[3] yet a resonable measure in strength. If I could win a

[1] What does he say? That I am like the angels?

[2] Yes, truly, save your grace, thus he says.

[3] I cannot versify or dance well.

lady at leap-frog, or by vaulting into my saddle with
my armour on my back, under the correction of
bragging be it spoken, I should quickly leap into a
wife. Or if I might buffet for my love, or bound my
horse for her favours, I could lay on like a butcher,
and sit like a jack-an-apes, never off. But before God, Kate,
I cannot look greenly,[1] nor gasp out my eloquence, nor
I have no cunning in protestation; only downright
oaths, which I never use till urged, nor never break
for urging. If thou canst love a fellow of this temper,
Kate, whose face is not worth sun-burning, that
never looks in his glass for love of anything he sees
there,—let thine eye be thy cook. I speak to thee
plain soldier:[2] if thou canst love me for this, take
me; if not, to say to thee that I shall die, is true,—
but for thy love, by the Lord, no; yet I love thee too.
And while thou livest, dear Kate, take a fellow of
plain and uncoined constancy;[3] for he perforce must
do thee right, because he hath not the gift to woo in
other places: for these fellows of infinite tongue,
that can rhyme themselves into ladies' favours, they
do always reason themselves out again. What! a speaker
is but a prater; a rhyme is but a ballad. A
good leg will fall; a straight back will stoop; a
black beard will turn white; a curled pate will grow
bald; a fair face will wither; a full eye will wax
hollow; but a good heart, Kate, is the sun and the
moon; or, rather, the sun, and not the moon,—for it
shines bright, and never changes, but keeps his
course truly. If thou would have such a one, take

[1] Like a novice in love.
[2] Like a plain soldier.
[3] Pure.

me: and take me, take a soldier; take a soldier, take a king: and what sayest thou, then, to my love? speak, my fair, and fairly, I pray thee.

Kath. Is it possible dat I should love de enemy of France?

K. Hen. No; it is not possible you should love the enemy of France, Kate; but, in loving me, you should love the friend of France; for I love France so well, that I will not part with a village of it; I will have it all mine: and, Kate, when France is mine and I am yours, then yours is France and you are mine.

Kath. I cannot tell vat is dat.

K. Hen. No, Kate? I will tell thee in French; which I am sure will hang upon my tongue like a new-married wife about her husband's neck, hardly to be shook off. *Quand j'ai la possession de France, et quand vous avez la possession de moi,*—let me see, what then? Saint Denis[1] be my speed!—*donc votre est France et vous estes mienne.* It is as easy for me, Kate, to conquer the kingdom, as to speak so much more French: I shall never move thee in French, unless it be to laugh at me.

Kath. *Sauf votre honneur, le François que vous parlez est meilleur que l'Anglois lequel je parle.*[2]

K. Hen. No, faith, is 't not, Kate; but thy speaking of my tongue, and I thine, most truly falsely, must needs be granted to be much at one.[3] But, Kate, dost thou understand thus much English,—Canst thou love me?

Kath. I cannot tell.

K. Hen. Can any of your neighbours tell, Kate?

[1] The patron saint of France.

[2] So please your honor, the French you speak is better than the English I speak.

[3] Much the same.

I'll ask them. Come, I know thou lovest me: and at
night, when you come into your closet, you'll question
this gentlewoman about me; and I know, Kate, you
will to her dispraise those parts in me that you
love with your heart: but, good Kate, mock me
mercifully; the rather, gentle princess, because I love
thee cruelly.[1] If ever thou beest mine, Kate,—as I
have a saving faith within me tells me thou shalt,—I
get thee with scambling,[2] and thou must therefore
needs prove a good soldier-breeder: shall not thou
and I, between Saint Denis and Saint George, compound
a boy, half French, half English, that shall go to
Constantinople and take the Turk by the beard? shall
we not? what sayest thou, my fair flower-de-luce?

Kath. I do not know dat.

K. Hen. No; 'tis hereafter to know, but now to
promise. How answer you, *la plus belle Katharine
du monde, mon très chère et divine déesse?*[3]

Kath. Your *majesté* have *fausse* French enough to
deceive de most *sage demoiselle* dat is *en France.*[4]

K. Hen. Now, fie upon my false French! By
mine honour, in true English, I love thee, Kate: by
which honour I dare not swear thou lovest me; yet
my blood begins to flatter me that thou dost,
not-withstanding the poor and untempering effect of
my visage. Now, beshrew my father's ambition! I was
created with a stubborn outside, with an aspect of
iron, that, when I come to woo ladies, I fright them.
But, in faith, Kate, the elder I wax, the better I
shall appear: my comfort is, that old age, that ill

1 I love thee very much.

2 Contention.

3 The most beautiful Katharine in the world, my dear and divine goddess?

4 Your majesty has false French enough to deceive the wisest maiden in France.

layer-up of beauty, can do no more spoil upon my face: thou hast me, if thou hast me, at the worst; and thou shalt wear me, if thou wear me, better and better:—and therefore tell me, most fair Katharine, will you have me? Put off your maiden blushes; avouch the thoughts of your heart with the looks of an empress; take me by the hand, and say,—Harry of England, I am thine: which word thou shalt no sooner bless mine ear withal, but I will tell thee aloud,—England is thine, Ireland is thine, France is thine, and Henry Plantagenet is thine; who, though I speak it before his face, if he be not fellow with the best king, thou shalt find the best king of good fellows. Come, your answer in broken music,—for thy voice is music, and thy English broken; therefore, queen of all, Katharine, break thy mind to me in broken English,—wilt thou have me?

Kath. Dat is as it shall please de *roi mon père.*

K. Hen. Nay, it will please him well, Kate,—it shall please him, Kate.

Kath. Den it shall also content me.

K. Hen. Upon that I kiss your hand, and I call you my queen.

Kath. *Laissez, mon seigneur, laissez, laissez: ma foi, je ne veuz point que vous abaissez vostre grandeur en baisant la main d'une vostre indigne serviteur; excusez moi, je vous supplie, mon très puissant seigneur.*[1]

K. Hen. Then I will kiss your lips, Kate.

Kath. *Les dames et demoiselles pour être baisées devant leur noces, il n'est pas la coutume de France.*

K. Hen. Madam my interpreter, what says she?

1 Forbear, my lord, forbear, forbear; my faith, I do not wish that you lower your greatness by kissing the hand of your unworthy servant; do not, I beg you, my very great lord.

Alice. Dat it is not be de fashion *pour les* ladies of France,—I cannot tell vat is *baiser en* English.

K. Hen. To kiss.

Alice. Your majesty *entendre* bettre *que moi.*

K. Hen. It is not a fashion for the maids in France to kiss before they are married, would she say?

Alice. *Oui, vraiment.*

K. Hen. O Kate, nice[1] customs court'sy to great kings. Dear Kate, you and I cannot be confined within the weak list[2] of a country's fashion: we are the makers of manners, Kate; and the liberty that follows our places stops the mouth of all find-faults, —as I will do yours for upholding the nice fashion of your country in denying me a kiss: therefore, patiently and yielding. [*Kissing her.*] You have witchcraft in your lips, Kate: there is more eloquence in a sugar-touch of them than in the tongues of the French council; and they should sooner persuade Harry of England than a general petition of monarchs. —Here comes your father.

READING: *Antony and Cleopatra*

Act I, scene iii: Cleopatra's palace. Characters: Antony, Cleopatra, Charmian.

1 Start with the suggested preparation for Shakespearean scenes. Read Plutarch's life of Marc Antony.

2 Compare the degrees of love between Romeo and Juliet, Henry and Katharine, Antony and Cleopatra. Who is more like Romeo—

[1] Fastidious.

[2] Narrow limit.

Henry or Antony? How is Cleopatra different from Katharine and Juliet? In age? In experience?

In relation to this last question, beware the advice to "go out and get more experience." You cannot force experience. That kind of "experience" has no emotional rationale and is useless. Life will inevitably endow you with plenty of experience. In the meantime you don't have to murder to play a murderer, and you can play Antony or Cleopatra without having been a debauchee or a sybarite.

ACT 1, SCENE iii

Enter CLEOPATRA, CHARMIAN, (IRAS, *and* ALEXAS).

Cleo. Where is he?[1]

Char. I did not see him since.

Cleo. See where he is, who's with him, what he does:—

I did not send you:[2]—if you find him sad,

Say I am dancing; if in mirth, report

That I am sudden sick: quick, and return.

[*Exit* ALEXAS.

Char. Madam, methinks, if you did love him dearly,

You do not hold the method to enforce

The like from him.

Cleo. What should I do, I do not?[45]

Char. In each thing give him way, cross him in nothing.

Cleo. Thou teachest like a fool,—the way to lose him.

Char. Tempt him not so too far; I wish, forbear:[3]

1 Marc Antony.

2 Actually Cleopatra speaks to her servant, Alexas, who then exits. Speak to a servant at the door who is imaginary.

3 Here, "you would" is eliptically understood before "forebear"; or "wish" may be used in the sense it sometimes bore of "recommend."

In time we hate that which we often fear.
But here comes Antony.
Cleo. I am sick and sullen.

Enter ANTONY

Ant. I am sorry to give breathing to my purpose,—
Cleo. Help me away, dear Charmian; I shall fall:
It cannot be thus long, the sides of nature
Will not sustain it.
Ant. Now, my dearest queen,—
Cleo. Pray you, stand farther from me.
Ant. What's the matter?
Cleo. I know, by that same eye, there's some good news.
What says the married woman?[1]—You may go:
Would she had never given you leave to come!
Let her not say 'tis I that keep you here,—
I have no power upon you; hers you are.
Ant. The gods best know,—
Cleo. Oh, never was there queen
So mightily betray'd! yet at the first
I saw the treasons planted.
Ant. Cleopatra,—
Cleo. Why should I think you can be mine and true,
Though you in swearing shake the thronèd gods,
Who have been false to Fulvia? Riotous madness,
To be entangled with those mouth-made vows,
Which break themselves in swearing!
Ant. Most sweet queen,—
Cleo. Nay, pray you, seek no colour for your going.
But bid farewell, and go: when you sued staying,
Then was the time for words: no going then;—

[1] Antony's wife, Fulvia, in Rome, from whence he has heard.

Eternity was in our lips and eyes,
Bliss in our brows' bent; none our parts so poor,
But was a race of heaven:[1] they are so still,
Or thou, the greatest soldier of the world,
Ant. How now, lady!
Cleo. I would I had thy inches; thou shouldst know
There were a heart in Egypt.
Ant. Hear me, queen:
The strong necessity of time commands
Our services awhile; but my full heart
Remains in use[2] with you. Our Italy
Shines o'er with civil swords: Sextus Pompeius
Makes his approaches to the port[3] of Rome:
Equality of two domestic powers
Breeds scrupulous faction: the hated, grown to strength,
Are newly grown to love: the condemn'd Pompey,
Rich in his father's honour, creeps apace
Into the hearts of such as have not thriv'd
Upon the present state, whose numbers threaten;
And quietness, grown sick of rest, would purge
By any desperate change: my more particular,
And that which most with you should safe my going,[4]
Is Fulvia's death.
Cleo. Though age from folly could not give me freedom,
It does from childishness:—can Fulvia die?[5]
Ant. She's dead, my queen:
Look here, and, at thy sovereign leisure, read

1 No part of us but seemed made of heavenly materials.
2 Remains in trust, or in pledge.
3 Gate.
4 Excuse my going.
5 Can it be true that Fulvia is really dead?

The garboils[1] she awak'd; at the last,—best,—
See when and where she died.

Cleo. Oh, most false love!
Where be the sacred vials[2] thou shouldst fill
With sorrowful water? Now I see, I see,
In Fulvia's death, how mine receiv'd shall be.

Ant. Quarrel no more, but be prepared to
know
The purposes I bear; which are, or cease,
As you shall give the advice: by the fire
That quickens Nilus' slime, I go from hence
Thy soldier, servant; making peace, or war,
As thou affect'st.

Cleo. Cut my lace, Charmian, come;—
But let it be:—I am quickly ill, and well;
So Antony loves.[3]

Ant. My precious queen, forbear;
And give true evidence to his love,[4] which stands
An honourable trial.

Cleo. So Fulvia told me.
I pr'ythee, turn aside, and weep for her;
Then bid adieu to me, and say the tears
Belong to Egypt:[5] good now, play one scene
Of excellent dissembling; and let it look
Like perfect honour.

Ant. You'll heat my blood: no more.

Cleo. You can do better yet; but this is
meetly.

Ant. Now, by my sword,—

[1] Turmoils.

[2] Referring to the small bottles filled with tears the Romans placed in the tomb of a dead friend.

[3] As long as Antony loves.

[4] Bear true testimony to his love.

[5] And say the tears belong to Cleopatra, Queen of Egypt.

Cleo. And target.—Still he mends;
But this is not the best:—look, pr'ythee, Charmian,
How this Herculean Roman[1] does become
The carriage of his chafe.[2]
Ant. I'll leave you, lady.
Cleo. Courteous lord, one word.
Sir, you and I must part,—but that's not it:
Sir, you and I have lov'd,—but there's not it;
That you know well: something it is I would,—
Oh, my oblivion[3] is a very Antony,
And I am all forgotten.[4]
Ant. But that your royalty
Holds idleness your subject[5] I should take you
For idleness itself.
Cleo. 'Tis sweating labour
To bear such idleness so near the heart
As Cleopatra this. But, sir, forgive me;
Since my becomings kill me, when they do not
Eye well to you:[6] your honour calls you hence;
Therefore be deaf to my unpitied folly,
And all the gods go with you! upon your sword
Sit laurel'd victory! and smooth success
Be strew'd before your feet!
Ant. Let us go. Come;
Our separation so abides, and flies,
That thou, residing here, go'st yet with me,

[1] Marc Antony traced his descent from Hercules.

[2] Makes his chafed (angry) bearing become him.

[3] Defective memory.

[4] Has the double meaning of "I am entirely forgotten," and "I am entirely forgetful."

[5] You make trifling subservient to your purposes, so I know you are not trifling yourself.

[6] The moods you admire in me are offensive to me when you do not like them.

And I, hence fleeting, here remain with thee.
Away!

[*Exeunt.*

READING: *The Taming of the Shrew*

Act II, scene i: Baptista's home. Characters: Petruchio, Katharine, Baptista, Katharine's father.

1 Start with the suggested preparation for Shakespearean scenes.

2 This scene requires strict attention to the fast tempo, but beware: don't play the tempo itself. The necessary quickness must be a result of the actions played by the protagonists. See *Twelfth Night!*

3 Don't get lazy and play for emotions! Remember, the emotions must be the result of the action beats. Action beats lead to emotions which lead to a fast tempo.

4 "But use all gently; for in the very torrent, tempest, and as I may say, whirlwind of passion, you must acquire and beget a temperance that may give it smoothness. . . . Be not too tame neither, but let your own discretion be your tutor: suit the action to the word, the word to the action. . . ."

ACT II, SCENE i

Pet. . . . I will attend her here,— . . .
And woo her with some spirit when she comes.
Say that she rail; why, then I'll tell her plain,
She sings as sweetly as a nightingale:
Say that she frown; I'll say, she looks as clear
As morning roses newly wash'd with dew:
Say she be mute and will not speak a word;
Then I'll commend her volubility,
And say she uttereth piercing eloquence:
If she do bid me pack, I'll give her thanks,

As though she bid me stay by her a week:
If she deny to wed, I'll crave the day
When I shall ask the banns and when be married.—
But here she comes; and now, Petruchio, speak.

Enter KATHARINA.

Good morrow, Kate; for that's your name, I hear.

Kath. Well have you heard, but something hard of hearing:
They call me Katharine that do talk of me.

Pet. You lie, in faith; for you are call'd plain Kate.
And bonny Kate, and sometimes Kate the curst;
But, Kate, the prettiest Kate in Christendom,
Kate of Kate Hall, my super-dainty Kate,
For dainties are all cates,[1]—and therefore, Kate
Take this of me, Kate of my consolation;—
Hearing thy mildness prais'd in every town,
Thy virtues spoke of, and thy beauty sounded
(Yet not so deeply as to thee belongs),
Myself am mov'd to woo thee for my wife.

Kath. Mov'd! in good time: let him that mov'd you hither
Remove you hence: I knew you at the first,
You were a movable.

Pet. Why, what's a movable?

Kath. A joint-stool.

Pet. Thou hast hit it: come, sit on me.

Kath. Asses are made to bear, and so are you.

Pet. Women are made to bear, and so are you.

Kath. No such jade as you, if me you mean.

Pet. Alas! good Kate, I will not burden thee;
For, knowing thee to be but young and light,—

[1] Dainty foods.

Kath. Too light for such a swain as you to catch;
And yet as heavy as my weight should be.
Pet. Should be! should buz.[1]
Kath. Well ta'en, and like a buzzard.[2]
Pet. Oh, slow-wing'd turtle; shall a buzzard take thee?[3]
Kath. Ay, for a turtle,—as he takes a buzzard.[4]
Pet. Come, come, you wasp; i'faith, you are too angry.
Kath. If I be waspish, best beware my sting.
Pet. My remedy is then, to pluck it out.
Kath. Ay, if the fool could find it where it lies.
Pet. Who knows not where a wasp does wear his sting?
In his tail.
Kath. In his tongue.
Pet. Whose tongue?
Kath. Yours, if you talk of tails: and so farewell.
Pet. What, with my tongue in your tail? Nay, come again,
Good Kate; I am a gentleman.
Kath. That I'll try. [*Striking him.*
Pet. I swear I'll cuff you, if you strike again.
Kath. So may you lose your arms:[5]
If you strike me, you are no gentleman;
And if no gentleman, why then no arms.
Pet. A herald, Kate? Oh, put me in thy books!
Kath. What is your crest? a coxcomb?

[1] Buzz—making a pun of be (bee).
[2] Exactly the kind of joke a dunce would make!
[3] Shall a buzzard (which you have called me) take you, turtle-dove?
[4] Yes, as a dunce takes a buzzard for a turtledove.
[5] His limbs and his coat of arms.

Pet. A combless cock, so Kate will be my hen.
Kath. No cock of mine; you crow too like a craven.[1]
Pet. Nay, come, Kate, come; you must not look so sour.
Kath. It is my fashion, when I see a crab.[2]
Pet. Why, here's no crab; and therefore look not sour.
Kath. There is, there is.
Pet. Then show it me.
Kath. Had I a glass, I would.
Pet. What! you mean my face?
Kath. Well aim'd of such a young one.
Pet. Now, by Saint George, I am too young for you.
Kath. Yet you are wither'd.
Pet. 'Tis with cares.
Kath. I care not.
Pet. Nay, hear you, Kate: in sooth, you 'scape not so.
Kath. I chafe you, if I tarry: let me go.
Pet. No, not a whit: I find you passing gentle.
'Twas told me you were rough, and coy, and sullen,
And now I find report a very liar;
For thou art pleasant, gamesome, passing courteous;
But slow in speech, yet sweet as spring-time flowers:
Thou canst not frown, thou canst not look askance,
Nor bite the lip, as angry wenches will;
Nor hast thou pleasure to be cross in talk;
But thou with mildness entertain'st thy wooers,
With gentle conference, soft and affable.
Why does the world report that Kate doth limp?

1 A degenerate, cowardly cock.
2 A wild apple, harsh and rough; also a morose-tempered person.

Oh, slanderous world! Kate, like the hazel-twig,
Is straight and slender; and as brown in hue
As hazel-nuts, and sweeter than the kernels.
Oh! let me see thee walk: thou dost not halt.

Kath. Go, fool, and whom thou keep'st command.

Pet. Did ever Dian so become a grove,
As Kate this chamber with her princely gait?
Oh, be thou Dian, and let her be Kate;
And then let Kate be chaste and Dian sportful!

Kath. Where did you study all this goodly speech?

Pet. It is extempore, from my mother-wit.

Kath. A witty mother! witless else her son.

Pet. Am I not wise?

Kath. Yes; keep you warm.

Pet. Marry, so I mean, sweet Katharine, in thy bed:
And therefore, setting all this chat aside,
Thus in plain terms:—your father hath consented
That you shall be my wife; your dowry 'greed on;
And, will you, nill you, I will marry you.
Now, Kate, I am a husband for your turn;
For, by this light, whereby I see thy beauty
Thy beauty, that doth make me like thee well,
Thou must be married to no man but me;
For I am he am born to tame you, Kate,
And bring you from a wild Kate[1] to a Kate
Conformable, as other household Kates.
Here comes your father: never make denial;
I must and will have Katharine to my wife.

Re-enter BAPTISTA, (GREMIO, *and* TRANIO).

Bap. Now, Signior Petruchio, how speed you with my daughter?

[1] Wild cat.

Pet. How but well, sir? how but well?
It were impossible I should speed amiss.
Bap. Why, how now, daughter Katharine! in your dumps?
Kath. Call you me daughter? now, I promise you.
You have show'd a tender fatherly regard,
To wish me wed to one half lunatic;
A mad-cap ruffian, and a swearing Jack,
That thinks with oaths to face the matter out.
Pet. Father, 'tis thus:—yourself and all the world,
That talk'd of her, have talk'd amiss of her:
If she be curst, it is for policy,
For she's not froward, but modest as the dove;
She is not hot, but temperate as the morn;
For patience she will prove a second Grissel,[1]
And Roman Lucrece for her chastity:
And to conclude,—we have 'greed so well together.
That upon Sunday is the wedding-day.
Kath. I'll see thee hang'd on Sunday first. . . .
Pet. 'Tis bargain'd 'twixt us twain, being alone,
That she shall still be curst in company.
I tell you, 'tis incredible to believe
How much she loves me: oh, the kindest Kate!—
She hung about my neck; and kiss on kiss
She vied[2] so fast, protesting oath on oath,
That in a twink she won me to her love.
Oh, you are novices! 'tis a world to see,[3]
How tame, when men and women are alone,
A meacock[4] wretch can make the curstest shrew.—

1 The patient Griselda, of Chaucer's "Clerk's Tale."
2 Proffered in competition.
3 It is wonderful to see.
4 Timorous, too-yielding.

Give me thy hand, Kate: I will unto Venice,
To buy apparel 'gainst the wedding-day.—
Provide the feast, father, and bid the guests;
I will be sure my Katharine shall be fine.
Bap. I know not what to say: but give me your
hands;
God send you joy, Petruchio! 'tis a match.
Pet. Father, and wife, and gentlemen, adieu;
I will to Venice; Sunday comes apace:—
We will have rings, and things, and fine array:
And, kiss me, Kate, we will be married o' Sunday.
[*Exeunt Petruchio and Katharine severally.*

READING: *Richard III*

Act I, scene ii: A street. Characters: Richard, Duke of Gloucester, Ann, two pallbearers.

1 Start with the suggested preparation for Shakespearean scenes.

2 The tempo-rhythm here is funereal. Once again, don't let results lead to causes. Anne must make a real emotional preparation for this scene. Remember, she is a young widow in deep mourning. If you act her and have never had the misfortune of losing someone you loved, substitute the memory of another experience, the loss of a loved pet, or a separation that hurt terribly.

3 Do not over-intellectualize. It is possible to think yourself right out of this play. Anne: "If I loved my husband so very much, how can Richard talk me out of my grief and woo me successfully? Evidently I don't really love my husband so much, and therefore my mourning ought not to be really full or genuine after all." To solve this problem, give up being omniscient. Do not know the scene's ending at its beginning. Play the necessary action. First lament your husband's death. Do not anticipate Richard's action, which is to woo you. Act one beat at a time.

4 The best and in fact the only possible rule in playing the villain is to make him as nice as possible. Don't grab the cliché. In the preceding scene, Richard has explained

> And therefore, since I cannot prove a lover,
> To entertain these fair well-spoken days,
> I am determined to prove a villain. . . .

For the sake of balance in your characterization, you should accept this speech to mean that Richard must overcome what is good in him to prove a villain. Thus, in working on your psychological preparation from the given circumstances, seek out all the good qualities that can be found even in a villainous heart. The lines will prove you villainous enough. Play against them.

5 Richard needs a clearly worked out physical defect.

6 Denominate some prop for the husband's corpse and use that object during the playing of the scene.

7 Again use costumes and props as early as possible.

ACT I, SCENE ii—LONDON. *Another street.*

Enter the corse of KING HENRY the Sixth, *borne in an open coffin,* Gentlemen *bearing halberds to guard it; and* LADY ANNE *as mourner.*

Anne Set down, set down your honourable
load,—
If honour may be shrouded in a hearse;—
Whilst I awhile obsequiously[1] lament
Th' untimely fall of virtuous Lancaster.—
Poor key-cold[2] figure of a holy king!
Pale ashes of the house of Lancaster!
Thou bloodless remnant of that royal blood!

[1] With funereal observance.
[2] Deadly cold.

Be it lawful that I invocate thy ghost,
To hear the lamentations of poor Anne,
Wife to thy Edward, to thy slaughter'd son,
Stabb'd by the selfsame hand that made these
wounds!
Lo, in these windows, that let forth thy life,
I pour the helpless balm of my poor eyes:—
Oh, cursèd be the hand that made these holes!
Cursèd the heart that had the heart to do it!
Cursèd the blood that let this blood from hence!
More direful hap betide that hated wretch,
That makes us wretched by the death of thee,
Than I can wish to adders, spiders, toads,
Or any creeping venom'd thing that lives!
If ever he have child, abortive be it,
Prodigious and untimely brought to light,
Whose ugly and unnatural aspèct
May fright the hopeful mother at the view;
And that be heir to his unhappiness![1]
If ever he have wife, let her be made
More miserable by the death of him,
Than I am made by my young lord and thee!—
Come, now towards Chertsey with your holy load,
Taken from Paul's to be interrèd there;
And still, as you are weary of the weight,
Rest you, whiles I lament King Henry's corse.
[*The* Bearers *take up the corse and advance.*
Enter GLOCESTER.

Glo. Stay, you that bear the corse, and set it
down.

Anne What black magician conjures up this
fiend.
To stop devoted charitable deeds?

[1] Heir to his disposition to mischief.

Glo. Villains, set down the corse; or, by Saint Paul,
I'll make a corse of him that disobeys!
First Gent. My lord, stand back, and let the coffin pass.
Glo. Unmanner'd dog! stand thou, when I command:
Advance thy halberd higher than my breast,
Or, by Saint Paul, I'll strike thee to my foot,
And spurn upon thee, beggar, for thy boldness.
[*The* Bearers *set down the coffin.*
Anne What! do you tremble? are you all afraid?
Alas! I blame you not; for you are mortal,
And mortal eyes cannot endure the devil.—
Avaunt, thou dreadful minister of hell!
Thou hadst but power over his mortal body,—
His soul thou canst not have; therefore, be gone.
Glo. Sweet saint, for charity, be not so curst.[1]
Anne Foul devil, for God's sake, hence and trouble us not;
For thou hast made the happy earth thy hell,
Fill'd it with cursing cries and deep exclaims.
If thou delight to view thy heinous deeds,
Behold this pattern[2] of thy butcheries.—
Oh, gentlemen, see, see dead Henry's wounds
Open their cóngeal'd mouths and bleed afresh![3]—
Blush, blush, thou lump of foul deformity;
For 'tis thy presence that exhales this blood
From cold and empty veins, where no blood dwells;
Thy deed, inhuman and unnatural,
Provokes this deluge most unnatural.—

1 Shrewish.
2 Example.
3 It was believed that a murdered body bled afresh in the presence of the murderer.

O God, which this blood mad'st, revenge his death!
Oh, earth, which this blood drink'st, revenge his death!
Either, heaven, with lightning strike the murd'rer dead;
Or, earth, gape open wide, and eat him quick,[1]
As thou dost swallow up this good king's blood,
Which his hell-govern'd arm hath butcherèd!

Glo. Lady, you know no rules of charity,
Which renders good for bad, blessings for curses.

Anne Villain, thou know'st no law of God nor man:
No beast so fierce but knows some touch of pity.

Glo. But I know none, and therefore am no beast.

Anne Oh, wonderful, when devils tell the truth!

Glo. More wonderful, when angels are so angry.—
Vouchsafe, divine perfection of a woman,
Of these supposèd evils, to give me leave,
By circumstance, but to acquit myself.

Anne Vouchsafe, diffus'd[2] infection of a man,
For these known evils, but to give me leave,
By circumstance, to curse thy cursèd self.

Glo. Fairer than tongue can name thee, let me have
Some patient leisure to excuse myself.

Anne Fouler than heart can think thee, thou canst make
No éxcuse current, but to hang thyself.

Glo. By such despair, I should accuse myself.

Anne And, by despairing, shalt thou stand excus'd;

[1] Swallow him alive.
[2] Uncouth.

For doing worthy vengeance on thyself,
That didst unworthy slaughter upon others.
Glo. Say that I slew them not?
Anne Then say they were not slain:
But dead they are, and, devilish slave, by thee.
Glo. I did not kill your husband.
Anne Why, then he is alive.
Glo. Nay, he is dead; and slain by Edward's hand.
Anne In thy foul throat thou liest: Queen
Margaret saw
Thy murd'rous falchion smoking in his blood;
The which thou once didst bend against her breast,
But that thy brothers beat aside the point.
Glo. I was provokèd by her sland'rous tongue,
That laid their guilt[1] upon my guiltless shoulders.
Anne Thou wast provokèd by thy bloody mind,
That never dreamt on aught but butcheries:
Didst thou not kill this king?
Glo. I grant ye.
Anne Oh, he was gentle, mild, and virtuous!
Glo. The fitter for the King of heaven, that
hath him.
Anne He is in heaven, where thou shalt never
come.
Glo. Let him thank me, that holp[2] to send him
thither:
For he was fitter for that place than earth.
Anne And thou unfit for any place but hell.
Glo. Yes, one place else, if you will hear me
name it.
Anne Some dungeon.
Glo. Your bed-chamber.

[1] The guilt of his brothers.
[2] Helped.

Anne Ill rest betide the chamber where thou liest!

Glo. So will it, madam, till I lie with you.

Anne I hope so.

Glo. I know so.—But, gentle lady Anne,—
To leave this keen encounter of our wits,
And fall somewhat into a slower[1] method,—
Is not the causer of the timeless deaths
Of these Plantagenets, Henry and Edward,
As blameful as the executioner?

Anne Thou wast the cause, and most accurs'd effect.[2]

Glo. Your beauty was the cause of that effect;
Your beauty, that did haunt me in my sleep
To undertake the death of all the world,
So I might live one hour in your sweet bosom.

Anne If I thought that, I tell thee, homicide,
These nails should rend that beauty from my cheeks.

Glo. These eyes could not endure that beauty's wreck;
You should not blemish it, if I stood by:
As all the world is cheerèd by the sun,
So I by that; it is my day, my life.

Anne Black night o'ershade thy day, and death thy life!

Glo. Curse not thyself, fair creature; thou art both.

Anne I would I were, to be reveng'd on thee.

Glo. It is a quarrel most unnatural,
To be reveng'd on him that loveth thee.

Anne It is a quarrel just and reasonable,
To be reveng'd on him that kill'd my husband.

[1] Less vivacious.

[2] Perhaps, "Thou was the cause, and this the most cursed effect."

Glo. He that bereft thee, lady, of thy husband,
Did it to help thee to a better husband.
Anne His better doth not breathe upon the earth.
Glo. He lives that loves thee better than he could.
Anne Name him.
Glo. Plantagenet.
Anne Why, that was he.
Glo. The selfsame name, but one of better nature.
Anne Where is he?
Glo. Here. [*She spits at him.*] Why dost thou spit at me?
Anne Would it were mortal poison, for thy sake!
Glo. Never came poison from so sweet a place.
Anne Never hung poison on a fouler toad.
Out of my sight! thou dost infect mine eyes.
Glo. Thine eyes, sweet lady, have infected mine.
Anne Would they were basilisks, to strike thee dead![1]
Glo. I would they were, that I might die at once;
For now they kill me with a living death.
Those eyes of thine from mine have drawn salt tears,
Sham'd their aspècts with store of childish drops:
These eyes, which never shed remorseful[2] tear,
No, when my father York and Edward wept,
To hear the piteous moan that Rutland made,
When black-fac'd Clifford shook his sword at him;
Nor when thy warlike father, like a child,

1 Basilisks were legendary serpents with lethal breaths and glances.
2 Pitiful.

Told the sad story of my father's death,
And twenty times made pause, to sob and weep,
That all the standers-by had wet their cheeks,
Like trees bedash'd with rain; in that sad time
My manly eyes did scorn a humble tear;
And what these sorrows could not hence exhale,
Thy beauty hath, and made them blind with weeping.
I never su'd to friend nor enemy;
My tongue could never learn sweet smoothing[3]
word;
But, now thy beauty is propos'd my fee,
My proud heart sues, and prompts my tongue to
speak. [*She looks scornfully at him.*
Teach not thy lip such scorn; for it was made
For kissing, lady, not for such contempt.
If thy revengeful heart cannot forgive,
Lo, here I lend thee this sharp-pointed sword;
Which if thou please to hide in this true breast,
And let the soul forth that adoreth thee,
I lay it naked to the deadly stroke,
And humbly beg the death upon my knee.
[*He lays his breast open.*
Nay, do not pause; for I did kill King Henry,—
[*She offers at his breast with his sword.*
But 'twas thy beauty that provoked me.
Nay, now dispatch; 'twas I that stabb'd young
Edward,—
[*She again offers at his breast.*
But 'twas thy heavenly face that set me on.
[*She lets fall the sword.*
Take up the sword again, or take up me.
Anne Arise, dissembler: though I wish thy
death,

[3] Ingratiating.

I will not be thy executioner.
Glo. Then bid me kill myself, and I will do it.
Anne I have already.
Glo. That was in thy rage:
Speak it again, and, even with the word,
This hand, which, for thy love, did kill thy love,
Shall, for thy love, kill a far truer love:
To both their deaths shalt thou be accessary.
Anne I would I knew thy heart.
Glo. 'Tis figur'd in my tongue.
Anne I fear me both are false.
Glo. Then never man was true.
Anne Well, well, put up your sword.
Glo. Say, then, my peace is made.
Anne That shalt thou know hereafter.
Glo. But shall I live in hope?
Anne All men, I hope, live so.
Glo. Vouchsafe to wear this ring.
Anne To take, is not to give.
[*She puts on the ring.*
Glo. Look, how my ring encompasseth thy finger,
Even so thy breast encloseth my poor heart;
Wear both of them, for both of them are thine.
And if thy poor devoted servant may
But beg one favour at thy gracious hand,
Thou dost confirm his happiness for ever.
Anne What is it?
Glo. That it may please you leave these sad designs
To him that hath most cause to be a mourner,
And presently repair to Crosby Place;[1]
Where,—after I have solemnly interr'd,

[1] The residence of Richard in London.

At Chertsey monastery, this noble king,
And wet his grave with my repentant tears,—
I will with all expedient duty see you:
For divers unknown reasons, I beseech you,
Grant me this boon.

Anne With all my heart; and much it joys me too,
To see you are become so penitent.—

Glo. Bid me farewell.

Anne 'Tis more than you deserve;
But since you teach me how to flatter you,
Imagine I have said farewell already. (*Exit Anne*)

Glo. Sirs, take up the corse.

Gent. Towards Chertsey, noble lord?

Glo. No, to White Friars; there attend my coming.
[*Exeunt the rest with the corse.*
Was ever woman in this humour woo'd?
Was ever woman in this humour won?
I'll have her;—but I will not keep her long.
What! I, that kill'd her husband and his father,
To take her in her heart's extremest hate;
With curses in her mouth, tears in her eyes,
The bleeding witness of her hatred by;
Having God, her conscience, and these bars against
me,
And I no friends to back my suit withal,
But the plain devil and dissembling looks,
And yet to win her,—all the world to nothing![1]
Ha!
Hath she forgot already that brave prince,
Edward, her lord, whom I, some three months since,
Stabb'd in my angry mood at Tewksbury?
A sweeter and a lovelier gentleman,—
Fram'd in the prodigality of nature,

[1] The chances were everything to nothing against his winning her.

Young, valiant, wise, and, no doubt, right royal,—
The spacious world cannot again afford:
And will she yet abase her eyes on me,
That cropp'd the golden prime of this sweet prince,
And made her widow to a woful bed?
On me, whose all not equals Edward's moiety?
On me, that halt and am mis-shapen thus?
My dukedom to a beggarly denier,[1]
I do mistake my person all this while:
Upon my life, she finds, although I cannot,
Myself to be a marvellous proper man.
I'll be at charges for a looking-glass;
And entertain a score or two of tailors,
To study fashions to adorn my body:
Since I am crept in favour with myself,
I will maintain it with some little cost.
But first I'll turn yon fellow in his grave;
And then return lamenting to my love.—
Shine out, fair sun, till I have bought a glass,
That I may see my shadow as I pass. [*Exit.*

1 A French coin of the lowest possible denomination.

11

Style

It cannot be emphasized too much that the Method is not a style. Style in the theatre depends on the nature of the play presented, the production ideas and temperament of the director and the performing company. The Method is technique, a method for the training of the actor so that with experience over the years he may develop a technique for the most complete use of himself as an interpreter of parts in plays.

HAROLD CLURMAN[1]

Dictionaries define *style* as the way in which something is said or done, as distinguished from its substance. Consider for a moment one of the more difficult styles for American actors: the style of Restoration comedy. If you were to play the fop in one of these plays, the correct style of the period would be involved in the character *how* (your movement, diction, habitual gestures—in fact, all your habits, mental assumptions, basic psychology), as well as in the where and

1 From the introduction to Robert Lewis, *Method or Madness* (New York: Samuel French, 1958).

when of the given circumstances. You would have to know a great deal about the late seventeenth century in England—in the country, as well as in London. You would have to know your own attitude toward everything around you. You would have to be able to alter everything about your own natural speech and movement, and you would have to be able to accommodate yourself to a whole new set of unfamiliar clothing and small props.

No amount of careful work on the first three questions of the given circumstances, no amazing psychological discoveries, no rare acting moments could save you from failing in the part if you did not master the external elements that make up style.

As I have said in the Preface, the Method practitioners in America, under the influence of Stanislavski's earlier book, *An Actor Prepares,* trained actors to work on their "inner feelings" and neglected to train them adequately in the externals of diction and body movement so essential for acting in different styles. Therefore it was thought that classical plays, and Shakespeare in particular, were totally incompatible with the Stanislavski System. In fact, Stanislavski went on to solve the problem by tackling the acting externals. The technique of mastering various styles, he found, depended on the voice, the diction, relaxation, and body movement.

The Stanislavski System, if fully utilized, is as valuable in playing the plays of other periods as it is in playing the plays of our own. In the exploration of the character how, in finding the answers to where and when of the given circumstances, the actor needs to find the fullest possible answers, covering all the essential information about the period.

If the Old Vic wanted to do Clifford Odets' *Waiting for Lefty,* its members would have to do research on the America of the thirties. The company members would have to absorb the mood of America, the time and place, as well as the speech patterns, which in this case would involve using frontal speech. They would have to speak in a fast, flat staccato, almost in the manner of a riveting machine.

Perhaps the best method of getting down a foreign style is through the study of films. This would be an easier matter for the English company doing *Waiting for Lefty* than it would be for the American company doing Wycherley, but there are actually many good costume films which could be found and studied with profit by a company about to embark on a production which demands a difficult style. Actors might also do improvisations from paintings of the period, read history books, and find a professional who really knows the particular period.

The Juilliard School of Acting in New York, which has given birth to the Juilliard Company, really trains its actors in the style of different periods. There actors are trained in appropriate speech, body movement, the handling of costumes and props. This particular company and its expertise in handling various styles owes an important debt to Michel St.-Denis, and his book, *Theatre: The Rediscovery of Style,* which all student actors must study. (St.-Denis, perhaps not coincidentally, was director of the Old Vic School, and consulted at the Canadian National Theatre School as well as at the Juilliard School.) I have seen the young Juilliard Company do a *Women Beware Women* (Middleton, ca. 1620) and a *School for Scandal* (Sheridan, 1777) which I had not previously believed possible from *any* American company. They were truly excellent.

It is impossible for me to attempt to teach acting style through words. You must have recourse to speaking, moving models to teach you the actual diction and movement involved. But I will outline some of the major periods which have contributed dramas still represented in our repertory.

Greek plays were originally played in immense outdoor theaters, the actors elevated on platform shoes and wearing masks with built-in megaphones. This is obviously not a style for mumblers and mutterers, nor is it a style in which the lifting of an eyebrow is particularly significant. The trap, of course, is to fall into patterns of declamation. Blasting and bellowing speeches would be a grave fault at any time, and are a fault in Greek drama too. To find your proper actions is just as important here as in any modern play.

It is important to know that the Greek plays were born out of religious ceremonies, and always came to grips with universal problems, such as the individual and his conscience versus the state and its rights. Oedipus and Electra are famous examples of universal types found in Greek plays.

When the medieval drama emerged, it is not surprising to find that it too derived from religious ceremony. The characters in medieval plays, like those in Greek plays, also tend to represent universal types. The actor in the medieval play also worked in the open air, and had a voice projection problem. Actions, as in Greek plays, were large, and heroic, nothing on a small, subtle scale.

But both Greek and medieval plays lend themselves to the use of the given circumstances, the discovery of the play's spine, the spines of the characters, and the characters' individual action beats.

The action or beat, whether performed on a scale larger than life or on a scale true to life, grows out of the given circumstances, and if the proper actions are not discovered and performed, then the acting—whether heroic or realistic in style—is hollow, flimsy, and indicated. In *any* style the nucleus of good acting is the living truthfully under the given circumstances.

You should be acquainted with the epic dramas written by Marlowe in the sixteenth century, *Tamburlaine* and *Dr. Faustus;* they include grand, passionate, virtuoso parts. But here, too, you must be prepared to work from a truthful foundation upon which you can build your role, albeit with full voice and with full passion!

Shakespeare's style defies classification. His drama can be defined as realistic, naturalistic, or poetic. He mixed comedy, tragedy, and history. I have devoted an entire chapter to Shakespeare in this book because the fact is that if you can act Shakespeare really well, you can act anything—always provided you study the manners and speech of your period! Many different skills are required to act Shakespeare, depending upon whether you have drawn a clown, a king, a country lover, a villain, a courtier, a scold, an ingenue, and so on.

Jacobean tragedy is still occasionally acted, but can be handled by any company that can do Shakespeare. *Women Beware Women* belongs to this period.

The next important period is that of Restoration comedy, for the tragedy of that era is no longer acted. These comedies include the works of Congreve and Wycherley, still hardly less delightful than when they were written. To act in a Restoration play you must be able, depending on your sex, to use a fan, turn with a cape, handle long dresses, take snuff elegantly, wear heavy skirts and wigs, silk stockings and lace cuffs, salute, make an obeisance, curtsey, or bow. The tempo is swift, the acting must be etched in fine, satiric details, the dialogue must be crisp, and the inflection, inevitably, should be British.

These comedies are called the Comedy of Manners, and style is so quintessentially important here that it dictates social position. There are certain requisite manners at this time, which are a literal way of life. Those who exaggerate manners, and go too far, become fops and are laughed at for over-doing. Those who are ignorant of the manners are country bumpkins or people of ill-breeding and are laughed at for under-doing. Only the heroes and heroines of the piece know exactly how to behave and demonstrate to us how it is really to be done. How could knowing the style be more important?

Eighteenth century comedy, including the works of Colman and Garrick, Goldsmith and Sheridan, is very similar to Restoration comedy, from which it derives, though it is generally better-natured. In fact, once you have mastered the difficult technique of Restoration comedy, you will be able to play all drawing-room comedy, down through Oscar Wilde and Noel Coward.

The next important stylistic change came with naturalism, represented by such playwrights as Chekhov, Strindberg, and Ibsen. The characters are now middle-class and have internal problems to solve. The descendants of these playwrights are Odets, Inge, Williams, and Miller, and the style is still pretty much the same. This is the style in which you, of course, feel most at home. Here too, Stanislavski's System, first tested on the plays of Chekhov, is easiest to apply. Now at last we are on familiar ground, with the average man in his everyday home, speaking just like any human being, sighing, pausing, and just being real. The characters of naturalistic and realistic drama are true-to-life individuals, with histories you can fill in easily enough.

However, a new kind of drama, the Theater of the Absurd, has emerged, demanding a different style. The characters of the absurd play are once again, as in the Greek and medieval theater, symbolic, universal types. Estragon and Vladimir of *Waiting for Godot* have more in common with Everyman than with Willie Loman. How do you fill in the given circumstances for Everyman, Estragon, or Vladimir?

If you are acting in a play by Ionesco, Genet, Beckett, Pinter, Kopit, or Gelber, you must grasp the meaning of the play and must carefully act within the concept intended by the playwright. If you are determining the given circumstances for Vladimir, Estragon, or for the old man in *The Caretaker,* you must concentrate less on individual particulars, and more on universals. Estragon is Man, representing all men. What he wants is answers about his condition. He wants those answers because he doesn't like not knowing, and he intends to get them in the only way he can think of, which is to await the sending of his answers by the authority. In the meantime, he plays games with Vladimir, to fill in the time. The when and the where are deliberately vague, because the play's time is all times; the place, everywhere. The entire play is symbolic of man's universal position.

Pinter's *The Caretaker* does not take place in such a purely symbolic landscape; his setting is more particularized and so are his characters. Nevertheless, the character of the caretaker must be handled in somewhat the same manner as Vladimir and Estragon, even though particulars about him are known. Who is he? He, too, represents Man. What does he want? A living, security, a safe corner. Why does he want it? He must have it to live. How is he going to get it? By moving in one someone else's corner, an inch at a time. Isn't that how we all get what we have? The place and the time, though carefully detailed, are also universal. The apartment is brilliantly designed to represent one particular collection of flotsam and jetsam *and* also the universal flotsam and jetsam collected by Man. It is both precious to its owner and, in actuality, junk.

You will need more, not less, of yourself to play this kind of character. It is a character which Ionesco has described as psychologically empty; but it is symbolically full. A universal scream, one that represents all mankind, may have to emanate from your gut, or it may have to be suppressed into a high-pitched giggle which is just as terrifying. You must, in any case, be totally prepared to use your total instrument. Are you ready to move like an acrobat, or an old man; to squeal like a newborn infant; to bellow like a bull? Do you have any ideas or feelings about the human condition? Can you even understand what the Absurdists are trying to tell us?[1]

I can think of no better way to end this discussion than to emphasize once more the importance of using the Stanislavski System carefully on any style of play. There is no better way to play an Absurdist play successfully than to find the spine of one's character, and work one's action beats. In fact, for every different style discussed, there is always the imperative necessity to work from a system of truthful given circumstances that are fully particularized and expressed through a series of truthfully performed actions.

[1] An excellent text discussing the Absurdists is Martin Esslin's *The Theatre of the Absurd* (Garden City: Doubleday & Co., 1969).

12

What are you going to do now?

Anyone planning a trip into unfamiliar territory should be equipped with a road map. The information that follows is just that: a road map to guide you to your final destination, an acting job!

What do you know about landing an acting job? Try to remember that acting, especially in America, is really a business, and the more you know about that business, the more successful you will be. Knowledge about the unions, the agents, the professional publications, the preparation of resumés, and showcase opportunities should help you. Try to land as many interviews and auditions as possible. Many people try acting but quit before they have given themselves a fair chance. If you are going to try to become an actor, at least give yourself the satisfaction of knowing that you did everything you could to succeed.

There are three major unions for the actor: Actors' Equity Association (AEA) for the legitimate stage, the American Federation of Television and Radio Artists (AFTRA) for television and radio, and the Screen Actors' Guild (SAG) for films. You do not have to be a member of any of these unions to begin your life as an actor, but at the moment when you are offered a job with a union contract, you can and must join. At present the initiation fee for each of the unions is the same: $300. However, once you have joined one union, you can join the others, even without a contract, for half the fee.

You may wonder why actors are saddled with three unions. Actors' Equity, the oldest of the three, decided that the stage was separate from radio, screen, and television, when these media grew popular. Because Equity decided to have nothing to do with that suspicious new form, movies, the actor now has to pay his union fees in triplicate, and there are no plans at present for remedying the situation.

Many young actors can hardly wait to be members of Equity; until this moment arrives they hardly, even though they have been paid for their work, feel like true professionals. Remember that when you work under an Equity contract, you can and must join the union; from that time on you must abide by its rules. You will be given an Equity rule book, and you would do well to study it. You will learn where you can and cannot work (being a member of Equity will close many showcase opportunities to you). You may even have to change your name (rules are that only one member of Equity may use a particular name, and if a retired musical comedy actor of the twenties has yours, you'll have to use another one!). Equity members can never rehearse or perform in an Equity company without a contract. You must notify Equity when you do sign a contract, and you must send Equity a copy. You may perform with a non-Equity company only with permission from Equity. When you are not working, you may apply for a temporary withdrawal card so that you will not be required to pay annual dues of $42.00, but even with a temporary withdrawal card, you cannot work in a non-Equity company without union permission. If you do apply for permission to work in a non-Equity company and are turned down, it is dangerous to change your name and do the part under an assumed name. If you are reported for this infraction—and Equity sends deputies around to uncover just this sort of thing—you may incur a fine and suspension from the union, which could end by hurting your career.

In these circumstances, do not take the attitude that your first professional requirement is an Equity card. Aim for experience first; if you get that, the Equity card will probably follow. Actors' Equity provides statistics on the employment of its union members which are distinctly depressing. As of January 1973, approximately 3.4 percent of the union membership of 17,500 were working on Broadway. Including all other varieties of legitimate theater, 12 percent were employed.

Members working on Broadway	598
Members working off-Broadway	142
Members in road shows (touring companies)	513
Members working in regional theater	634
Members working in dinner theater	381
	2,268

Dinner theaters, listed above, can be found scattered throughout the United States. They are actually night clubs which offer as entertainment mini-versions of Broadway hits, mostly musicals. The productions are limited greatly in terms of sets, stage effects, and cast.

Equity does help its members by setting wage minimums for specified jobs. Minimums depend on the income that can be grossed by the theater in which your play is housed. At the beginning of your career, you will always be offered minimum. In fact, in this and in all matters of professional relationships, remember that the law of supply and demand being what it is, you can be replaced with very little trouble on the part of the management. Do not, therefore, indulge in temperament, make demands, or get an inflated idea of your own consequence just because you are working. Minimum salaries rise with inflation, but as of January, 1973, these figures pertained:

Equity minimums on Broadway

Houses that can gross $24,000 and over weekly	$182.00
Houses that can gross $12,000 to $24,000	$157.55
Houses that can gross $6,000 to $12,000	$140.95
Houses that can gross $6,000 and under	$117.50

Equity minimums off-Broadway

Houses that can gross $7,500 to $8,500	$155.00
Houses that can gross $6,500 to $7,500	$145.00
Houses that can gross $5,500 to $6,500	$135.00
Houses that can gross $5,500 and under	$125.00

Off-off-Broadway is not unionized and therefore no figures are available. Off-off-Broadway is to off-Broadway what off-Broadway was originally to Broadway. When off-Broadway first started, it paid from nothing to $25.00 a week. The tendency is, obviously, for Equity to step in and regulate; just as obviously, young producers on a shoe-string will find they have to go to a loft or a cellar where union salaries do not have to be paid.

Examination of the figures above will lead even the youthful dreamer to realize that it is not wise to go into acting because he wants a swimming pool. Even if you had the statistically improbable luck of working at the top Broadway minimum of $182.00 for a full year, you would find yourself at the end of that year, after the deduction of taxes, with something like $7,500, whereas a Transit Authority subway patrolman begins at about $10,000 a year.

Besides Equity jobs on and off Broadway, there are also Equity stock companies which usually, but not always, operate mostly in the summer months. Stock companies, before the advent of the movies, provided entertainment all over the country. Operating year round, they were an excellent training ground for young actors. But especially after the talkies came in, stock companies began to diminish. For a long time they remained a summer tradition in this country, but television has now caused a serious decline of summer stock theaters, from over 200 in 1963 to only 98 today. Part of the blame may also lie with the decrease in good Broadway plays and musicals which can be repeated in stock, and in the rise in popularity of the rock festival.

Stock salaries are also based on the capacity of the theater which houses the company.

Equity minimums in stock

X Companies (in houses that can gross over $13,500 weekly)	$150.39
Y Companies (in houses that gross $7,500 to $13,500)	$122.56
Z Companies (in houses that gross less than $7,500)	$111.40

Stock companies are made up of a basic nucleus of a leading man, a leading woman, an ingenue, and a juvenile, a character man and woman. Minor parts can be played by apprentices, or by other non-union actors. However, a given proportion of the actors in any Equity production must be Equity members. Sometimes, if there is a large cast in the play, additional Equity jobbers have to be hired for that one production. X Company jobbers get $150.39 a week, and Y and Z company jobbers get $139.28.

There is nothing like working in a stock company to give the young actor experience. In addition, spending two summers as an apprentice in an Equity stock company is the surest way to get your Equity card. Union rules state that in your second summer, you get a card and a contract with your fourth part. But be sure the theater will give you four parts before you choose this road to Equity membership!

Remember, however, that in stock you play one show at night and rehearse the next show during the day. This goes on for ten weeks and can be very hard on some people. There are excellent actors who cannot do stock because they cannot memorize a play a week. If you feel that stock is not your cup of tea, though, you can still try out for a summer touring package. With a package you travel all summer, from theater to theater, doing the same role. This is certainly not as demanding as stock, but neither is it as conducive to your growth as an actor.

For stock jobs, get the *Summer Stock Directory,* sold at newsstands in the 42nd Street area. The Directory lists all the summer theaters and provides the addresses of producers. The usual procedure is to send in your photo and resumé to the producer, requesting an interview. Most producers come to New York every spring, hire an audition room, and audition actors.

Equity also regulates the salaries for a lucrative but less-rewarding acting engagement, a part in an industrial show. Industrial shows are produced by large corporations to promote their products.

Minimum weekly salaries in industrial shows

For an employment period of seven calendar days . . $324.30
For an employment period of two weeks or more . . . 256.30

The union of the television or radio actor is AFTRA, which you can join either when you have a contract for a television or radio part, or after you are a member of one of the other two unions. Dues are $47.50 per year.

AFTRA offers a dismal employment picture; over the years, approximately 90 percent of its membership is unemployed at any one given time. Currently there are more jobs in television on the West Coast than on the East, but because there are also more actors there, the unemployment rate remains the same.

The daily afternoon soap operas offer the actor steady employment for at least a time, and really good pay, but it is extremely difficult to break into what is known as a contract cast. Its members are those regulars who appear on the show steadily, at least until the actor tires and wants to leave, or the director or producer decides he wants to get rid of him, at which point the actor is written out of the show. Each daily show is preceded by a ten-hour rehearsal period; the actor gets paid a minimum of $175.00 per show. Actors with under five lines get $85.50 per day, and the extra without lines gets $48.00 for a day, which includes a four- or five-hour rehearsal period.

The rules for membership in the Screen Actors' Guild (SAG) are like those for Equity and AFTRA. Here again, chances of employment are not good. Far fewer movies are being made than in the past. For 1973, six films were scheduled for shooting in New York City, and forty in California.

SAG salaries are $138.00 per day, or $483.00 per week for five lines or more, and $35.65 per day for extras.

SAG will permit its members to work for a non-union film unit provided it is university or institution-connected. However, if the film is ever released commercially, then the actor must be paid scale wages for the time he spent working on the film.

Television commercials can be made under the jurisdiction of either SAG or AFTRA. Payment is a flat fee, "plus residuals," which means that the actor gets an additional payment each time the commercial is shown. An actor can make thousands from one good commercial.

Now let us suppose that you are about to pit yourself against the commercial theater. You probably will head for either "the East

Coast" or "the West Coast"—New York or Hollywood. These instructions are slanted largely towards the young actor who wants to try for the legitimate theater of Broadway. If you are headed for the studios of Los Angeles, adapt the instructions, with this difference: In New York it is traditional for the young actor to spend his free time, "making the rounds"—that is, visiting all the casting offices, production offices, and agents to make himself known, to leave a photo and resumé for their files, to make a favorable impression, to remind them of his existence, to check up on rumors about casting, and, not least important, to mingle with other actors in hopes of hearing some good tips. On the West Coast, where the theater area is far more vast and spread out, making the rounds isn't feasible. The actor simply has to depend on a good agent, and therefore an agent is proportionately more important to the Hollywood actor, while the New York actor often can do perfectly well without one.

Having an agent is a little like having an Equity card. At a certain point in your career it may be a necessity, but to have one (just for the sake of having one) too early may turn out to be a drawback. An agent will sign you up if it looks like you're at all "hot," or going to be hot. But in the meantime you'll be out getting jobs on your own, too, or through other contacts, and you'll have to pay your agent 10 percent from every job you do, regardless of how you landed it. He has to work hard for you to justify his share. Of course, if you're on the West Coast, you're going to need an agent anyway. But beware of the "personal manager"—the unions forbid the agent to take more than 10 percent of the actor's salary, but the personal manager can get 25 percent. Sign up mistakenly with a personal manager, and you could find yourself with an unscrupulous parasite who gets a quarter of all you make, while you are paying another 10 percent to the other agents who happened to send you up for jobs that you landed.

In all your dealings with agents, try to find out what kind of reputations they have, and behave accordingly. Remember that an agent refers to his actor clients as his "stable." While you imagine that the agent is working for you, the agent, perhaps with reason, believes that you and your fellow actors are working for him.

Now for some practical advice about your move to New York.

Write ahead to a Y for a cheap room reservation, so you'll have a place to stay, at least until you can meet some other actors and rent an apartment together. If you're female, look into the for-women-only hotels, like the Barbizon.

Bring a good address book and a good appointment book. In the address book, plan to keep an accurate record of agents' names and phone numbers, casting offices, and so forth. In the appointment book keep a clear record of all appointments, interviews, and readings that you land.

Plan to have a good photo taken of yourself as soon as you arrive. Out-of-town photographers usually don't make good theatrical photographs, so better not risk it. Buy a trade newspaper (in New York, *Show Business* or *Back Stage*) and look at the photographers' ads. You'll find someone whose work you like. By looking through the trade papers, you will also get an idea of what kind of photograph you need. Some people use a head shot. Others use a composite, a photograph showing four or more shots of the actor in different character roles. A dancer, who wants to show a head shot and a dancing photograph of the whole body, will find a composite useful. Know what kind of photos you want taken of yourself when you go to the studio, and take any props, costumes, or makeup required.

After you have had the photographs taken, resist the temptation to choose a flattering shot that doesn't resemble you. What's the use? You'll only waste the time of both the casting office and yourself. Pick good honest shots.

Now that you have your photographs, take them with your resumé to a photo-reproduction company. (A sample resumé is given below.) You can have the resumé worked up before you leave home. Your calling card, in your new trade, is a reproduced photo with your resumé printed neatly on the back. The photo-reproduction company will reproduce a hundred of your new photos for you quite cheaply, and print the resumé on the back for you. The photo-reproduction company will also make up your composite for you, if you want one.

If you study the model resumé, you will see that your name, address, phone number (or numbers), union affiliations, and social security number, are printed in capital letters, or large, easy-to-read *type*. Do not print or write. Limit the resumé to one page.

If is important not to pad your resumé with false facts, even

Resumé form

Height:		DAVID GARRETT	AFTRA-SAG-AEA
Weight:		390 3rd Avenue	SS. 111-00-3133
Hair:		New York City, N.Y. 10019	
Eyes:	*Call:*		
Age range:		(Answering service number)	Voice: (if you sing)
			Dance: (what kind?)
		(Home number)	Dialects: (list)
		(Work number)	
	Agent:	(if you have one)	

EXPERIENCE:

Stage:

(Where played)	(Name of play)	(Role)

(Here list all the parts in all the plays you have done, the latest first.)

Television:

(Name of program)	(Name of play)	(Role)

Films:

(Name of company)	(Name of film)	(Role)

T.V. commercials:

(Name of agency)	(Commercial)

though you will begin, inevitably, embarrassed by your meager background. Liars are easily exposed, and the smart director or producer will ask you for programs, newspaper reviews, or production photographs, or chat with you about the names of the director or the other actors in the show. Don't risk embarrassment of this kind.

Do, however, get a good photograph album, and put into it any production shots from shows that will build up your background favorably, both from your pre–New York and your New York days. Neatly print the names of the plays and where they were done under each photograph. If you have a favorable review, add it. Sometimes a director will give you a chance at a role he didn't think you were right for after you have shown him a character photo of yourself in costume and makeup.

As soon as you have your photos reproduced, take a head shot over to *Player's Guide*, 165 W. 46th St. The *Guide* is a New York institution, a directory containing photos of actors broken down into categories: leading man, leading woman, ingenue, juvenile, and so forth. No casting office or agent is without a *Guide*, and a lot of producers and directors use it in a pinch, so get your picture into it as soon as possible. The fee is reasonable, especially considering the possible benefits.

Get yourself an efficient phone-answering service. For the best services, check with other more knowledgable actors, whom you will meet at the agents' offices and on casting calls. A phone-answering service is essential; with it, you can go out to make the rounds or on a job and know that you won't miss that one important break. Get your answering service number onto your resumé, in a good prominent position.

Then you must check with your service regularly, if they are not calling you at home.

Some answering services provide other benefits. They may have bulletin boards with casting calls on them. They are good places to meet other actors who are making the rounds, who may lead you to a part right for you, not for them. Your operator, who takes calls about casting all day, is a goldmine of information—but don't expect her to betray secrets meant for other actors.

Buy the trade papers as soon as they appear on the newsstands in the Times Square area. Try and find out just when they first appear so that you get casting information first. *Show Business, Back Stage,* and *Variety* are particularly important. If you read these papers carefully, you will gather much useful information about who is doing what, when, and where. Warning: you will sometimes find inaccurate or outdated casting news. If a casting notice tells you not to phone, but just to send your photo and resumé, then do just that. Don't try to impress anyone by a cute trick. With your photo and resumé, send a polite note, pointing out any particular qualifications you think you have for the part, and requesting an appointment or an audition. Be specific about the part and the play you have in mind. Do not get personal; always try to keep your acting contacts professional.

Keep a record of casting information that interests you, along with a record of what action you have taken. You don't want to waste your photo-resumé by sending out duplicates. Don't mail it to every casting notice listed; be selective. What good is an appointment with an agent who does lots of casting for trick dogs? Don't continue mailing your resumé to offices to which you have already sent it, either. A lot of your photos will be thrown away; try to keep this waste to a minimum.

Drop into the union offices. You will find a lot of real production activity there. Friendly actors may tell you where a job is waiting. While at Equity, pick up a copy of the *Digest*. It contains a list of all the New York franchised—approved—agents. This is a valuable list, for it tells you when and how an agent will see you. Some agents list their days and times of appointments. Write to these people, asking for an interview on that day at that time. The *Digest* also lists producers of industrial shows, producers of children's theater, producers of year-round stock companies, off-Broadway producers, and of course, Broadway producers.

The *Digest* has other uses. Let us say that you find a production blurb in the *New York Times*. It will say that X is about to produce Y's play. Look up X's name in the *Digest*, and drop him a polite note, or drop into his office and find out if there's a part for you.

Always watch your behavior while making the rounds. Try to be modest, efficient, and considerate of those who seem to be in control of the jobs that you want. Let them see that you realize they have tough jobs and that you aren't trying to crowd them. They will be far more likely to remember you favorably than if you make an entrance like the music man's, or try to charm the receptionist, who has seen too much professional charm in her time. Never try to crash a line. Be polite and courteous and save your energy for the audition.

Once you have an audition date, don't panic. Don't try to figure out a gimmick to call special attention to yourself. You don't have to help along the imagination of the casting agent or director by getting into period costume. Your talent will speak louder than any gimmick you can think of.

Do, however, ask if there will be time for you to study the material before you audition. If it's a new script, at least get it overnight.

If you are called in and asked to read the script cold, ask for a minute to look it over. If the director is there, ask him what he wants from the actor doing the part. This will not only flatter him, and give him a good opinion of your maturity and willingness to take direction, it will also help you to give him what he is looking for and may win you the part.

In most auditions you will find yourself acting with an exhausted, cold, and indifferent stage manager. While you studied the script you went over the lines with a vivid person in mind, only to find yourself now confronted by a stage manager who is not going to act with you at all. What can you do?

You must act. Pretend the stage manager is not what he is. Use whatever you can of him. Relate to him. *Don't* try to play to the director, or to act alone. It is true that if the stage manager gives you nothing, you are, in effect, alone—but still, if you try to *use* him, bad as he is, he's better than nothing.

When the audition is over, *leave*, efficiently, quietly, and *considerately*. Don't hang around asking people who don't care, "How did I do?" This will not get you a part; in fact, it may ruin your chances. When you do leave, you will be anxious. "We'll let you know," "Don't call us, we'll call you," will ring in your ears. Don't go home and sit by the phone for hours waiting for word. Some offices never do let you know. Get busy, do other things, look for more work, study, but don't wait around thinking about how the audition could have gone better. Don't tell audition stories. Actors don't realize how terribly boring these stories are, even to other actors, who don't care about why you didn't get a part, or what some important director said. Tell yourself it's all just an ego trip, and forget it.

Face your limitations as an actor. In college or community theater you may have played a ninety-year old person, or a middle-aged lead, and no doubt you were great. But in professional theater, directors will not use you unless you are right, and right means close to the actual age or type. They will not pad a thin person if they want a fat person; they will hire a fat person. They will not age you if they want an old person; they will hire an old person. Type casting is a necessary evil in commercial theater. Don't fight it. You won't win, and you'll make enemies.

You need to study acting, probably for years, to become truly professional. There are many excellent schools of acting and teachers of acting in New York, ranging from full time to a couple of hours a week, from expensive to very reasonable. Be careful before committing yourself to a teacher. Ask around. Find out who is most respected by the young actors you most respect. Then enroll with a teacher and work hard. This will be important to you in the long run. You will meet other actors who may help you in your classes, and some acting classes present showcase productions.

Most important of all, though, act, act, act, and be seen. Join groups and act. Act for nothing, if there's no pay; but act. When the production is ready, invite agents, using the Actors' Equity *Digest* list. You must be seen, and seen again. An actor needs exposure. Never feel too grand to work in a church, a cellar, a loft, or for nothing. Such an attitude will lead nowhere. If you are having trouble getting into a group, form your own group, put on your own plays, find an inexpensive loft or a free church basement, share the expenses among you, and act!

When you do get a job in a play, don't ever consider yourself too good for the group you're with. Don't look critically at the drab, dirty environment. (Wait until you've seen a Broadway theater's dressing rooms). Don't hold back in enthusiasm, energy, or sincerity. Your approach should never differ, whether you are acting in an off-off-Broadway loft or in a large Broadway theater. You are a professional actor; behave like one. That first role in New York City may be an important step in a successful career. It could lead to a good agent. Work on your role truthfully, and build your given circumstances. Never criticize your fellow actors or the director, just because the group you joined doesn't use your method of work. Never announce that you cannot work with a non-Method director who speaks in results and clichés. If you are smart, you will learn now that your method should help you to act under any working conditions whatsoever. Don't expect the world to conform to your standards. Learn flexibility, tact, and patience. Respect the other man's method, or lack of it. A negative attitude will hurt you and the play, and chances are that the director will never use you again, and will tell others that you are a troublemaker.

Remember that acting is a serious and honorable profession. Don't waste your energy in petty seductions or flirting with all comers. You don't have to prove your attractions through daily conquests. Save your energies for the stage. Put your work first and respect yourself and others. Dust off the word *integrity,* and use it. There isn't enough integrity around today; if you provide a little, you and everyone else will be glad you did. And you'll get more roles that way, too.

Watch your manners in every possible way. Be early to all rehearsal calls; lateness in the theater is unpardonable and will be held against you. Do not talk during rehearsals. Do not smoke on stage. Never leave the rehearsal area without telling the stage manager. Never touch or eat props that are not yours. Be ready to help your fellow actors when they *ask* for help. Do not challenge your director during rehearsals. If you must discuss your role with him, arrange to do it privately, after rehearsal.

Professional manners need to be applied off stage, too. Don't be critical of another actor who is competing with you for a job; if you can't say anything nice, don't say anything. Don't let more than one agent put you up for a part; if the agents find out about this, you will lose both of them for the future. Share your job tips with others; they will reciprocate. Be modest; don't assume a false modesty, but have the real self-confidence to examine yourself critically and analyze your faults and mistakes. You will grow as an actor.

See as much theater as possible. Equity has a supply of free tickets daily, for its membership. Twofers, or coupons with which you can buy two tickets nearly for the price of one, are in plentiful supply in the Broadway area. If you're really broke, you can play the time-honored actor's trick of waiting till the first theater intermission, mingling with the crowd, and moving back into the theater, but don't try it with a sell-out production! You should be acquainted with all the current shows and know which parts you could play. Then you'll be ready when they cast the road company.

New York City is currently benefiting from a theatrical renaissance that is coming from the off-off-Broadway movement. This movement is a serious effort by thousands of people of all ages to give their artistic lives a chance. Not since the old dramatic stock days has there been so much varied theatrical activity. The movement is so powerful that an organization, known as the Off-off Broadway Alliance has been formed, with headquarters at 245 W. 52nd St. Not all off-off-Broadway theaters or companies are members, but the published list of members numbers sixty-nine active companies, of which twenty-seven have touring companies.

Remember, with all this activity going on, actors don't have to sit around waiting for lightning to strike. Make your own opportunities. Join groups, read the trade papers, use union showcases such as the Equity Library Theater, and *act.* If you really want to practice your profession, you can do it in a cellar, a church, an empty store, or a garage—all of which are currently being used by highly successful groups. Put your life and training to work—now!

Suggested readings in the theater

Cole, Toby, and Chinoy, Helen Kirch, eds. *Directing the Play*. Indianapolis: Bobbs-Merrill, 1953.

Cole, Toby, comp. *Acting: A Handbook of the Stanislavski Method.* New York: Crown, 1955

Edwards, Christine. *The Stanislavski Heritage.* New York: New York University Press, 1965.

Fergusson, Francis. *The Idea of a Theatre*. Princeton: Princeton University Press, 1951.

Gorchakov, Nikolai. *Stanislavski Directs,* trans. Miriam Goldina. New York: Funk & Wagnalls, 1954.

Grotowski, Jerzy. *Towards a Poor Theatre*. New York: Simon and Schuster, 1969.

Lewis, Robert. *Method—or Madness?* New York: Samuel French, 1958.

Marowitz, Charles. *The Method as Means: An Acting Survey*. Herbert Jenkins, 1961.

Stanislavski, Constantin. *An Actor Prepares,* trans. Elizabeth Reynolds Hapgood. New York: Theatre Arts Books, 1936.

Stanislavski, Constantin. *Building a Character,* trans. Elizabeth Reynolds Hapgood. New York: Theatre Arts Books, 1949.

Stanislavski, Constantin. *Creating a Role,* trans. Elizabeth Reynolds Hapgood. New York: Theatre Arts Books, 1961.

Stanislavski, Constantin. *My Life in Art,* trans. Elizabeth Reynolds Hapgood. New York: Theatre Arts Books, 1948.

Stanislavski, Constantin. *Stanislavski on the Art of the Stage,* ed. and trans. David Magarshack. New York: Hill and Wang, 1961.

Stanislavski, Constantin. *Stanislavski's Legacy,* trans. Elizabeth Reynolds Hapgood. New York: Theatre Arts Books, 1968.

St.-Denis, Michael. *Theatre: The Rediscovery of Style.* New York: Theatre Arts Books, 1960.

INDEX

Accents, 70
Actions, 118
Actor Prepares, An, 149, 222
Actors' Equity Association (AEA), 228–32
Agent, 234
American Federation of Television and Radio Artists (AFTRA), 228, 233
Antony and Cleopatra, 197–203
Arena Stage, 7
Aristotle, 107, 108, 109, 122, 154
Arkin, Alan, 6
Articulation, 71
"As if," 162, 121
Auditions, 238–39

Beats, 111
Beclch, 7
Bergman, Ingmar, 96
Bernstein, Aline, 97–98
Blank verse, 157, 159
Boswell, James, 124
Bottoms, Timothy, 5
Bow (yoga exercise), 25, 27
Breathing, controlled deep, 15, 16, 17, 19
Broadway, 6
Brustein, Robert, 6
Building a character, 134
Building a Character, 149

Candle (yoga exercise), 34
Caretaker, The, 226
Carroll, Lewis, 74–75, 82–83
Character how, the, 131–32
Characterization, 128–39
Chekhov, Anton, 109
Chest voice, 66–67
Clurman, Harold, 131, 221
Cobra (yoga exercise), 24–25
Comedy of Manners, 225
Concentration, 50–53
Contrast, 11–14
Craig, Gordon, 93

Demian, 96–97
Diction, 69
Digest, 238
Drawing-room comedy, 225
Dr. Faustus, 224

Economics of the theater, 5–6
Edwards, Christine, 16
Emotional problems, 121–27
Empty chair exercise, 126–27
Eye exercises, 44

Fantasticks, The, 6
Ferrer, Jose, 5
Film acting, 5
Folded candle (yoga exercise), 36–37
Folded leaf (yoga exercise), 29
Frontal voice, 65–66

Ghelderode, Michel de, 94, 119
Goose, Mother, 80
Greco, El, 119–20
Greek drama, 223, 224
Gregory, Andre, 7
Grotowski, Jerzy, 57
Guiness, Alec, 3

Hamlet, 150, 151, 152, 153, 156, 157–59
Hamlet, 4
Head stand (yoga exercise), 38
Head to knee (exercises), 40
Head voice, 67–68
Henry V, 85–92, 191–97
Hesse, Hermann, 96–97
Hoffman, Dustin, 132

Imagination, 93–95
Imitation, 107–8
Improvisations for emotional problems, 125–27
Incident at Vichy, 131
Industrial shows, 232
International Phonetic Alphabet (IPA), 70
Ionesco, Eugene, 226

Johnson, Dr. Samuel, 124, 160
Journey of the Fifth Horse, 132
Julius Caesar, 172–75
Julliard Company, 223
Julliard School of Acting, 223

Kazan, Elia, 130
Kerr, Walter, 56
King Henry V, 85–92, 191–97

Last Picture Show, The, 5
Lear, Edward, 73–74, 75–76, 79–80, 83–85
Lewis, Robert, 9, 10, 133–34
Lip exercises, 72–76
Listening, 70
Listening exercises, 100–2
Lotus (yoga exercise), 46

Macbeth, 163–72
Macbeth, Lady, 156
Marlowe, Christopher, 224
Marowitz, Charles, 109
Massage, 14–15
Masters, Edgar Lee, 136, 137–49
Medieval drama, 223–24
Meditation, 53–55
Memory, 95–97
Method or Madness, 9
Meyerhold, Vsevolod, 112–13
Modified lotus (yoga exercise), 48
Moore, Sonia, 122
Motives for choosing acting career, 1–8
My Life in Art, 149

Nasality, 63–65
Naturalism, 225
New York Shakespeare Festival, 7
New York Times, 56
Nonsense Cookery, 83–85
"Notebook for *A Streetcar Named Desire,*" 130

Odet, Clifford, 222
Off-Broadway, 6
Off-off Broadway Alliance, 242
Olivier, Laurence, 131
One-beat problem, 114–18
Othello, 155–56
Owens, Rochelle, 7

Pavlov, Ivan Petrovich, 95
Period, 133
Photographs, 235
Pitch placement (voice), 60–62
Plato, 81–82
Player's Guide, 237
"Playing the objective," 112

Preparation for head stand (yoga exercise), 33
Professional manners, 241
Props, 133–34
Proust, Marcel, 95–96, 97
"Psychologic gesture," 131
Psycho-physical, 122
Pygmalion, 70–71

Questions to be asked in characterization, 130–34

Rag doll (voice exercise), 58–59
Regional theaters, 6–7
Relaxation, 9–49
Remembrance of Things Past, 95–96, 97
Restoration comedy, 224–25
Resumé, importance of, 235–36
Reverse folded leaf (yoga exercise), 31
Richard III, 209–20
Rocket (vocal exercise), 61–62
Romeo and Juliet, 183–90

Salvini, Tomasso, 51, 131
Saxon, O. Glenn, 6
Schechner, Richard, 7
School for Scandal, 223
"Scoring" a day, 110
Screen Actors' Guild (SAG), 228, 233
Seagull, The, 109
Seeing exercises, 98–100
Sense memory exercise for characterization, 136
Sense memory exercises, 103–6
Senses, 97–106
Shakespeare, William, 85–92, 149, 150–57, 159–61, 163–220, 224
Shaw, George Bernard, 70–71
Smelling exercises, 103
Soliloquies, 156
Spoon River Anthology, 136, 137–49
Stanislavski, Constantin, 4, 10–11, 16, 50, 51, 52, 53, 56, 69, 93, 94, 95, 101, 109, 111, 113, 121, 122, 124, 131, 149–62, 222
St.-Denis, Michael, 10, 223
Stock companies, 6, 231–32
Stomach lift (exercises), 42
Style, 221–27

Tamburlaine, 224
Taming of the Shrew, The, 203–9
Tasting exercises, 103
Tempo, 163
Theater of the Absurd, 225–27
Theatre of the Living Arts, 7
Theatre: The Rediscovery of Style, 223
Tongue exercises, 76–92
Touching exercises, 102–3
Towards a Poor Theatre, 57
Tree (yoga exercise), 20
Twelfth Night ,159, 175–83
Tyrone Guthrie Theater, 7

Unions for actors, 228–33, 238

Vocalizing with deep breathing, 59–60
Voice: diction, 69–92; placement, 132; production, 56–68

Waiting for Godot, 225
Waiting for Lefty, 222
Wild Strawberries, 96
Winter's Tale, The, 154
Women Beware Women, 223, 224

Yoga exercises, 10, 16–49